AN ART TOUR

TO

RUSSIA

AN ART TOUR

TO

RUSSIA

BY

J. BEAVINGTON ATKINSON

WATERSTONE · LONDON
HIPPOCRENE BOOKS · NEW YORK

Waterstone & Co. Limited
49 Hay's Mews
London WIX 7RT
Hippocrene Books, Inc.
171 Madison Ave.
New York, NY 10016

First published in Great Britain in 1873 as
An Art Tour to Northern Capitals of Europe

This edition first published by
Waterstone & Co. Limited 1986

UK ISBN 0 947752 47 1
US ISBN 0 87052 303 1

Front cover: Russian Brocatelle *c.* 1870
Reproduced by courtesy of the Board of
Trustees of the Victoria and Albert Museum

Cover design by Michael Head

Printed and bound in Great Britain by
Richard Clay (The Chaucer Press) Ltd.,
Bungay, Suffolk

CONTENTS.

CHAPTER X.

CHAPTER XI.

CHAPTER XII.

CHAPTER I.

ABO, HELSINGFORS, AND WIBORG.

IN the middle of the summer month of July I left
Sweden for Russia. The steamer loosed from her
moorings somewhat after midnight, yet daylight still
lingered in the sky. The track lay around the lovely
environs of Stockholm ; islands and wooded headlands,
studded with villas, or crowned with churches, loomed on
the eye as shadows visible and yet half invisible. The
evening of the first day brought me within Russian
territory. Before the sun had quenched his fever fire
in the western waters, the boat was moored under the
shadow of the castle and the cathedral of the ancient
capital of Finland. Abo is finely planted, but her
ancient glory has departed. Fire desolated her public
buildings, her university was removed, her trade lost.
The streets are wide and deserted, the chief edifices form
together less of a society than of a solitude. Indeed, as
I subsequently found to be common within the confines
of the vast Russian empire, an infinite space seemed to
be placed at the disposal of an infinitesimal population.
It is said that Abo with only 20,000 inhabitants, covers
an area equal to Dresden with her 150,000 souls. An
artist would find in the city and neighbourhood little
material for his sketch-book. But interest can scarcely
fail to be felt in the venerable cathedral which served in

these parts as the cradle of Christianity.   The architecture wears that uncouth and anomalous aspect, which
seems to tell how Gothic styles lost their way, and
wandered far adrift ere they reached these utmost
confines ; how symmetry, beauty, finish, gave place to
a barbaric grandeur which may be supposed to comport
with granite rocks, pine forests, snow, ice, and the dark
shadows of the wintry nights, which hang in melancholy
sadness over life.   The insanity known to come over
peoples long immured in villages and huts, snow-covered
and night-shrouded, ever and anon peers out from
beneath the art which in Scandinavia and Russia
struggles into hard and half-starved existence.   The
cathedral of Abo is as a twin sister to the cathedral of
Upsala : each stands on the furthermost frontier of
civilisation : each is the historic representative of piety,
learning, rank ; and each too, in point of art, may be
comparable to a huge antediluvian creature cast on a
desert shore, or imprisoned in Siberian snows.

The interest of this, the oldest ecclesiastical structure
in Finland, lies not in its exterior but within its gloomy
brick-built walls.   The crypt is by its contents a curiosity:
here for centuries the first families were buried, and now
into this ghastly charnel-house the visitor is permitted to
clamber and crawl in order to see, as in the Capuchin
Church in Rome, the sleeping and silent dead dressed as
the living.   The gloomy caverns might have suggested
to Rembrandt ideas for 'The Raising of Lazarus'; and
to Decamps, Gustave Doré, and other sensational artists
in France, these robed remnants of humanity would
serve as tempting models.   The internal structure of
this large and massive cathedral is not without nobility,
the nave and aisles are lofty, the vaulting fine, and the
octagonal shafts at the east end imposing.   There is no

triforium, and the collective effect has been greatly marred by a wholesale wash of colour, which proves that the Fins were no better than the English at the time when the practice was to whitewash and colour all Gothic interiors. Here at Abo, as at Upsala, the traveller is not beyond the boundary of wall-paintings ; frescoes indeed, though proverbially frail and sensitive, can live like the Alpine rose on the confines of the snow. A series of consecutive decorations, six in number, range in subject from the Nativity to the Resurrection. Some have suffered severely, others are so fresh as to appear repainted. The style is the usual modern version or rather perversion of the Raphael manner ; the handling, as might be anticipated, is coarse ; the effort made is considerable, some of the compositions cannot be less than fifteen feet long. On a higher range are two historic scenes, also in fresco ; in merit these works are not above mediocrity. It is said that certain of these wall-paintings are due to Ekman, a Finnish artist. The statement has probability on its side. Finland produces painters, as will subsequently appear. I have not been able to ascertain anything certain as to this artist except that he derived his education, as indeed might be supposed, from Germany. The painter who introduced frescoes into the cathedral of Upsala in like manner learnt the process within German territory. Thus explained, the apparition of frescoes among Swedes or Fins, is less strange and startling. Wall-painting in fact has been making its way northwards for centuries. Perhaps at Abo it has for the present reached its utmost limit, at all events the monumental art of fresco can hardly live where there exist no monuments to decorate.

Helsingfors, sometimes termed the Gibraltar of the

North, presents an imposing aspect when approached from the sea. Effective sketches might be taken inside and outside the town. Architecture at all events has here assumed pretensions developed since Russia made this stronghold the capital of her much-petted province of Finland. The streets are systematically named in three languages, Finnish, Russian, and Swedish; the native tongue, when in a few years it shall by existing educational enactments have supplanted the Swedish, will become the official language of the Grand Duchy. We may be sure, however, that the constructional, plastic and pictorial arts will continue to be modelled on Russian standards. All the new parts of the city have been laid out on an ambitious scale : the streets are straight and rectangular, the squares ample and imposing; in short, the railway now open which brings St. Petersburg within easy distance, will import wholesale Russian arts and manners into Helsingfors. The public buildings, such as the Senate House and the University, assume that pomp in pediments, that array of lofty columns and parade of granite steps, which constitute the invariable resource of Imperial architects. In scale and material, outlay and labour, the architecture of Russia is akin to the ancient structures of Imperial Rome: and yet while Rome is now old and venerable, Russia in her art creations seems juvenile and impertinent : while Rome too built for eternity, Russia runs up some false construction, some showy façade which melts like snow in the sun, or crumbles as stucco in the frost.

Wiborg, the next town of importance in the Gulf of Finland, and now a favourite summer resort of the well-to-do people of St. Petersburg, has one of those magnificent approaches from the water common to the tideless seas of the Baltic and of the Mediterranean. In fact here once again under a hot sun and a cloudless sky in midsummer, I was reminded of the blue waters which environ Italy and Greece. Scarcely more picturesque are the approaches to Genoa, Naples, Smyrna, and Constantinople, than the entrances to Stockholm, Helsingfors, Wiborg, and St. Petersburg. The number of days however in the year when a sailor along the coasts of Finland can imagine himself in a southern sea are naturally but few. On penetrating inland of course the character of the vegetation at once dispels all delusion—yet Finland would seem to be no exception to the rule, that where there is excellent fishing there is good sketching. Hills and lakes abound—indeed it is said that with the exception of some parts of North America, no country exists that is so much covered with inland waters. Finland will probably become, at least in its most accessible parts, the sketching-ground of St. Petersburg. The railway, as it extends from point to point on the northern shores of the gulf, will carry well-to-do merchants to their country boxes ; excursions with inevitable picnics will be made into the interior, and thus favoured spots, such as the waterfall at Wiborg, must find their way into picture-galleries. It may easily be understood that Finland has hitherto done little for the arts. Ekman, a Fin painter, worked, as we have seen, at fresco in the cathedral of Abo ; and Arsenius Mestschersky, as will appear in the sequel, rendered with rare fidelity the snow and the ice of the Finnish winter. I was interested to find that Mestschersky learnt to paint winter not in Finland but in Switzerland. He was a pupil indeed of Calame, who in turn had studied under Francis Danby. Thus it would appear that our English Danby made Swiss Calame, and that Calame then created Russ Mestschersky. This is but one of

the many instances of how national schools in Europe
are, and always have been, linked together by personal
bonds and the innate affinities of genius. That the
most faithful painter of ice and snow in the northernmost
provinces of Russia should have learnt his art among
the Alps, may appear less strange if it is remembered
that when Mr. Cooke, R.A., painted the ships Hecla and
Terror, ice-bound within the arctic circle, he used studies
made, not at the North Pole but among the lakes
and mountains of Switzerland. Snow and ice are in
fact the same all the world over, which may be one
reason why winter scenes are much alike, whether
painted in Russia or England, in Germany or Switzerland.

In a journey which I took for the purpose of judging
of the art capabilities of Russia, my first experience was
not on land but upon the sea, and I soon found that
these Russian waters do not yield much material for the
pencil. Yet the traveller's impressions are novel, and
the aspects of nature exceptional. The steamer threads
her way among fiords, headlands, and innumerable
islands, or rather rocks ; yet the scenery may be
summed up in the three words, 'sea, granite, firs.'
Altogether the landscape loses by comparison with the
neighbouring and analogous coasts of Norway, Sweden,
and Scotland. Granite rocks from which the rugged
angles have been abraded, heaps of granite stones, some
minute and others gigantic, all made round and smooth
as pebbles by the ceaseless beating of angry waves,
have but a puerile effect when transferred to a sketch-
book. Pine-trees too, though noble beings when they
shoot up to the sky with stout trunk and wide sweeping
branches, as in the sheltered plains and valleys of
Sweden, assume a mean and poverty-stricken aspect

when growing precariously on the thin soil of these arid
rocks. The remaining pictorial elements in the Gulf of
Finland—the sea and the sky—naturally change with
the season. In the winter an army with bag and
baggage has been marched across the ice from shore to
shore, but in midsummer the sun is so hot and the sky
so clear that the traveller might fancy himself, as already
supposed, on the blue waters of the Mediterranean.
Still I have always found while sailing on northern seas
a chilling suspicion of half departing or quick returning
winter. The craft upon the waters float not as in the
Adriatic, like brightly coloured butterflies; they glide
not with the light wing of the swallow, but are heavy,
dark, and dirty, as traders doing hard work. The coasts
too, which the steamer hugs, are not like the shores of
Ravenna, one grand table-land of stone pines, or as the
bays of Naples and of Salerno, fragrant with orange
groves. Thick snows, biting frosts, and keen cutting
ice, have stunted nature in her growth, and blanched her
in her colour. The artist indeed would almost do better
had he the courage, to portray these savage lands, these
uncivilised peoples, in their winter attire: yet have I
invariably found that such sketches, though startling in
effect, are circumscribed alike in material as in mental
sphere. The imagination however cannot fail to be
moved deeply when a picture seizes with appalling
reality some great catastrophe, such as the loss of a
family or a caravan in the snow drift, or the overthrow
of an army in retreat. The retreat of Napoleon from
Moscow, as depicted by the French artist Yvon, is a
scene unparalleled for tragic horror. And once more I
would suggest that the landscape and marine painter
may be able to turn to account the grandly panoramic
sunsets of these northern latitudes. Specially novel, as

already found in Scandinavia, are the effects during the few weeks when the sun scarcely dips below the horizon, but maintains a golden and saffron twilight even into midnight and into morning. Midsummer, too, is subject to sudden atmospheric vicissitudes, such as sea mists, silvery under the sun and soft as moonlight. On my way to Helsingfors the steamer had to cast anchor twice, and in sailing on the Neva in July, the speed of the boat was slackened, so perplexing and impenetrable were the fogs, which came as a cloud before the wind and as swiftly as a cloud were swept away. But the atmospheric effects were on the whole disappointing; even Turner would have found it hard to illumine these mists, or to turn into gold these leaden skies. The sun had no iridescent colour or rainbow panoply: weak and blanched as the moon, his power was not like that of the sun in Palestine, described by the Psalmist as a giant rejoicing in his strength.

CHAPTER II.

ST. PETERSBURG.

CRONSTADT, the strong fortress which stopped the advance of the English squadron in the last Russian war, is as the water-gate of St. Petersburg. A bright July sun made no unpleasing picture of the huge hulks of the men-of-war, and of the many-masted merchant ships which lay within the harbour, or behind the fortifications. Passing Cronstadt the capital soon comes in sight : the water is so smooth and shallow, and the banks are so low, that I was actually reminded of the lagoons of Venice. Far away in the distance glittered in the sunlight cupola beyond cupola, covered with burnished gold or sparkling with bright stars on a blue ground. The river, stretching wide as an estuary, was thronged with merchandise as the Tagus or the Thames : yachts were flying before the wind and steam-tugs laboured slowly against the stream, dragging behind the heavily-laden lighter. Warehouses and wharfs and timber-yards now begin to line either bank ; yet the materials for a sketch-book are scanty and uninviting : an artist who, like Mr. Whistler, has etched at Battersea and Blackwall, would find by comparison on the Neva the forms without character, the surfaces without texture, the masses without light, shade, or colour. As the boat advances the imperial city grows in scale and pomp. The river view becomes imposing, the banks are lined on either side by granite quays, which for solidity, strength, and area, have no parallel in Europe. Beneath the bridges the unruly river rushes, bearing along rafts and merchandise, and in the broad-laid streets people hurry to and fro, as if the day were too short for the press of business : only in great commercial capitals, the centres of large populations, is life thus rapid and over-burdened.   Throughout Russia generally time hangs heavily, but here at the seat of empire, the focus of commerce, life under high pressure moves at full speed.   I know of no European capital, excepting perhaps London and Vienna, which leaves on the mind so strong an impression of power, wealth, and ostentation, as the city of St. Petersburg.

Possibly the first idea which may strike the stranger on driving from the steamer to the hotel, is the large scale on which the city has been planned ; the area of squares and streets seems proportioned to the vast dimensions of the Russian empire : indeed the silent solitudes of the city may be said to symbolise the desert tracks of central Russia and Siberia.   Only on the continent of America is so much land at command, so large a sweep of territory brought within the circuit of city life.   In the old world, Munich offers the closest analogy to St. Petersburg, and that not only by wide and half-occupied areas, but by a certain pretentious and pseudo-classic architecture, common to the two cities alike : the design for the Hermitage in fact came from Munich.   St. Petersburg, like Munich too, has been forced into rapid growth ; indeed while looking at the works raised by successive Tsars, I was reminded of the boast of Augustus that he found Rome of brick and left her of marble.

St. Petersburg, though sometimes decried as a city of shams, is certainly not surpassed in the way of show

by any capital in Europe. As to natural situation she
may be said to be at once fortunate and infelicitous :
the flatness of the land is not redeemed by fertility, the
monotony of the panorama is not broken by mountains ;
the city rides as a raft upon the waters, so heavily
freighted as to run the risk of sinking. And yet I
know of no capital more imposing when taken from the
strong points of view. Almost beyond parallel is the
array of palaces and public buildings which meets the
traveller's eye in a walk or sail from the English quay
up to the Gardens of the Summer Palace. The structures it is true tend a little too much to what may be
termed buckram and fustian styles ; indeed there is
scarcely a form or a detail which an architect would
care to jot down in his note-book. And yet the general
effect is grand : a big river rushing with large volume
of water through the arches of bridges, along granite
quays and before marble palaces, is a noble and living
presence in the midst of the city life. The waters of
'the great Neva' and of 'the little Neva' appear as an
omnipresence ; the rivers are in the streets, and great
buildings, such as the Admiralty, the Fortress, and the
Cathedral of St. Peter and St. Paul, ride as at anchor
on a swelling flood. The views from the three chief
bridges—Nicholas Bridge, Palace Bridge, and Troitska
Bridge—are eminently palatial and imperial. The
Academy of Arts, the Academy of Sciences, St. Isaac's
Cathedral, the Admiralty, the Winter Palace, the
Hermitage, and the fortress and cathedral of St. Peter
and St. Paul, give to the stranger an overpowering
impression of the wealth and the strength of the empire.
The Englishman, while standing on these bridges, will
naturally recall analogous positions on the river Thames ;
such comparison is not wholly to the disadvantage of

the northern capital, yet on the banks of the Neva rise no structures which in architectural design equal St. Paul's Cathedral, Somerset House, Westminster Abbey, and the Houses of Parliament. Indeed, with the exception of the spire of the Admiralty, I did not find in St. Petersburg a single new idea.

Of the famous Nevski-Prospekt, the chief street in St. Petersburg, it may be said as of our London Regent Street, that it can stand neither weather nor criticism. As to style of architecture, strictly speaking the Nevski-Prospekt has none: the buildings, consisting of shops, interspersed with a few churches and public edifices, so much partake of the modern and mongrel Italian manner, that the traveller might easily fancy himself in Paris, Brussels, or Turin. Few cities are so pretentious in outside appearances as St. Petersburg, and yet the show she makes is that of the whited sepulchre : false construction and rottenness of material, façades of empty parade, and plaster which feigns to be stone, constitute an accumulative dishonesty which has few parallels in the history of architecture. Classic pillars and porticos, which have been thrust in everywhere on slightest pretext, are often built up of brick covered with cement and coloured yellow. Columns, here the common and constant expedient, are mostly mismanaged; they are as it were gratuitous intrusions, they seem to be stuck on, they fail to compose with the rest of the building. Neither do the architects of St. Petersburg understand mouldings or the value of shadow, there is scarcely a moulding in the city which casts a deep, broad or delicate shadow : hence the façades look flat and thin as if built of cards. In the same way the details are poor and treated without knowledge; it thus happens that conceptions bold and grand are carried out incompletely.

The great mistake is that the architects have made no attempt to gather together the scattered elements of a national style. With the noteworthy exception of the use of fine, fanciful and fantastic domes, often gilt or brightly coloured, the architecture in Russian capitals is either Classic or Renaissance of the most commonplace description.

A practice I have adopted in Rome I found wise and pleasant in St. Petersburg ; I made it a rule never to pass a church without looking in at the door. This daily habit, when extended over a few weeks, brings much observation of ecclesiastical structures and modes of decoration, of rituals and church music, of picturesque worshippers in paintable attitudes and costumes. I shall defer any description of religious ceremonies in the Greek Church until I reach Moscow and 'Kief, the city of pilgrimage.' And I shall not think it worth while to dwell on the very many churches which adorn the northern capital, because, with few exceptions, there is nothing in point of art which merits to be recorded. Yet I can scarcely refrain from again referring to the fine fantasy played by many-coloured domes against the blue sky. The forms are beautiful, the colours decorative. The city in its sky outline presents a succession of strange pictures, at one point the eye might seem to range across a garden of gourds, at other positions peer above house-tops groups which might be mistaken for turbaned Turks ; and when the sun shines vividly, and throws glittering light on the 'patens of bright gold,' over these many-domed churches, a stranger might almost fancy that above the city floated fire balloons or bright-coloured lanterns. The large cupola of St. Isaac, covered with copper overlaid with gold, has been said to burn on a bright day like the sun when

rising on a mountain top.   I can never forget the sight
when I returned to St. Petersburg from the most brilliant civic and military spectacle I ever witnessed, the
fête of the Empress at Tsarskoé Sélo.   It was still dark,
but before I reached my hotel for the short repose of
a night which already brightened into morning, every
cupola on the way was awakening into daylight ; the
sun, hesitating for a moment on the horizon, announced
his coming as by electric light on the golden stars
which shone on domes more blue than the grey sky of
morning.   In Moscow we shall find that church cupolas
play a part in the city panorama still more conspicuous
than in St. Petersburg.

The Cathedral of St. Isaac will fall under notice when
I come to speak of the modern mosaics and pictures
which adorn the interior.   But a word may here be
given to the exterior and to the general construction of
this the most costly and pretentious of Russian churches.
The noble edifice has the advantage of a commanding
situation ; not, it is true, as to elevation—for that is impossible in a city set throughout on a dead level—but
the surface area in its wide sweeping circuit at all
events contrasts strikingly with that cribbed and cabined
church-yard of St. Paul's in London, which the Englishman may have just left behind him.   Yet St. Isaac's can
scarcely venture on comparison with St. Paul's, though
the style of the two buildings is similar.   The great
Cathedral of St. Petersburg has, however, the advantage
of that concentration which belongs to the Greek as
distinguished from the Latin Cross, a distinction which
has always been to the disadvantage of St. Peter's in
Rome.   A cross of four equal arms, with columned
porticos mounted nobly on steps at the four extremities,
the whole composition crowned by central and sur-

rounding cupolas, is assuredly an imposing conception, of which the French artist M. Montferrand has known how to make the most. I may here, by way of parenthesis, remark that the two works which do most honour to St. Petersburg, the Cathedral of St. Isaac and the adjacent equestrian statue of Peter the Great, are severally due not to Russian but to French artists. This is one example among many of the foreign origin of the arts in Russia. But at all events let it be admitted that the materials used, as well as the ideas often brought to bear, are local or national. For example, the grandest of all architectural conceptions, the idea of a dome, is here glorified in true Russian or Oriental manner, not so much by magnitude of proportion as by decorative splendour, heightened to the utmost by a surface of burnished gold. Then the four porticos which terminate each end of the Greek cross with stately columns and entablatures of granite from Finland, albeit in design mere commonplace compilations, are wholly national in the material used. I do not now stop to mention the large and bold reliefs in bronze, which though French in design were, I believe, cast in St. Petersburg: indeed here, as in Munich, the government makes that liberal provision which only governments can make, for noble but unremunerative art. The great dome is said to be sustained by iron; indeed the science of construction brought to bear is great, yet again it must be acknowledged that whether the material be iron, bronze, or stone, the art, the skill, and even the commercial capital, are not Russian but foreign, and often English. Russian workmen, however, are employed as mechanics or machines, partly because their rate of wages is low, but also because in copyism and mechanism Russian artisans cannot throughout Europe be surpassed. When I got to

St. Petersburg I could scarcely believe the statement
to be true that the 'English Magazine' and not any
Russian factory had executed the eight stupendous malachite pillars within the church, weighing about 34,000
pounds and costing £25,000 sterling.   Yet while the
organisation might be English, the operatives were
Russians. These unsurpassed malachite pillars combine
in the grand altar-screen with columns of lapis-lazuli :
the latter are said to have cost per pair £12,000
sterling. I need scarcely observe that this parade of
precious materials partakes more of barbaric magnificence than of artistic taste; indeed these columns of
malachite and lapis-lazuli, which to the eye present
themselves as solid and honest, have been built up as
incrustations on hollow cast-iron tubes.   Thus hollow
are the most precious arts of Russia.   Justice, however, demands that I should speak hereafter in fair
appreciation of the interiors of Russian churches,
whereof the Cathedral of St. Isaac is among the chief.
Nevertheless, material rather than mind, money rather
than art, is the governing power ; malachite, lapis-lazuli,
gold, and other precious substances are heaped together
profusely, yet no architect in Europe of the slightest
intellectual pretensions, would care to look a second
time at the constructive or decorative conceptions which
the churches of St. Petersburg display.   St. Isaac's in
fact is miraculous only in its monoliths.   I could
scarcely believe my eyes when first I stood beneath the
stately porticos and looked from top to bottom of the
very many columns, seven feet in diameter and sixty
feet high, all polished granite monoliths from Finland.
Already I had made the assertion that there was
nothing new in St. Petersburg when these granite
monoliths at once compelled a recantation.

The monoliths in St. Petersburg are so exceptional in number and often so gigantic in dimension as to call for special mention. The monolith obelisks of ancient Egypt are scarcely more remarkable. In addition to the magnificent columns, each sixty feet high, which sustain the four porticos of the cathedral of St. Isaac, are fifty-six monoliths, also of granite from Finland, thirty-five feet high in the Kazan Cathedral; likewise the noble entrance-hall of the Hermitage is sustained by sixteen monoliths, and the magnificent room which receives the treasures from the Cimmerian Bosphorus has the support of twenty monoliths. But the greatest single block of modern times stands in front of the Winter Palace, as a monument to Alexander I. The height is eighty-four feet, and the weight nearly four hundred tons. The story goes that the contractor in Finland, finding that he had exceeded the required length, actually cut off ten or fifteen feet. The vast granite quarries of Finland supply the Tsars with these stupendous columns, just as the granite quarries at Syene on the Nile furnished the Pharaohs with obelisks. These enormous masses are too heavy to be conveyed on wheels, the only practicable mode of transit is on rollers. In this way each of the sixty-feet columns for St. Isaac's was transported across country all the way from Finland. Each column represents so incredible an amount of labour as to make it evident that monoliths are luxuries in which only emperors can indulge. And even when these heavy weights have reached their destination the difficulty next occurs how to secure a solid foundation. St. Petersburg was once a swamp, and so rotten is the ground that it would be quite possible for a monolith to sink out of sight and never more be heard of. To provide against such contingencies a forest of piles was driven into the earth at the cost of £200,000 as the foundation of St. Isaac, and yet the cathedral sinks. Like causes render the roads of St. Petersburg the worst in Europe; winter frosts, which penetrate several feet below the surface, seize on the imprisoned waters and tear up the streets. The surface thus broken is so destructive to wheels that I have known an Englishman, who, though he kept four carriages, had not one in a condition to use. The jolting on the roads is so great as to make it wise for a traveller to hold on fast, and when a lady and gentleman ride side by side, it is usual for the gentleman to protect the lady by throwing his arm round his companion's waist. This delicate attention is so much of a utilitarian necessity as in no way to imply further obligations.

St. Petersburg is considerably indebted to the art of sculpture: public monuments adorn her squares and gardens. Indeed the art of sculpture has, like the sister arts of architecture and painting, been forced into preternatural proportions. In the large area within sight of the church of St. Isaac and of the Admiralty, stands conspicuously one of the few successful equestrian statues in modern or ancient times, the colossal bronze to Peter the Great. The huge block of granite, which is said to weigh upwards of 15,000 tons, was conveyed from a marsh, four miles distance from St. Petersburg, by means of ropes, pulleys, and windlasses, worked by men and horses. A drummer stationed on the rock itself gave the signal for onward movement. It would seem that the methods used in Russia to this day for transporting granite monoliths, are curiously similar to the appliances of the ancient Egyptians for moving like masses. In point of art this equestrian statue, though grand in conception, is, after the taste of

barbarous nations, colossal in size. Peter the Great is
eleven feet in stature, the horse is seventeen feet high.
The nobility lies in the action, the horse rears on his
hind legs after the favourite manner of Velasquez in
well-known equestrian portraits of Ferdinand IV. The
attitude assumed by the great Emperor is triumphant,
the fiery steed has dashed up the rock and pauses
as in mid-air on the brink of the precipice. The idea
is that Peter the Great surveys from the height the
capital of his creation, as it may be supposed to rise
from the waters. His hand is stretched forth for the
protection of the city. This work, like many other
proud achievements in the empire, unfortunately is
not Russian. The design is due to the Frenchman Falconet; Marie Callot is said to have modelled the head,
and the casting was done by Martelli, an Italian.
Falconet, in order to be true to the life, carefully studied
again and again a fine Arab horse, mounted by a
Russian general who was famous as a rider : the general
day by day made a rush up a mound, artificially constructed for the purpose, and when just short of the
precipice the horse was reined in and thrown on its
hind legs. The artist watched the action and made
his studies ; the work accordingly has nature, movement,
vigour. I may here mention that I have nowhere found
such large masses of stone conveyed from place to
place here as in St. Petersburg. It is true I have seen
marble fresh from the mountains of Carrara tugged
along by teams of bullocks, but I have nowhere
witnessed so much power brought to bear as in the
transit of the granite used in the immense memorial
to the Empress Catherine.

The monument to the late Emperor Nicholas is a sad
falling off from the manly and heroic style of the

memorial to Peter the Great, the reason being that while the design of the latter is due, as we have seen, to a Frenchman, the equestrian statue of Nicholas, with surrounding bas-reliefs and emblematic figures, is the work of the Russian sculptor Baron P. Clodt. This productive, hard-working, but not original artist naturally proved himself wholly unequal to an undertaking so arduous. The style embodies weakness with affectation; the work, in short, is a failure, as all such art compilations in St. Petersburg or elsewhere are bound to be. Other public statues help to people the solitudes of the city: the Suwaroff monument, destitute, almost as a matter of course, of art merit, stands on the open space at the flank of the British Embassy. The monument to the Scotchman Sir James Wylie is in the court of the Imperial Academy of Medicine: the memorials to Field - Marshals Tolly and Koutousoff surmount pedestals opposite the Kazan Cathedral. Of these collective works, certainly not less than respectable, perhaps the worst that can be affirmed is that they but exchange servility to the Byzantine school for equal servility to classic and Italian styles. The misfortune of these Russian sculptors is that they seldom succeed in establishing an independent individuality or a distinctive nationality. The best means of escape from this dead-alive condition seems to be in the direction of naturalistic and pictorial treatment. As favourable exceptions to the dull conventionality of Russian sculpture may be quoted four groups of horses reined in by attendants: these compositions, which tell with admirable effect on one of the many bridges in St. Petersburg, are wholly exceptional in this local plastic art for free movement, bold action, and faithful transcript of nature. The sculptor, Baron Clodt, has deservedly won for himself renown. Also exceptional for manly, robust, and individual treatment is the bronze statue to the well-known popular fabulist Krilof, surrounded by bas-reliefs illustrative of his works. Here again Baron Clodt proves command of character, action, incident. The reliefs surrounding the figure illustrate Krilof's animal fables and other tales, which have recently been translated into English by Mr. Ralston. These reliefs are evidently most popular with the common people; indeed uneducated Russians I have found in no material degree to differ from the uneducated classes in England or other countries: all alike know a spade or a besom when they see one, and little more. Sculpture has always been to the illiterate of all nations a dead letter so far as it is an art.

Yet though the virtuous efforts made under imperial patronage to create a school of sculpture have not hitherto been crowned with signal success, yet I confess to have felt peculiar interest in watching the birth, the cradling, and the culture of plastic art in this the northernmost of art capitals. In the Academy of St. Petersburg I noted some few figures which, though modelled almost as a matter of course under Italian influence, showed that simple love for nature, that deliberate purpose to arrive at truth which can be the only hope of a nascent and native school. In the Paris Exhibition of 1867, among eighteen statues, 'The Infant Sculptor' by Theodore Kamehekin, deserves to be remembered as a pretty genre figure. Also I marked for merit by Matthew Tchijoff 'Le Messager de Kief, sujet tiré de la chronique de Nestor, appartenant au musée de l'Académie des Beaux-Arts.' This work, though rude and awkward, as often happens with an

honest but semi-barbaric period, displays the vigorous
motion and the vivacious motive which occasionally
serve as saving graces to this graceless northern art.

Sculpture in this ostentatious capital of Russia not
unnaturally assumes the imperial phase of bronzes. Emperors in fact, in sculpture as in the sister arts, went in for
utmost ostentation, spared no cost, and provided the
means whereby the city is made conspicuous for monuments in metal. Many of the works already mentioned
are in bronze. The compositions in high relief which
adorn the exterior of St. Isaac's would be memorable in
any capital in Europe ; yet the objection may be raised
that of all capitals they belong least to St. Petersburg, so little have they of Russian nationality. Like
objection holds to divers large bronze doors in sundry churches, though utmost toleration is due to the
servility which secured for St. Petersburg reproductions
from the bronze doors in the Baptistery of Pisa. Other
compositions cast in metal and mounted wholesale in
the midst of the most humdrum of architectural designs,
frequently boast of novelty rather than of merit. Indeed
in most such examples lavish expenditure is more
apparent than art talent. In fact talent did not come
in response to imperial cash. And yet I am bound to
say that in St. Petersburg, as also in divers exhibitions
in western Europe, I have found Russian bronzes which
by vigour and naturalism stand in favourable contrast
to the decadence and the debility that have become the
characteristic and the curse of all European schools of
sculpture since the days of Canova. Among these
Russian workers in bronze, I would mention M. Anto-
kolsky, born 1841, and educated in the Academy of
St. Petersburg. This native sculptor exhibited in the
last International Galleries, at Kensington, a life-size

statue of 'John the Terrible.' The character of the monarch who killed his own son in a paroxysm of rage, is here sketched to the life with trenchant detail; the hands are sinewy as griping talons, the eye. is keen like the eagle's, the head is darkened by vindictive vengeance. For once the manner becomes essentially northern, indeed the style shows points in common with that most Scandinavian of northern groups, 'The Wrestlers,' by Molin in Stockholm. Yet the modelling is sketchy and indecisive, a defect common to Russian artists from the want of knowledge essential to detail.

Baron P. Clodt, professor in the Academy of St. Petersburg, by whom a multitude of designs have fallen under my observation, seems equally in that embryo state which invariably marks these half-formed schools. Yet Baron P. Clodt, in common with his contemporaries, just saves himself by struggling into naturalism. 'A Study of a Mare and Foal,' with other like groups of animals and figures, now in the Imperial Academy of St. Petersburg, are closely modelled on nature; the touch is trenchant and sharp. Another worker in bronze is M. Nikolaus Lieberich, also a member of the Imperial Academy. When I wished, in search for art, to travel as far as St. Petersburg, I was led on by the promise of bronzes by this most picturesque of modellers. 'The Dead Roebuck on a Mat' is exquisite for detail and manipulation; the touch is tender, firm, and true. 'The Reindeer Sledge,' a favourite subject, is equally true, because within the artist's knowledge. Yet this realistic worker in bronze is too prolific for improvement; like most of the artists of Russia he stops just at the point when he promises perfection. After having made myself familiar with M. Lieberich in western Europe, I looked in vain in his native land

for new development, and yet I was glad to find in
models of reindeer, horses, sledges, peasants in costume,
that national character which constitutes the great value
of Russian art. M. Lieberich, though circumscribed,
has thrown into bronze the life of the peasant and of
the noble. And all people are ready to applaud a fur
cap or a horse's trappings as a triumph of the naturalism
which now rules throughout Europe.

I proposed to myself in visiting St. Petersburg to
examine into the state of arts and manufactures as
displayed in one of the national (not international)
Exhibitions which are held periodically in St. Petersburg
and Moscow. I was somewhat disappointed, inasmuch
as I found that in London and Paris, from 1851 downwards, the Russians had already made us familiar with
the best works which it was within their power to
produce. In the Exhibition at St. Petersburg nothing
appeared to compare with the malachite doors which
took London by surprise in 1851, nor with the figure
mosaics which in Paris in 1867 placed the Imperial
mosaic manufactory at St. Petersburg on an equality
with the Pope's famous establishment in the Vatican.
But here, on the spot, it was interesting to see the raw
materials used in these art manufactures. Large heaps
were displayed of native unwrought malachite, fresh
from the rock. In equal profusion as a peculiar product
of Russia appeared lapis lazuli, not cut or polished but
in the rough. Native iron ores were also piled together
in proof of the mineral riches of the empire. Iron
castings were also shown, which though, as a matter of
course, inferior in detail and delicacy to the castings of
Berlin, indicate how skilful is the Russian artisan in the
working of metals. Also in the precious metals, as
I shall again have occasion to remark, the Russians

display a cunning hand; Russian jewellery is excellent
in the chasing, also in the setting of the stones. I am
sorry to say, however, that the French style prevails;
yet some designs are Northern. Very interesting are
the reproductions from the Finnish or Scandinavian
remains in the museums of Northern Europe. Such
jewellery is in form and ornament closely allied to the
modern Irish replicas from ancient models in the
Museum of Irish Antiquities in Dublin. I was glad to
notice in St. Petersburg that the adaptations from the
old Finnish forms were eagerly bought up.

Russia, like Scandinavia, makes herself, for obvious
reasons, conspicuous in woodwork. She has been and
still remains in the period of wood; in times past we
are told there have been successive ages of stone,
bronze, and iron, but wood as distinguished from these
other materials seems perennial. There is a wooden
church near the cottage of Peter the Great which stands
as the most ancient sacred structure in the capital.
Then whole villages are of wood, also of wood are the
villas which well-to-do merchants and others in St.
Petersburg take to as pleasant suburban retreats during
the heat of summer months. Wood was also chosen
as the material of the central court in the last Exhibition
at St. Petersburg; here, in fact, as in the Russian Court
of the Great Exhibition in Paris, carved wood was used
structurally and decoratively; indeed the forms and
the carvings reminded me of the bargeboards and other
wood-fabrics which I have known in Shrewsbury,
Coventry, Chester, Hereford, Southampton, and other
English towns. In fact, along the whole of Northern
Europe, wood was universally used for domestic
dwellings. While stone and brick have supplanted
more primitive appliances elsewhere, in Scandinavia

and Russia timber cut from the forest is still the favourite resource. Indeed wood for dwellings possesses certain advantages, it is said to dry after winter wet more speedily than stone, also it is found in summer cooler. For these and other reasons wooden huts and houses are likely long to survive. That wooden floors also, in the form of tarsia-work, decorative in design as in colour, are favourite fashions in the art of furnishing, might be seen by many large and elaborate specimens in the Exhibition of St. Petersburg as well as in its predecessors in London and Paris. These inlays of coloured woods are used not only in palaces but in private dwellings. The Picture Galleries of the Hermitage are laid with tarsia; the effect is decorative, yet subdued, the floors keep down in their places quietly; moreover they are cool in summer, warm in winter, and always cleanly. Tarsia, or marquetry, has advantages over carpets; the use of such wood mosaics has extended in England of late years, and the Royal Academy, like the Hermitage, is with advantage thus floored. The Exhibition gave other interesting samples of the state of arts and manufactures within the empire. Specially to be commended were the cheap calicos printed in oriental designs allied to the Indian shawl-patterns, and really glorious in intensity and harmony of colour. These fabrics followed me all through Russia, from St. Petersburg to Moscow down to Kief, and on to the western frontier as far as Poland. In Cracow the peasants in the market-place were gay as pheasants and peacocks; in fact, the Poles, as the Russians, show themselves oriental in their love for colour. In an art point of view, the value of figures thus brilliantly illuminated can scarcely be over-estimated; in cities and villages, as well as in fields, men, women, and children, thus apparelled, are as jewels shining on a grey or golden ground. Great provision is made in the bazaars of St. Petersburg and Moscow to meet the ornate tastes of the people on cheap terms. Besides calicos there are cashmeres, not woven in colours, but printed. I seldom could ascertain with absolute certainty where these cotton and woollen fabrics had been made; sometimes, no doubt, they belonged to Russian territory, but often, clearly, they came from beyond the frontier; in fact, Russians are supposed to be under much obligation to Manchester for cottons and to Birmingham for hardware. In like manner the railway carriages, with railway ambulances, which were paraded as of Russian manufacture, had been imported in pieces from England, little or nothing being Russian except the putting together. I cannot, however, but regard as praiseworthy the efforts thus made in many directions to place the semi-barbarous empire in the front rank of European civilisations. There is, in short, scarcely an art or a manufacture that the government has not stimulated into rapid growth. In addition to mosaics, of which I shall speak in detail, there are factories for glass and porcelain; yet it must be admitted that the works produced are not up to the highest standards reached by foreign nations; the ornament is mostly poor; styles which approach the oriental it will easily be understood are the best. Of the Russian school of sculpture I have already treated, and of the truly national products from the Government School of Art in Moscow I shall hereafter speak. It remains to add that modern examples of ecclesiastical art possessed exceptional interest as illustrations of the faith and the ritual of the Greco-Russian Church. The best, as also the worst of this art, is of Byzantine origin; Byzantine pictures are always degraded, but Byzantine ornament, on the contrary, is usually true to the immutable laws of art decoration. The loan collection of ancient Russian art—mostly ecclesiastical—was unique in its way. But, on the whole, the contributions to this exhibition, whether ancient or modern, induced the conclusion, since confirmed, that Russian arts are most circumscribed; the ideas embodied are few and oft repeated: in short, art in Russia seems doomed to stagnation rather than destined to progression.

The art collections in St. Petersburg may give the traveller pleasant occupation for several weeks; indeed if the tourist be an art student he will find work for months. The Winter Palace, adjoining the Hermitage, on the Neva, is like the palace at Versailles, conspicuous for rooms or galleries commemorative of military exploits. Here are well-painted battle-pieces by Willewalde and Kotzebue, also naval engagements by Aivasovsky, highly coloured as a matter of course. Likewise are hung the best battle-pieces I have ever seen, by Peter Hess, the renowned Bavarian painter, who appears to less credit here in Munich than in the Winter Palace, St. Petersburg. Also may be noted the portrait of Alexander I by Dawe, the Englishman, who worked much in Russia. Here likewise is the imperial gallery of portraits of all the sovereigns of the reigning Russian house. I pass over these multitudinous works thus briefly, because, though the collection is of importance in the history of the empire, it has little value in art.

'The Crown Jewels' I shall not attempt to describe; no description of jewels can be worth much. I may venture to say, however, that after seeing all the royal jewellery in Europe, I found these Russian crowns,

sceptres, &c. richer in diamonds than any other. Also
pearls, rubies, Siberian aqua-marines, &c. add colour and
splendour to the imperial treasure. The comparison on
the spot, which I not unnaturally instituted, was with
the imperial treasury at Vienna. Next, a word may
be given to the room in which the proud, stern, and
unrelenting Nicholas died, where all is kept intact
as he left it. I have seldom been more impressed
than with this small, simple, and almost penurious apartment, so striking in contrast with the splendour of the
rest of the palace. Silence, solitude, and solemnity
all the more attach to the spot from the statement to
which credence is given that the great emperor, on
learning of the reverses in the Crimea, here committed
suicide. In other words, it is said that he directed his
physician to prepare a medicine which after having
taken he died. The sword, helmet, and grey military
cloak are where he laid them. Here lies a historic
tragedy which remains to be painted : one of the most
dramatic pictorial scenes in Europe, the death of
Wallenstein in Schiller's drama, painted by Professor
Piloty, and now in the new Pinakothek, Munich, might
in the death of the great Nicholas find a parallel. The
emperor lies buried with all the sovereigns of Russia
since the foundation of St. Petersburg, in the cathedral
fortress of St. Peter and St. Paul. Nothing in Europe
is grander in the simplicity and silence which befit a
sepulchre—not even the imperial tombs in Vienna—
than this stately mausoleum of the Tsars. The Emperor Nicholas lies opposite to Peter the Great. In
the Hermitage, or rather in the Winter Palace, is a
gallery illustrative of the life and labours of Peter the
Great. The collection, besides turning-lathes and other
instruments with which the monarch worked, contains

curiosities, knicknacks, as well as some works of real art value: the connecting point of the whole collection is in Peter himself. An analogous collection was some years ago opened in the Louvre as the Museum of Napoleon I. Dynasties all the world over thus seek to perpetuate their memories.

The Academy of Fine Arts is a noble institution, imposing in its architecture, and richly endowed. I shall have occasion to speak of its contents and functions in the sequel. The Corps des Mines must also be visited, the collection of minerals proves the amazing riches of European and Asiatic Russia. I wish I had knowledge and space to describe this unexampled collection, which though not falling within my art province has direct art relations. Nothing beauteous or wondrous in nature lies beyond the sphere of art ; the forms of crystals, the colours of precious stones are specially objects of delight to the artist's eye. The Imperial Public Library is one of the richest libraries in Europe; its literary treasures can hardly be overrated ; I regret that I cannot enter on its contents. Private collections, though scarcely numerous, are choice; the celebrated Leuchtenberg Gallery, formerly in Munich, is the richest. The royal residences of Peterhof and Tsarskoé Sélo I also found to contain much in the way of art, and yet scarcely of sufficient importance to need special description.

The Foundling Hospital I can hardly trust myself to speak of ; I have never witnessed a sadder sight. It is said that about 6000 children are admitted annually, and that the daily average number of inmates is from 700 to 800. In the space of an hour I saw, I should say, fully 800, between the room where infants were of a few hours old, to the sick room or hospital where they were dying. I think I may venture to say that the most unpleasant and painful scene I ever witnessed was in the apartments where the feeding from the breast is conducted wholesale. Wet nurses happened to be unusually scarce, so that the hired women served one child after another in quick succession. There is in maternity a sanctity, in infancy a beauty, to which these Foundling Hospitals do outrage. The matron who took me round said that she thought England happy in having abolished the system. The holy art of Italy specially sanctifies the relationship of mother and child. A painter in search of subjects for his pencil would flee from a spot which proclaims in hideous aspect and giant proportion that illicit intercourse between the sexes which in Russia is unusually rife.

St. Petersburg and its immediate neighbourhood are not tempting to the landscape painter. Yet the grand river rolling through the midst of the city, laden with craft and lined with palaces, might evoke a Canaletto. Accordingly there is a certain F. J. Alexieff who has earned for himself the title of the Russian Canaletto. Perhaps of St. Petersburg it may be said without disparagement, that she is far too fine to be painted; as well might a Prout plant his sketching stool in the smartest quarters of Paris. And just as our new embankment has swept away from the Thames many a picturesque warehouse and shed, so have imperial quays reduced the banks of the Neva to stately monotony. Yet in the environs among 'the Islands,' whereon villas, gardens, and plantations congregate, I have walked amid sylvan nooks, picturesque bridges, jetties and boat-houses which would tell with pictorial effect in a sketch-book. And travellers are accustomed to drive to a promontory which stretches beyond wooded islands towards the

western sun, a spot where I have seen the whole
sky on fire. St. Petersburg is not wanting in romance
at such times, although the accessories to sunsets are
mostly meagre. Neither mountains nor temples are
present to compare with the jagged heights of the
Apennines as seen from San Miniato, or with the historic structures ·of Rome as looked down upon from
the Pincian, or with the gardens of olive and orange, of
ilex, chestnut, and walnut-trees, as seen from Castela-
mare and Palermo. In warm summer weather the artist
may unawares stroll near to open waters where the
Russian women come down to bathe. In the rocky
bays at Wiborg, and along the branches of the Neva,
mothers and young daughters, after the simple manner of
their eastern ancestors, enter the water undraped. The
practice has scarcely been reflected into the art of the
country as freely as might have been anticipated. I
cannot recall any picture worthy of comparison with
Diana and her Nymphs, by Domenichino, in the Borghese
Palace, Rome. The bathing scenes, by the Russian
painter Neff, which are more often copied than any
other works in the Hermitage, are derived rather from
Italy than from the rivers or lakes of Russia. I did not
observe that Muscovite artists had taken due advantage
of the liberty allowed to nations emerging from barbarism,
it is only among primitive peoples that painters are
permitted the privileges which pertained to the first
occupants of the garden of Eden. In Paris I remember
to have seen a truly artistic composition, full of fire and
movement—horses wild, as if caught from the prairie,
ridden by unclothed riders along a hill-girt shore into
the open sea. The replica of such a scene is now before
me in a photograph taken from the life. Russian
peasants cast aside their scanty garments as do fellahs

on the banks of the Nile, they leap into their seats on the horses' backs, and so, as centaurs, they ride over land and through water. But Russian painters and sculptors can scarcely with full advantage avail themselves of such incidents, until they submit to the training which enabled the old Greeks to model a race of godlike heroes, and to raise to the ideal the common incidents of daily life.

CHAPTER III.

ST. PETERSBURG.   THE HERMITAGE.

THE Imperial Hermitage alone repays a journey to
St. Petersburg; for a whole fortnight I visited almost
every day the picture and sculpture galleries of this
vast and rich museum, and in the end I left with the
feeling that I had done but inadequate justice to these
valuable and exhaustless collections.   I am tolerably
well acquainted with the great museums in the south
and west of Europe, and I was interested to find that
the Hermitage does not suffer by comparison with the
Vatican, the Museum of Naples, the Galleries of Florence,
the Louvre in Paris, or the great Picture Gallery in
Madrid.   In some departments, indeed, St. Petersburg
has the advantage over other capitals : the collection of gold ornaments from Kertch is not surpassed
by the goldwork in the Etruscan room of the Vatican ;
the coins are not inferior to the numismatic collections in Paris, or in the British Museum ; the Dutch
pictures are not to be equalled save in Holland or in
Dresden ; the Spanish school has no competitor save in
Madrid and Seville ; the portraits by Vandyck, and the
sketches by Rubens, are only surpassed in England and
Bavaria.   It is thus obvious that the collective strength
of these assembled collections, is very great.   The
picture galleries contain more that 1500 works ; the
number of drawings is upwards of 500, the coins and
medals amount to 200,000, the painted vases are

above 1700, the ancient marbles number 361, and the collection of gems is one of the largest in existence. The Hermitage has been enriched partly to the prejudice of other cities or palaces. From the Tauris palace came classic sculpture. Tsarskoé Sélo also furnished contributions. The policy has been to make one astounding museum, which shall represent not a capital but an empire, and stand before the world as the exponent of the wealth, the resource, and the refined taste of the nation and its rulers.

Before I enter into detail as to the contents of the Hermitage it may be as well to describe the building, which by its art style and its palatial magnificence has brought great éclat to St. Petersburg. When I say that Ritter von Klenze, of Munich renown, was the architect, the reader may be able to picture to himself the structural and decorative aspect. Klenze has written his name in sufficiently large and legible characters on the face of modern Europe, in the Walhalla at Ratisbon, also in the old Pinakothek, the Glyptothek, the Ruhmeshalle, and the Allerheiligen Kapelle, severally at Munich. No architect in one century has revived so many dead traditions, or given such grandiloquent expression to worn-out commonplaces. Klenze had already won his laurels in the service of King Ludwig of Bavaria, when he was summoned, in the year 1839, by the Emperor Nicholas, to St. Petersburg. His duties became onerous; he had to carry out the interior arrangements of the Cathedral of St. Isaac, and he was entrusted with the design and construction of the Hermitage, a work of ten years, begun in 1840, completed in 1850, and formally opened in 1851. Previous structures had to be swept away which dated back to the time of Catharine II, who here made for herself a refuge

from burdens of government called the Hermitage. The
palatial Museum, which takes the place of the previous
structure, shows itself in every sense span new ; from
toe to top, from basement to roof, it is bedizened
with ornament and polichrome, after the manner which
has become notorious in Munich.   The style is bastard
Grecian, degenerating in the portico and the interior
into the grotesque and florid renaissance.   The portico
is sustained by ten caryatides, tortured in form, and of
more than usual dimension.   These monolith colossi
were cut in granite by the Russian sculptor Terebènieff,
from a small model by the Munich sculptor Halbig.
Niches in the walls are occupied by statues of historic
artists ; the sculptures at the sides are by Schwanthaler.
The collective effect, though far from mean, wants
character and originality.   The stranger may safely
reserve his emotions for the interior.   The entrance-hall
presents a truly noble appearance : the roof is supported
by sixteen monoliths of the finest granite from Finland,
and the whole interior boasts of an aggregate of no fewer
than 140 granite monoliths.   A stately flight of marble
steps, second only to the monumental Treppenhaus in
the New Museum, Berlin, conducts from the basement to
the picture galleries.   The visitor when he reaches the
summit finds himself on a plateau adorned with modern
French and Italian sculpture, and supports for candelabra
of violet jasper from Siberia.   The traveller feels that
he is no longer in a museum but in an imperial palace ;
the Pitti Palace in Florence is in comparison small and
simple.   Yet the architectural ideas are not so striking
for novelty, as the decorative materials are astounding
for boundless expenditure.   It is easy to see whence the
conceptions have been borrowed ;—Klenze in fact not
unnaturally thought he might steal from himself without

charge of larceny, accordingly the sculpture galleries on the basement are indebted to the Glyptothek in Munich, while the picture galleries are a free and florid adaptation from the Old Pinakothek.   The three large central galleries severally assigned to the Spanish School, to the Italian School, and to Rubens and Vandyck, are crowned by coved ceilings, enriched with gold and polichrome, and lighted from the top.   Blinds are needed in the Russian summer as in the dog-days in Burlington House.   The side rooms which branch off as in the Old Pinakothek from the lofty central halls, are of the nature of cabinets suited to small pictures ; here the windows are on the side, screens intrude in the centre, the light, as in Munich, is capricious and poor.

The decorations of the galleries, cabinets, and corridors, may astound strangers not accustomed to the elaborate ornamentation of galleries and palaces in Munich. Mural colouring is known to have been reduced by Germans to a system or science, and Klenze being a painter as well as an architect, has heightened by his brush the work of his chisel.   But he had less occasion for the use of paint, by reason of the richness and the variety of the solid materials at his command.   Whoever has visited the Mineralogical Museum in St. Petersburg, the richest in the world, with perhaps the single exception of the collection in the British Museum, must have been astounded with the amazing mineral wealth of the Russian empire.   From Finland in the north, to the Ural Mountains southward, and to Siberia stretching towards the east, supplies reach St. Petersburg from quarries and mines which yield granites, marbles, malachite, lapis lazuli, crystals, precious stones, gold, and other metals.   With these materials in lavish profusion

it is not surprising that Klenze was able to throw into
the decoration of the Hermitage an opulence in excess
of even the ornate Bavarian interiors.   Moreover in
staircases and other large surfaces and spaces, he has
seen no objection to the use of scagliola, and thus an
unbroken aspect of marble halls is maintained throughout.   Klenze, in the design and the decoration of the Old
Pinakothek, and of the Glyptothek, had learnt the
utilitarian distinction between a picture and a sculpture
gallery, and accordingly, when he came to St. Petersburg,
he wisely kept his basement, which was to be reserved
for ancient marbles, solid and comparatively sombre,
while the topmost story, devoted to the pictorial arts,
naturally assumed a more festive and aerial aspect.
Yet the architect has shown his knowledge and discretion in keeping down any undue splendour in his
materials and appliances, thus, although each part is
forced up to the highest pitch, the whole is balanced
and brought into tone, so as to enhance rather than to
militate from the effect of the pictures hung on the
walls.   The background of silk hangings, against which
the gold frames rest, inclines to a uniform scarlet red.
But any monotony involved in this invariable colour of
the wall linings, is relieved by the variety thrown into
doors, ceilings, and floors.   The floors, the only wood in
the building, are of marquetry, of which we have a
comparatively humble example in our Royal Academy.
In some of the rooms the patterns both in arrangement
of form and of colour, are highly effective.   Marquetry
may almost be deemed in Russia a national manufacture;
when treated as in the Hermitage, in the flat, and not
in relief of light and shade, the flooring keeps its place
well on the ground, and does not intrude itself upon the
pictures on the walls.   Another point worthy of observa-

tion is, that while the whole interior is kept in sufficient harmony, the component parts, like the different rooms in the Munich palace of King Ludwig, occasionally pass from style to style; thus Pompeian decoration may be divided only by a door from Italian. A corridor has been decorated with good effect in emulation of the Raphaelesque arabesques in the Loggia of the Vatican.

It remains to notice that the galleries are furnished with a taste and magnificence in keeping with the structure. The chairs and couches are covered like the walls with rich silks. The vases and tables of porphyry and malachite, the candelabra of violet jasper and of rhodonite, the tazzas of lapis lazuli, syenite and aventurine, have the value of scientific specimens as well as of art products. These mineralogical monuments are in fact the only strictly national works in the Hermitage, except Russian pictures. But I need not here dwell on a thought which I fear will have to be oft repeated in this volume, that the arts are in Russia exotics imported from afar. The Hermitage happens to be in St. Petersburg only because there was money to rear it. As I have already signified the structure has been transported from Munich, the contents are foreign, and the style is but the usual eclecticism from Italy.

Commencing with the picture galleries it will be found that two considerable collections form the nucleus : first the Crozat Collection and second the Walpole Gallery. I refrain from including as usual a third collection, 'the Choiseul,' as a chief component part of the Hermitage, because I find it to be quite subordinate. The Crozat Gallery, which took its name from a celebrated amateur in Paris, enjoyed a European reputation before it reached St. Petersburg. The 400 pictures from this gallery now in the Hermitage, had been gathered together during the

last century from some fifteen collections in France and
Italy.   The magnificent cabinet of gems, forming part
of the Crozat treasures, was first sold to the Duke of
Orleans, and then purchased for the Hermitage.   The
Crozat Gallery now yields to the Hermitage 65 Italian
pictures, 145 works of the German styles, and 60 examples of the French school.   Of these the most famous
are two pictures by Raphael, a 'Holy Family' and
'St. George'; many oil sketches by Rubens; a number
of portraits by Vandyck, including the sketch for the
Herbert family picture at Wilton, together with some
first-rate examples of Rembrandt.   Next in importance
among the component parts of the Hermitage, is the
Walpole Collection, formed by the minister of George I
and George II, and described by his son, the author
of 'The Anecdotes of Painting.'   This collection passed
to St. Petersburg in 1779, for the moderate sum of
£35,000 :   under the amazing rise of prices it were
hazardous to estimate its present monetary worth.   The
pictures thus acquired from Houghton Hall are 198 in
number, of which 89 are Italian, 75 German, 7 Spanish,
22 French, and 5 English.   Of these the most famous
are a female portrait by Da Vinci, an entombment by
Parmigianino, 'The Adoration of the Shepherds,' and
'The Dispute of the Fathers on the Immaculate Conception,' both by Guido.   To these must be added 6
works by Salvator Rosa, 5 by Carlo Maratta, 4 by Murillo, 13 by Rubens, 4 by Teniers, and 12 by Vandyck.
Among the last are portraits acquired by Walpole from
the heirs of the Marquis of Wharton.   It is a calamity
that portraits, essentially English, should ever have left
our shores.   It is hard for an Englishman to see exiled
in a foreign gallery, Charles I and Henrietta his wife,
Archbishop Laud, Inigo Jones, &c.

The treasures of the Hermitage were further augmented by many minor purchases. For instance, in the month of April, 1772, took place a sale of the cabinet of the Duke of Choiseul, minister of Louis XV, whereat an agent of Catharine II chose eleven pictures, chiefly of the Dutch school, which certainly are master-works in their way. The sum paid was 107,904 livres, being for eleven pictures a fourth part of the product of the entire collection of 147 works. Such statements show that the Hermitage in this, as in other instances, secured for herself the lion's share. The secret in fact of the riches here amassed, is that the sovereigns of Russia entered with hot ardour and a full purse into the picture mart of Europe, at a time when the works of Da Vinci, Raphael, Rembrandt, Vandyck, Rubens, Ruysdael, &c., could be got, to use a vulgar expression, for a mere song. Other collections were weeded or taken possession of *en masse*. All emperors and empresses, from Peter the Great down to Nicholas, strained their resources to add riches to the Hermitage. Peter the Great had in the course of his foreign travels picked up pictures, chiefly Dutch or Flemish, which for the most part naturally show that, whatever vocation he might have for ship-building, he was without knowledge in art. Catharine II employed agents throughout Europe, and in addition to the purchases already mentioned, gathered treasures from Langlier and Lebrun, from Braamcamp of Amsterdam, and Dezalier d'Argenville. Catharine, moreover, to whom has recently been raised in gratitude a vast monumental effigy in St. Petersburg, engaged the services of renowned living artists for the decoration of palaces, and otherwise. Among native Russians may be mentioned Anton Lossenko, Féodor Alexéiew, Féodor Matwéiew, &c. and among foreigners stand conspicuously Raphael Mengs, Angelica Kauffmann, and Sir Joshua Reynolds. The number of pictures added by Paul I to the collection formed by his mother, was not considerable. Then followed Alexander I, who among some not unimportant additions made, in 1814, the acquisition .of thirty-eight pictures from the Malmaison collection, formed by the Empress Josephine. This choice gallery added further wealth to the Dutch school, already opulent. The Emperor Nicholas, to whom Russia is indebted for the new Hermitage, was scarcely more mindful of the building than of the jewels the casket held. In the year 1829 were bought, at the cost of £7000, thirty pictures from the gallery of Queen Hortense, mother of Napoleon III. The late Tsar added to the Hermitage no less than 350 pictures, among which is conspicuous 'La Madonna d'Alba,' by Raphael, from the banker Coesvelt, of Carlton Terrace, London. Also the 'Descent from the Cross,' a magnificent work by Sebastian del Piombo ; a portrait known as 'La Colombina,' by Luini ; 'The Annunciation,' by Jan Van Eyck, and 'The Coronation of the Virgin,' by Quintin Matsys, all from the collection of the late king of Holland, and obtained through M. Bruni, the wellknown painter and keeper of the Hermitage. The Emperor Alexander further employed M. Bruni to buy at the Soult sale, also from the Count de Morny. Thus specially was enriched the already ample collection of Spanish masters. The present Emperor Alexander II made, as is well known, important purchases from the Campana collection in Rome, among which may be mentioned frescoes which, though falsely assigned to Raphael, are undoubtedly of the school. Also as late as 1866 was added to the Hermitage one of the most lovely and consummate works of Da Vinci, 'La Madonna Litta,' purchased from the Palazzo Litta, known to all travellers in Milan. Such is a brief history of the gallery of the Hermitage. I have often heard an expression of surprise that a capital so far removed from art centres as St. Petersburg, and a nation so recently emerged from barbarism, should be in possession of so magnificent a collection. The causes which account for any such anomaly I have endeavoured to assign. Successive monarchs who strove to advance Russia from the rear to the front of European civilisation have used the arts as potent agents in their designs.

The pictures now in the Hermitage are a selection from 4000 works acquired, as already related, by Catharine II, and her successors. The surplus has been distributed in various directions, Moscow having obtained, as was her due, a considerable share. Of the pictures reserved as worthy of the Hermitage, about 331 belong to the Italian, 117 to the Spanish, 949 to the Flemish, Dutch, and German, 172 to the French, 8 to the English, and 67 to the modern Russian schools. A further analysis shows that the Italian pictures come principally from the already-named Crozat and Walpole Collections ; that the Spanish works have been gathered chiefly from the Crozat, Walpole, and Choiseul Collections ; that the Flemish school is mostly indebted to the Crozat, Gotskowsky, Choiseul and Walpole Collections ; that the Dutch pictures come greatly from the Crozat and the Brühl Collections ; and that the French masters are due mainly to the Crozat and Walpole galleries.

The Hermitage, though scarcely as yet brought to the knowledge of the English-reading public, has been pretty fully described and illustrated in foreign languages. In the year 1774 the first catalogue was published by order of the Empress Catharine : it contained an inventory of 2080 pictures.   In 1773 a catalogue raisonné was compiled for the Empress by Count Ernst of Munich ; two volumes were finished by 1783, and in 1786 the third volume was ready.   This catalogue, which is preserved in the Hermitage, was never printed : it described 2658 pictures, but is said to have fallen into grave historical blunders.   Many inferior pictures were included, some of which have been drafted off to the palaces of Tsarskoé Sélo, of Péterhof, and of Gatchina, others were presented by Catharine to gentlemen of her court, and some were as late as the year 1853 sold by order of the Emperor Nicholas.   The intention always has been to reserve for the Hermitage works of only first-class merit.   The Emperor Paul ordered an inventory to be made of all objects in the Hermitage.   This new catalogue, in two volumes, included 3996 pictures.   In 1838 appeared a catalogue in French, 1683 pictures are described, but no classification into schools is attempted. In 1860 was published the first catalogue after the removal into the new buildings.   Three years later the present director of the gallery, Baron de Köhne, brought out a more complete and critical catalogue than had been before attempted.   A second edition of the first part was called for in 1869, and of the second instalment in 1870.   In the introduction we read that the descriptions have been made as complete as possible, that all the pictures have been again carefully examined, the signatures verified, new signatures found, and rectifications in the attribution of some pictures consequently made.   The description of each work includes its pedigree, the name of the collection whence it has come, also the measurements, likewise the engravings, if any, that have been published.   The catalogue is on the ' raisonné' principle—the works of each master are thrown together, and the list is headed by the artist's name, his place and time of birth, &c. The numbers have the great advantage of running continuously from Number 1 onwards : how great is the consequent convenience to students, any one can tell who has tried to work with the catalogue of our National Gallery, which is rendered all but unusable in consequence of the numbers not being consecutive either in the catalogue or upon the walls, an obvious blunder which has strangely been allowed to exist over a period of many years.

Several non-official works have also been published. In the year 1805 appeared 'The Gallery of the Hermitage,' with historical descriptions, and engravings from seventy-five principal pictures. In 1845 and 1847 were brought out two volumes of lithographs from 120 pictures executed by French artists. More recently a series of photographs has been taken, accompanied by an explanatory text in Russian, French, and German. A few critical works have also been devoted to the Hermitage. One by Louis Viardot has little value. A work of much more weight is Dr. Waagen's volume, large octavo, 448 pages, now in its second edition. The doctor was commissioned by the late Emperor to examine, verify, and in some measure to arrange, the pictures in the newly reared Hermitage. Thus Russia had recourse to Germany both for an architect and a critic, so little of art and of erudition can be found within her own borders. Dr. Waagen remained in St. Petersburg during 1861 and 1862. The disquisitional essay, interwoven with the catalogue, is distinguished by the doctor's usual traits. It is a little prolix and prosy, but on the other hand it displays knowledge, thoroughness, and impartiality.

I will now give a short account of the pictures,
beginning with the Italian school. The notes I made
before the works will be my chief guide ; I shall also
receive help from Dr. Waagen's volume, likewise from
the careful and critical catalogue of the Director of
the Gallery. The Hermitage has no examples of the
early Italian masters ; Giotto, Orcagna, and others, are
wholly absent. This deficiency is natural when it is
remembered that the collections were formed at a
period when the archæology or the early history of
art was little cared for, the motive then being to
procure pictures which were showy and pleasing.
Consequently the Hermitage begins at a late date.
Dr. Waagen sums up the strength and the weakness
of the Italian department relatively to other European
galleries in the following proportions. The Italian
school numbers 327 pictures, of which a few examples
only are of the early epoch, from 1400 to 1500 ; then
comes a moderate collection of good works of the
finest period, between 1500 and 1580 ; lastly, of the
time of the decadence, from 1580 to 1640, there is a
large number of very important pictures. The Hermitage in the early epoch is inferior to the galleries
of Berlin, Florence, Paris, London, Munich, and Vienna,
but stands on a level with Dresden and Madrid. In
the time of highest perfection St. Petersburg yields to
Paris, Dresden, Florence, and Madrid, but claims
equality with Munich, Vienna, Berlin, and London.
In examples of the decadence the Hermitage surpasses
the Louvre as well as the galleries of Berlin, Munich,
Vienna, and Dresden.

I find my notes on the pictures in the Hermitage
much in excess of the space at my command. Moreover, I fear the general public could take little or no

interest in detailed criticisms which, at the distance
of many hundred miles, they are not able to verify,
or scarcely to appreciate. The utmost, then, which
I shall venture to attempt, is to give a general sketch
of schools, masters, and works, as they appear within
the Hermitage. The classification which I shall adopt
will occasionally differ from that in the official catalogue; for instance, I shall transfer Da Vinci from
Florence to Milan, and Sebastian del Piombo from
Tuscany to Venezia and Rome.

Let us begin with the school of Milan at the time
when Da Vinci was its leader. 'La Madonna Litta'
(130), which is one of the earliest pictures painted by
Leonardo in Milan, is certainly in the artist's finest,
simplest, and most careful style. The type is lovely,
and the details have the utmost delicacy. 'The Holy
Family' (14) is also a marked work of this rare
painter; indeed, among the many pictures assigned to
Leonardo there are few in Europe more important.
The heads, hands, and draperies, are studied and
matured throughout, and of special dignity and tenderness is the Madonna's head; the shadow cast by the
drooping eyelids throws a pensive sadness on the
countenance. To the same period as this Holy Family
Dr. Waagen assigns a portrait (15) of a lady slightly
draped, a chalk study of which is in the collection of
the Duc d'Aumale. The deep impression which these
earnest conceptions of one of the profoundest minds
of the middle ages cannot fail to make, receives con-
firmation in several choice works of the pupil Luini.
'The Portrait of a Young Woman' (74) was indeed
formerly assigned to the master, Leonardo, and is
worthy of him. The head, which is from a well-known
model, has passed under the several names of Colom-

bine, of Flora, and of Vanity. This lovely gem was
in the successive possession of Marie de Medicis, the
Duke of Orleans, and the King of Holland; the
Emperor Nicholas secured it for the Hermitage at the
cost of 40,000 florins: an ancient copy, a little varied,
is in the possession of Sir Thomas Baring. No head
can be more exquisite in delicate pencilling, in careful
detail, and in refined sentiment. I often think how
great would be the privilege to make the acquaintance
of the ladies who appear in Luini's pictures. One of
the artist's most lovely types is ' St. Catharine' (72): the
picture has suffered, like many others in the collection,
by the too lavish use of varnish. Also equally lovely
is ' The Virgin with the Infant Christ' (71). This picture
has been in the ateliers of the Hermitage transferred
from panel to canvas, always a hazardous operation.
' St. Sebastian,' nude (73), is supposed to be an actual
portrait of Maximilian Sforza, Duke of Milan. The
modelling is careful, but weak, after the manner of
the master; such works are exceptional, save at Lugano
and the church of San Maurizio, Milan, where severally
may be seen the figure of St. Sebastian in fresco.
Leonardo and Luini are the only masters of Milan
worthily represented in the Hermitage.

One object I had in visiting St. Petersburg was to
see the pictures of Raphael in the Hermitage. Perhaps
I was a little disappointed with the work which had
most raised my expectations, ' La Vierge de la Maison
d'Albe' (38). I had known the first sketch for this
faultless composition in the Albertina Collection in
Vienna; also I had seen a study for the Madonna in
the Wicar Museum, Lille. There are likewise said to
be cartoons for the picture in the Lateran, and at
Liége. The work is also known by old copies in the

Dudley Collection and elsewhere. The chief cause of my disappointment was the somewhat damaged condition of the picture; the surface is understood to have been considerably repainted, an almost inevitable penalty when, as here, a picture has been transferred from panel to canvas: nevertheless the student at once feels himself to be in the presence of a signal masterwork. The Madonna belongs to the middle or transition period, when Raphael had quitted Florence for Rome in the year 1508, it therefore still retains the spirituality, gentleness, and tenderness which are chiefly prized in the master's first manner; and yet it gains the firmness and force of full maturity. The modelling of the Infant Christ has never been surpassed for roundness and softness, and the articulations are well pronounced. The group is arranged with a symmetry and compactness suited to the circular form of the canvas: the Madonna seated in the centre, the children playing around, with a truly Raphaelesque landscape beyond, make a composition as musical in its lines as it is placid and blissful in its sentiment. The pedigree of the picture is somewhat singular. The Duchesse d'Albe, celebrated for her beauty and intrigues, gave this masterpiece, which graced the hereditary gallery, as a fee to the family physician who had cured her in a dangerous illness. This doctor, afterwards accused of poisoning the duchess, but acquitted on the trial, sold the picture to the Danish Count Bourke, who resold it to M. Coesvelt, from whom it was purchased for the Hermitage in 1836, for the sum of £14,000.

'The Holy Family,' with St. Joseph old and beardless (37), supposed to be two years earlier than the last-named work, is also disappointing by reason of the cruel treatment it has suffered; indeed, at first sight, I gave

but slight credence to the picture.   Here again the
barbarous process has been resorted to of taking the
surface of the picture from panel and then affixing
it to canvas — a measure like to the most perilous
operations in surgery, only to be justified as a last
resource when life cannot otherwise be saved.   The
authorities in the Hermitage, as at a former period
the experts in the Louvre, seem to have had a fatal
facility in such murderous manipulation ; of four
Raphaels three have been thus flayed alive.   But this
'Holy Family' had even previously undergone severe
trial, for we read in the work on the Crozat Gallery
how it was bought from the collection of the Duke of
Angoulême at a very moderate price, because no one
could any longer recognise the hand of Raphael, some
stupid restorer having repainted nearly the whole
picture.   Subsequently a more skilful artist succeeded
in removing the new paint ; in more recent days the
picture was again, as we have seen, subjected to severe
trial.   All this I narrate as an illustration of the common
fate of pictures in the Hermitage and other galleries
where the custom is so to repaint and polish, that
wrecks are restored to juvenescence.   Sometimes indeed
scarcely a square inch of the surface which the painter
had looked upon in his lifetime is left intact.   The
vicissitudes of the most famous pictures in Europe
have been wellnigh as tragic as the fate of families and
of empires.   A pretty romance might be penned on the
theme here suggested.

The little 'St. George' (39), by Raphael, is one among
the many instances of the interesting relationship
subsisting between our English collections and the
Hermitage.   This picture of the patron saint of England
galloping on a white horse, his lance piercing the dragon,

was commissioned by the Duke Guido Ubaldo of Urbino as a present to Henry VII of England. The Duke having been made a Chevalier of the Order of St. George, sent as an acknowledgment the picture to the king. On the left leg of St. George is the Order of the Garter with the word 'Honi,' as the commencement of the well-known motto. That the work was subsequently in the collection of Charles I is proved by the mark it bears. When that collection was sold by Cromwell this now priceless gem fetched only £150 sterling. The picture reached St. Petersburg on the acquisition of the Crozat Gallery. The subject was repeated by Raphael with variations, and copies, as well as one or more sketches for the composition, are in existence; a beautiful pen-drawing is in the Florence collection. The picture was painted at Urbino about the year 1506, Raphael being then twenty-three years of age; his father and mother were dead; he had entered the school of Perugino, had made his first visit to Florence, and then returned for a brief space to his native city in the Umbrian hills, apparently because his good parents had 'left his affairs in much confusion.' These few biographical details give a clue to the carefully wrought 'St. George.' The work belongs to what, with some appearance of paradox, may be termed the pre-Raphaelite period of Raphael; in other words it is almost identical with the works of his master. Indeed, Vasari expressly states that at this time Raphael imitated with such exactitude the manner of Perugino that the difference between the work of the master and of his pupil could not be discerned with any certainty. The 'St. George' must have been painted at Urbino just about the same time as 'The Agony in the Garden,' in the collection of Mr. Fuller

Maitland, exhibited this year among the Old Masters
in Burlington House. Both pictures are alike important,
because they represent Raphael before his great change ;
in fact they stand at the antipodes to the latest of all
representative works, ' The Transfiguration.'   Thus this
' St. George' in the Hermitage retains the simplicity, the
earnestness, and the devotion which characterise the
spiritual school of Umbria.   The Hermitage has an
advantage over most of the great galleries of Europe
in the possession of this exceptional work.

Raphael is further represented by contemporary copies
and some doubtful originals.   Among the latter I
incline to place ' A Portrait of an Old Man' in a black
dress with a black barretto and a white collar (40).
The work has been approved by those wholesale white-
washers of pictorial reputations, M. Passavant and Dr.
Waagen ; but the execution is certainly blundering and
slovenly, the handling is not expressive of form.   Yet it
is possible that these too obvious defects may be but
the dire results of that transfer from panel to canvas
against which I have ventured to inveigh.   Certain
frescoes attributed to Raphael must be held still more
dubious, though they are of value as characteristic works
of scholars, Giulio Romano and others, who preserved
as well as they could the sacred traditions of the master.
These nine compositions, arranged tastefully in one room,
treat chiefly of Venus, Cupid, and Adonis.   They remained
in the well-known Villa Mills on the Palatine Hill
until the year 1856, when they were detached from the
walls by the expert Succi for the Marquis Campana,
who bought them of the nuns to whom the villa had
passed   The Hermitage acquired these frescoes as part
of the Campana collection.   They have been engraved
by Marc Antonio and others ; thus they descend to our

times somewhat well accredited. 'The Rape of Helen'
is a famous design for which there are sketches in
Oxford and at Chatsworth, and Majolica plates in
various collections are painted from the same composition. This fresco, doubtless the work of a pupil, came
from the so-called Raphael's Villa, near the Porta
Pinciana, which was destroyed in 1848 during the siege
of Rome. My notes assert stoutly that not one of
these frescoes could possibly have been executed by the
hand of Raphael. I mark as the best 'Venus and
Cupid' (50), which obtains, I find, exceptional favour
from Dr. Waagen, as the possible work of Penni, the
pupil and friend of Raphael. But whoever may be
responsible for these pictures, I cannot doubt that the
Russian government acted most wisely in securing for
their northern capital these fairly good specimens of an
art which essentially pertains to the southern nations
of Europe. It is well known that Russian authorities
pronounced against fresco as unsuited to the climate of
St. Petersburg. These works serve in the Hermitage
as a witness to a truth for which I have always con-
tended, that in the express age and within the geographic
area of fresco, no process was more ready or rapid,
more easily practised by master and by pupil, or more
widely diffused, whether in the rich and intellectual city,
or in the poor and untutored hamlet. The Hermitage
is to be envied for these possessions.

The Hermitage, like other galleries, has surrendered
some great names under prevailing historic doubts, and
in accordance with the growing tendency to question
hearsay and to revert to documentary evidence. Dr.
Waagen, it is understood, lent his assistance in the re-
christening of pictures wrongly named. Two works have
been transferred from Da Vinci to Luini, and more

marvellous to relate, a ' Judith ' (112), which for long had
been attributed to Raphael, is now set down to Moretto
of Brescia.   The same figure when in the Crozat Gallery
was assigned to Giorgione ; such transfer of paternity is
analogous to the changed fate of the so-called 'Fornarina'
in the Florence Tribune, a lady who, having been for
long ascribed to the pencil of Raphael, is now usually
assigned to a Venetian master. I know of few figures of
greater grace, beauty, or gentleness, than this 'Judith':
Moretto is rare save in Brescia his native city.   In the
Dresden Gallery a lovely holy family in the clouds, and
a like composition in the National Gallery, bear the
name of this truly great though circumscribed artist.
Moretto is known to have been an ardent admirer and
an earnest imitator of Raphael, hence it is less remarkable that the Judith should have borne Raphael's name,
nothing in fact being more common in the history of art
than the transfer of a work by a disciple to the chief
master of the school.   Only in the more critical days on
which we have now entered has it become possible to
draw with an approach to accuracy the boundary lines
which separate a master from his scholars, and one
scholar from another scholar.

From Brescia it is easy to pass to Venice, indeed
between the two cities there grew up art sympathies,
and Moretto, whom I have just mentioned, in early days
fell under the influence of Titian. The Hermitage, from
some cause not very apparent, is weak in the Venetian
school.   One reason is that out of thirteen pictures
assigned to Titian, six are doubtful, at least to my eye.
' The Magdalen,' too (98), from the Barbarigo Collection,
is inferior to the famous figure in the Pitti, also ' The
Head of Lavinia ' (104), the painter's lovely daughter, is
not to be compared with other well-known versions of

the same lady. But for these deficiencies some amends
are made by three works which would not dishonour
Titian in Venice, Madrid, Dresden, or London. Commencing with the earliest, 'The Madonna and Child' (93)
probably belongs to the period when Titian was still
under the influence of his master Giovanni Bellini, or
the work may possibly pertain to the somewhat later
time, when Titian had adopted, as in an exquisite
example in the Belvedere, the style of Palma Vecchio.
Such early and exceptional products have a value
analogous to the works of Raphael before his advanced
manner. 'The Toilette of Venus' (99), another never-to-
be-forgotten Titian, though darkened, retains glory of
colour : the flesh painting is superb ; the head and the
torso are evidently taken from some magnificent creature
of the Venetian type. This celebrated composition is
known by many repetitions ; the original sketch is in
Dresden. Another oft-repeated subject is 'Danaë' (100).
Here the quality of the flesh painting is not equal to the
matchless Venus in the Florentine Tribune ; and yet the
figure relieves warmly and roundly from the cool drapery,
colour becomes triumphant in the sky, the robes, and
accessories. Of three examples of Palma Vecchio, 'The
Holy Family' (92) is the best : the female heads and the
two infants are distinguished by the specific beauty
peculiar to this beauty-loving artist. Of sixteen works
ascribed to Paul Veronese, two only are worth remember-
ing; one a small sketch, 'The Adoration of the Magi' (139),
the other, 'A Descent from the Cross' (145), which
reminds me of the signal composition by Mantegna in
Berlin. Accordingly the expression has unusual depth
and solemnity; the grey shadow thrown on the dead
body is grand. Not very remarkable are the examples
of Bonifacio, Bordone, Lotto, and Pordenone. By

Bernadino da Pordinone, however, is an 'Adoration of
the Magi' (119), a work from the Crozat Gallery, exceptional for the number of figures.   I must mention too,
'Jupiter and Io' (121), also from the Crozat Gallery,
as the best picture by Schiavone I can recall; the
fine landscape background is attributed by Dr. Waagen
to Domenico Campagnola ; the nude figures unite the
manner of Correggio and of Titian.

But the masters of Venice who merit in the Hermitage
most attention are Tintoret and Piombo.   By the former
is 'The Resurrection of the Saints' (133), a mere sketch
for the tremendous composition known in Venice as
'Il Paradiso,' yet displaying vast facility, extempore
power, command of colour and readiness in expressing
intention.   Genius here asserts itself incontestably.
'The Nativity of John the Baptist' (132), from the Crozat
Gallery, is hung high, and seems to have suffered, but
the composition is in Tintoret's most romantic and
brilliant style ; the conception of beauty is high and
truly Venetian, the colour of the flesh and of the
drapery can only be reached by the school which
reflected the radiant gold and blue of the Lagoons.
Again, for care and delicacy in the nude, for beauty in
form, and harmony in the play of line, nothing, even in
the Ducal Palace, Venice, can surpass 'The Deliverance
of Andromeda' (135).   In the presence of such glorious
achievements I could scarcely charge with extravagance
the eulogy passed by Mr. Ruskin on Tintoret.   But
perhaps the work which of all others in the Hermitage
took me most by surprise is 'The Descent from the
Cross' (18), by Sebastiano del Piombo.   The picture,
which is in good condition, was acquired at the sale
of the gallery of the King of Holland for 29,600 florins.
I will simply transcribe my notes : this, next to 'The

Raising of Lazarus' in our National Gallery, is the most important composition I know by Piombo. The forms are of the grand school of Michael Angelo, while the colour is Venetian, though more than usually solemn in tone. Thus the work fulfils the aspiration and accomplishes the purpose of the painter, who, born in Venice and dying in Rome, strove like his contemporary Tintoret to reconcile the colouring of Titian with the mighty forms of Michael Angelo. The landscape background which rises more than three-fourths up the canvas is truly Titianesque: as for the action it reaches tragic grandeur. Such a work is almost more than a picture, it moves the soul as music of the passions, it carries imagination to the before and after, and thus like an inspired narrative shadows forth the infinite. Pictures of this solemn character fulfil all the conditions of religious art.

The Florentine school is poorly represented. Fra Bartolommeo and Albertinelli make an insignificant appearance: Andrea del Sarto is seen by nothing better than an injured replica (24), with variations, of 'The Holy Family' in the National Gallery. But while thus recording my hostile verdict, I am bound in fairness to state that Dr. Waagen pronounces the picture in the Hermitage the original, and designates the work in the National Gallery as only a good school copy. The three pictures assigned to Ridolfo Ghirlandaio are doubtful. The best example of Florentine art at the end of the fifteenth or the beginning of the sixteenth century, is a 'Nativity' (22), which formerly went under the name of Perugino, and now in the catalogue is set down to that rare painter Francesco Granacci, notwithstanding that M. Cavalcaselle has attributed the work to Ridolfo Ghirlandaio. This is but one of the many examples of

the caprice rather than the knowledge under which
pictures have been named in the Hermitage and other
European galleries.   But the work itself is in spirit and
in technical merit worthy of the best period in Christian
art.   By Cardi da Cigoli, who lived into the seventeenth
century, there are some fairly good examples; also
Bronzino has some capital portraits; to Carlo Dolci and
to Sassoferrato are ascribed five pictures apiece : of this
total of ten, two are fairly good.

The Hermitage has three pictures by Correggio : 'La
Madonne del Latte' (81), nowhere surpassed, bears resemblance to 'La Vierge au Panier' in the National
Gallery.   The figures are liquid as gems, ripe as rich
fruit ; indeed, to borrow a saying sometimes applied to
Murillo, the colours might almost have been mixed with
milk and honey.   'The Assumption of the Virgin' (82)
appears as a hasty, careless, and by no means student-
like sketch for the fresco in Parma known as ' The Hash
of Frogs.'   'Apollo and Marsyas,' in four scenes (82ª),
adds another to the many works in the Hermitage
which have been transferred from panel to canvas.
One more picture so served out is a small but choice
specimen of Parmigianino, 'The Entombment' (86).   The
painter, in tribute to the merit of this work, was
created a Chevalier by the Duke of Parma.   The
composition, for which sketches exist, has been several
times engraved.

The Bolognese school of the Carracci and their
followers is strong in more than fifty examples, some of
which have seldom been surpassed by these eclectic
masters.   Ludovico Carracci, the father of the movement and the idol of Sir Joshua Reynolds, is present
in a grand though showy effort, ' Christ bearing the
Cross' (165).   Next comes the pupil Annibale, numer-

ously but not well represented ; a small 'Holy Family' (170) is highly finished, 'The Descent from the Cross' (172) is not quite the best of its kind. Il Domenichino is specially conventional, meretricious, showy and audacious in 'The Madonna carried to Heaven' (179). Guido is largely and well represented. The most famous of twelve samples of the master is 'The Dispute of the Fathers of the Church over the Immaculate Conception' (187). The work, while in the Walpole Collection, furnished our English engraver, William Sharp, with the subject for his well-known masterpiece. The picture on its way to England encountered a not unusual difficulty, it was stopped at Civita Vecchia, and all the influence of its purchaser, Lord Walpole, was needed to induce the Pope to take off the embargo. The original struck me as scarcely justifying its great reputation ; but Guido seldom satisfies critics or the public in these days of reaction from late to early masters. 'The Adoration of the Shepherds' (182), 'The Adoration of St. Francis' (185), 'The Seamstresses,' known also as 'The Youth of the Virgin' (191), and 'The Rape of Europa' (189), are all more or less fine examples of a master who, notwithstanding his conventionality, commends himself by ideal form and a silvery moonlight sentiment. Neither in this enumeration can I omit to name Albani, who takes us far into the seventeenth century. 'The Baptism of Christ' (203) is the nearest approach to the standard of high art permitted to this prettily frivolous painter. Among the masters too, who can be best judged in the Hermitage, is the coarse and meretricious but always powerful Guercino. 'God the Father' (237) is one of those impertinent and audacious attempts for which this master made himself notorious. This little short of blasphemous

picture reminds me of a head, 'Il Padre Eterno,' by the
same artist in Bologna, which it is said was painted over
night and hung up finished in early morning.   It is no
wonder that by the middle of the seventeenth century
sacred art became secularised.   'The Assumption of the
Virgin' (239) has by some been pronounced the master-
work of Guercino.   Also for showy effect and imposing
impetuosity hold conspicuous positions 'St. Jerome' (241)
and 'The Martyrdom of St. Catharine' (240).

As we approach and enter the period of decadence,
masterworks further multiply within the Hermitage.
In fact St. Petersburg, having no inheritance from the
remote past, as Florence, Sienna and Rome, or as Cologne,
Ghent, Bruges, and Nuremberg, reflects merely the prevailing fashions at the time when it pleased Catherine II
and the Emperors who followed to annex the arts as
decorative appurtenances to a vast empire and a utilitarian civilisation.   The tastes of the times, as well as the
ambition and the ostentation of governors, almost of
necessity tended to periods when art became florid,
corrupt, or grossly naturalistic.   Hence in these handsome and spacious galleries Pietro da Cortona, Carlo
Maratta, Luca Giordano, and others of the sort, take
their full fling.   By Pietro da Cortona, the painter of the
never-to-be-forgotten 'Saul struck Blind' in the church
of the Capuchins, Rome, are seven works which, though
good in their way, do not materially improve the artist's
position.   The best, 'The Martyrdom of St. Stephen'
(281), is scarcely above second rank.   No fewer than
twelve pictures attest the eclectic commonplace of that
effete Christian artist Carlo Maratta ; not a single one
of these compositions is anti-Christian, which is saying
much for a painter who worked under the resuscitated
paganism which had set in a century and a half
ago.   The pictures I have noted as the best are 'The

Holy Family' (299), tender and refined, 'The Virgin with the Infants Jesus and St. John' (302), a picture which agreeably recalls the manner of Guido, and 'The Repose in Egypt' (305), which is pretty and little more. But by far the best product of this painter's studio is the portrait of Pope Clement IX, Giulio Rospigliosi (307). Evidently the artist was greatly indebted to Raphael and Titian, hence naturally for once he surpassed himself. Again, Luca Giordano, a painter who brought upon himself contempt by hasty and reckless methods which won him the title of 'Fa presto,' proves himself the Rubens of Italy in 'The Judgment of Paris' (294); the forms are better, the colours worse than Rubens. Dr. Waagen cites a finer example of this work at Berlin. Worthy of more consideration is 'The Entombment' (291): parts are no doubt vulgar, such painters are bound to be common; yet coarseness is not unredeemed by force, and for once at least the artist, having submitted to rule and precedent, gains unity, even dignity; indeed the figure of Christ is little short of grand. I know of no work so well calculated to restore respect for this rash painter, who habitually rushes in where angels fear to tread.

Il Caravaggio, one of the most savage and brutal of men who ever wielded a brush, appears quite in his element in 'The Martyrdom of St. Peter' (216). This is perhaps the most terrific achievement of the basely naturalistic school. Dr. Waagen conjectures that this horrible composition inspired Rubens when he painted St. Peter crucified head downwards, a composition still to be seen in the church of St. Peter, Cologne. I remember to have met the spiritual painter, Overbeck, in front of this carnal work. The respectful, not to say the reverent way, in which Overbeck, the purest of purists stood before this rampant Rubens, seemed to

me a lesson of toleration and Christian love. Caravaggio
in the Hermitage has made the crucified St. Peter
jolly as a drunken Silenus. It is just possible that the
placidity of the saintly Overbeck would not have been
ruffled even in the presence of this gross impropriety.
It needs very much art—greatly more than survived
in this comparatively late period—to excuse a spirit
thus in open revolt against the true, the beautiful, and
the good. I believe that, if I could have my way, no
plea in favour of the manifestation of historic developments would hinder me from exorcising such works from
national museums, wherein the governing motive should
be the elevation and purification of the public taste.
Art can never be a teacher when she teaches the false.

Crespi, another painter of the decadence, depicts the
'Death of St. Joseph' (314) with repulsive realism. The
subject, as might be expected, is conceived coarsely,
yet with the power and originality seldom denied to
a time of lawlessness and rude nature. The Procaccini,
names now held perhaps in even too much contempt,
are here less than usually open to condemnation, especially in such compositions as 'The Holy Family' (262),
and 'The Marriage of St. Catharine' (264). Tiepolo,
born in Venice, and who died in Madrid scarcely more
than a century ago, brings this audacious art down
almost to our own times. 'The Feast of Cleopatra'
(317) a cap'opera, is clever and impudent, showy and
unscrupulous as the brilliant frescoes of the painter
in Venetian palaces. Canaletto, the contemporary of
Tiepolo, is seen in a magnificent composition, 'The
Reception of Count Gergi at Venice' (318). Here the
lineal and aerial perspective are truly marvellous ; for
once is merged the painter's matter-of-fact mechanism.
The pictorial management evinces more mental grasp

and art subtlety than the painter has credit for. Here again is a masterwork, though from a second-rate artist, which may serve to repay a visit to St. Petersburg. Salvator Rosa, painter, engraver, poet, &c., is yet another artist of the decadence, remarkably well represented in the Hermitage. Of eleven examples two are master-pieces. 'The Prodigal Son' (220), thrown on his knees imploring the divine forgiveness, from the Walpole Collection, is very striking in conception; the utter abandonment of the prodigal is most impressive. Salvator Rosa here shows himself a tragedian on canvas. Also from the Walpole Gallery comes another grand conception, 'Democrites and Protagoras' (222). The figures compose effectively with the trees and sky, a characteristic of Salvator in common with Titian.

The Spanish school, as I have before said, has no rival collection out of Spain : with the exception indeed of Madrid, there is no gallery equal to that of the Hermitage. The hundred and more works comprise all the four schools of Toledo, Seville, Valencia, and Madrid. There are nineteen pictures bearing the name of Murillo, and six of Velasquez. The galleries of Europe, in the strength of the Spanish school, are in the following order :—first Madrid, then follow St. Petersburg, Paris, London, Berlin, Dresden, Florence, Vienna. Sir Stirling Maxwell, after describing the 'Galerie Espagnole' of the King of the French writes as follows—

'Next in extent, and perhaps superior in importance to the Spanish collection of the King of the French, is that of the Emperor of Russia. To St. Petersburg and the vast Hermitage of the Czar fate has transferred 110 paintings of the Spanish schools, which once adorned the palace of Don Manuel Godoy, Prince of the Peace, on the Prado of Madrid. The gifts lavished on the minion of the Queen of Spain are appropriately lodged in the sumptuous halls where Catherine wooed her Orloffs and Potemkins. There, beneath gilded cornices and amongst columns of Siberian porphyry and vases of malachite, hang many fine and original works of Juanes, Tristan, Cespedes, Mayno, Velasquez, and Murillo—placed without method and catalogued with little accuracy.' *

The collection, though as a whole choice, comprises the usual sprinkling of spurious works. Thus the school of Andalusia commences with a 'Virgin and Child' (345), which Dr. Waagen assigns to the Netherlands, and the next work in the catalogue, 'The Martyrdom of St. Stephen' (346), which used to pass for Cespedes, 'the Spanish Raphael,' is now deemed doubtful; the German critic, however, lets it pass. To the honoured Roelas, the master of the still greater Zurbaran, is ascribed 'The Communion of St. Theresa' (347), though unlike the master's known works. To Zurbaran himself belong two pictures, the first of which, 'The Prayer of the Madonna' (348), comes, like many others in this de-partment, from the Coesvelt Collection. The figure is as charming for its simplicity as for its truth, and the handling is strong as it is tender. The Madonna is repre-sented as a young girl, clad in red and blue, seated on a chair; she has for a moment left the needlework on which she was engaged, and clasps her hands in prayer. The scene is all the more impressive because it has the persuasive power of nature; the artist, as we know, de-termined, in common with his contemporary Velasquez, never to paint without 'the life' before him. From the gallery of Marshal Soult came, at the cost of 3000 francs, 'St. Laurence' (394), robed in richest sacerdotal habits, his eyes cast towards heaven in contemplation of his martyrdom. Here Zurbaran scarcely escapes vulgarity, though in extenuation it may be pleaded that

---

* This was published in 1848 : the first edition of the present catalogue of the Hermitage appeared in 1863, and the second and corrected edition in 1869 ; therefore the above charge does not apply to the catalogue now in use.

the picture is meant to be seen a long way off. Waagen holds the figure as ' evidently a portrait.' Another famous, but, as far as I have observed, a rare painter even in Spain, Alonso Cano, is supposed to be present in no less than five works, none of which are mentioned by Sir Stirling Maxwell. That Alonso Cano has not left behind him a greater number of paintings, is better understood when the traveller in Spain finds how much of the artist's life was devoted to sculpture and architecture. Finest in quality of the five examples, also lovely and pure in sentiment, is ' The Virgin and Child ' (352). The composition, if I remember rightly, corresponds with ' Our Lady of Bethlehem,' in the cathedral of Seville, a work which for ' serene celestial beauty ' I always wish to associate with Alonso Cano. A large composition of five figures, once in the gallery of Charles IV of Spain, 'Apparition de Saintes à un Dominicain' (354), is comparatively of inferior quality. Cano was good in portraits : two, by no means bad, are in the Hermitage ; one of these is a likeness of the artist by himself (355). The picture differs from the head engraved in Sir Stirling Maxwell's ' Annals.'

Murillo, in the school of Andalusia, follows next with twenty reputed pictures. It is the fashion—to which, however, I have never conformed—to fall into ecstasies over every canvas which bears the name of Murillo. Of the twenty works in the Hermitage, about one half deserve to be remembered. This cutting down is but in accordance with a passage in ' the Annals,' wherein it is stated that Tobár and others ' produced amongst them more than one half of the works which pass current in Europe under the name of Murillo, whether in the galleries of royal collectors, like the Emperor of Russia, who grudge no price, or in the show-rooms of experienced dealers, like Marshal Soult, who have spared no pains to possess themselves of the most authentic specimens.' Yet Sir Stirling Maxwell thinks it worth while to mention thirteen of the works by Murillo in the Hermitage. I fear that the limited space at my command will compel me to make short work of the collection. I will commence with one of the most admirable examples of Murillo in the whole world, 'The Repose in Egypt' (369), from the Walpole Gallery. The Madonna seated, attended by angels, looks tenderly at the sleeping infant. St. Joseph, as usual, a little in the background, holds the ass by the bridle. The treatment is naturalistic and genre-like. The light has been finely thrown upon the child asleep, and rich deep browns and reds, relieved by blues and whites, bring the composition into agreeable harmony. I should suppose the work to belong to the painter's middle manner, for though the figures are seen in a vaporous haze, the forms are still firm. 'The Assumption of the Virgin' (371), from the Houghton Collection, is another exquisite gem ; though smaller, it is not inferior to 'The Assumption' from the Soult Collection in the Louvre. The cherubim are in the painter's happiest manner. The picture seems well preserved. 'The Vision of St. Anthony' (373), another charming composition, was purchased from the Soult Collection for 30,000 francs. The saint is on his knees ; above are angels, one bearing a lily ; a hilly landscape forms the distance : the story is well told ; the workmanship is good though sketchy : in fact this study is the first idea for the great altar-picture in the Cathedral of Seville. 'The Delivery of St. Peter from Prison' (372), is poorly painted, and scarcely worthy of its supposed antecedents, as one of the eleven works executed about 1674 to adorn the hospital of La Caridad in Seville. 'The Delivery of

St. Peter' is known to have hung for many years as a
campanion to Murillo's greatest composition, 'Moses
striking the Rock.' The famed hospital was robbed by
Soult, who sold 'Abraham receiving the Angels,' and
'The Return of the Prodigal Son,' to the Duke of
Sutherland; 'The Release of Peter,' which remained
'unsold on the hands of the plunderer,' was ultimately
acquired by the Hermitage at the cost of 151,000 francs.
'The Death of the Inquisitor Pedro Arbuez' (374),
formerly in the baptistery of Seville Cathedral, may be
accepted as an early work, though Dr. Waagen esteems
it doubtful: the manner is vigorous and dark. 'The
Adoration of the Shepherds' (363), from the Walpole
Collection, is similar in character. The remaining fourteen works display either that inequality which belongs to
Murillo himself, or that inferiority which specially stigma-
tises his imitators and followers. Very lovely are the
crowds of cherubim in 'The Annunciation' (361); also
eminently picturesque is 'Jacob's Ladder' (359), the
ladder, the clouds, and the angels, are well managed,
though the task is obviously arduous. 'The Benediction
of Jacob' (360) descends into mere genre; the accessory
landscape is what might be looked for from Teniers.
'A Young Peasant' (377) and 'A Young Peasantess'
(378) show Murillo in his naturalistic moods. In short,
no one of Murillo's successive manners is here wanting;
the painter passes from sacred to secular, from high
to low, with pleasing facility. The minor masters of
Andalusia are also present, such as Gomez, the Mulatto
servant and pupil of Murillo, Nuñez de Villavicencio,
another pupil of Murillo, Francisco Herrera, the son and
pupil of his father, Francisco Herrera the elder, Iriarte,
the pupil of Herrera the younger, Bocanegra the pupil
of Alonso Cano, and Tobár the imitator of Murillo. I

mention these painters chiefly to point to a distinctive
characteristic of this collection : other museums are
content with a few great names, such as Murillo, Velasquez and Zurbaran, but here in the Hermitage are
artists not often heard of beyond the Spanish frontier,
and thus the history of the school of the Peninsula is
given with unusual detail and fulness.   This complete-
ness is greatly due to the acquisition by the Emperor
Alexander of the Coesvelt Collection, which furnishes
fifty pictures to the Spanish Gallery.   M. Coesvelt had
profited by the Peninsular war : he was a banker, but not
being a soldier he purchased the pictures fairly by his
funds ; he did not, like Soult, acquire them foully by the
force of the sword.   From the Coesvelt Collection comes
' The Adoration of the Shepherds' (391), by Valdes Leal,
the ' Fa presto ' of Spain, who lived to be ' the last of
the better artists of Andalusia.'   Valdes Leal was too im-
patient of labour, too impetuous and opinionated to carry
out his ready conceptions with conscientious care.   Thus
Spanish art fell like Italian art, after the manner of the
rebel angels.   There came a time when Spanish and
Italian painters sought to take heaven by storm, but
they suffered overthrow, and with them perished the
Christian arts.

The school of Valencia is represented by three great
masters, Juan de Juanes, Ribera, and Ribalta.   ' St.
Anne' (328) is assigned to the spiritual-minded Juanes,
one of the few Spanish painters who, believing art to be
an inspiration from above, began a sacred work with
prayer and fasting.   This devout artist found his reward :
his pictures reflect the religious life.   The fine works
ascribed to the two Ribaltas, father and son, seem to
me, as usual, rather dubious.   But Ribera, surnamed
' lo Spagnoleto,' the pupil of Ribalta the elder, is present

with a power even unaccustomed to this most sledge-hammer of painters. 'The Martyrdom of Sebastian' (331), once in the collection of the mother of Napoleon III, is a subject much to the liking of this imitator of the savage and brutal Caravaggio. The theme is in replica, with variations, as is also another congenial composition, 'St. Jerome in the desert' (332–333). Little more than half a century intervened between Juanes and Ribalta; seldom even in the fitful and feverish history of the arts can be found within so short a period so dire an overthrow.

The third school of Spain, that of Castille, begins like the school of Valencia with a devout religious painter. In periods of decadence I have pointed out the analogy between Spain and Italy; in like manner, in the early rise of art, the two nations run in parallel lines. Religion in fact lies at the root of all early art. Thus in the Hermitage the school of Castille fitly opens with Morales' 'El Divino. 'But, unfortunately, doubt attaches to the authenticity of 'The Virgin and Child' (400). Upon no artist have been affiliated so many illegitimate off-spring; indeed it has been said that 'every head of our Saviour which came from Spain, and could not be called a Murillo, has been attributed without scruple to Morales.' Dr. Waagen, however, considers this 'Virgin and Child' most characteristic of Morales; he cites a small and paler replica in the Berlin Gallery (412). 'La Mater Dolorosa' (401), from the Coesvelt collection, may have greater claim to be genuine. The subjects of Morales are always devotional, likewise usually dark; devotion and darkness being inseparable from the Spanish school. In Italy pictorial art sprang out of darkness into light, just as the constructive art of architecture became from cavernous gloom a creature of the elements, a companion

of the sky. But Spanish art remained sombre to the
last ; and the key-note struck by Morales in ' La Mater
Dolorosa ' finds its echo even to the present day. In the
school of Castille are present sixteen artists, mostly
minor, whose names I must content myself simply to
record as follows :—Alonso Sanchez Coello, Claudio
Coello, Escalante, Becerra, Navaretta, Villoldo, Barroso,
Prado, Orrente, Tristan, Mayno, Collantes, Carducho,
Camillo Carreño de Miranda, Puga, Menendez. These
sixteen artists make themselves known in the Hermitage by twenty works—another proof of the zeal or the
good luck of Russian monarchs in their dealings with the
collectors of Spanish pictures. It were a dreary task to
treat of any but the salient products of the school. Yet
' El Mudo,' the Mute, I should be sorry to leave out,
though his only reputed work is ' St. John the Baptist in
Prison ' (404). This dumb artist travelled in Italy, and
worked in the house of Titian—a clue to his style : he
had genius, if only to overcome the difficulties which
nature threw in his path. Also, the Hermitage is
fortunate to enlist ' El Greco,' though he presents himself by one portrait only, that of the poet ' Alonso Ercilla
y Zuniga' (411). This artist, Greek by parentage, stands
as a characteristic example of the strange mixture of
races and styles found in the Peninsula. After dalliance
among minor artists, it is at last no small satisfaction to
arrive at Velasquez, in whose presence no debate can be
held as to supremacy. In the Hermitage Velasquez
happens to occupy a post second to Murillo. And yet,
as little short of a miracle in art, asserts itself a study
(418) for that portrait in the Doria Palace, Rome, well-
nigh the greatest in the world, the head of ' Innocent X.'
No painter but Velasquez could approach this work for
mastery. ' Philipp IV of Spain ' (419–420) is here re-

peated almost as a matter of course. 'A Young Peasant' (423), from the Coesvelt Collection, though clever enough, is certainly not of necessity by Velasquez. The Hermitage naturally stretches a point whenever possible : what is spurious in the Spanish collection is almost as a matter of course covered by great names; yet, after making every allowance, the Spanish Gallery in the Hermitage remains supremely strong in the works of Murillo and Zurbaran.

CHAPTER IV.

ST. PETERSBURG: THE PICTURE GALLERIES IN THE HERMITAGE (*continued*).

In the last chapter having described the leading works in the Italian and Spanish schools, we will now turn to the Galleries occupied by Flemish and Dutch masters. In the earlier period, from the fifteenth to the sixteenth century, the Hermitage is in the Netherlands inferior to other Galleries : a like deficiency has been already found in the early epochs of Italian art. And yet even in this era St. Petersburg is on an equality with London and Madrid, though inferior to Paris, Dresden, Vienna, Munich, and Berlin. But when we come to the seventeenth and the eighteenth centuries the Hermitage appears on a par with the three richest Galleries in the world, viz. Paris, Dresden, and Munich. Indeed in certain masters the picture palace on the banks of the Neva surpasses all other collections ; nowhere have I seen finer examples of Rembrandt, Potter, Berchem, Ruysdael, and Jan Steen ; indeed taken altogether I incline to think that the strength of the Hermitage lies in the Flemish and Dutch schools. I shall never forget my surprise and delight as I walked from room to room and counted up 60 pictures by Rubens, 34 by Vandyck, 24 by Snyders, 40 by Teniers, 50 by Wouvermans, 12 by Gerard

Dow, &c. In fact there is scarcely a master of note who is not worthily and indeed magnificently represented, while painters comparatively but little known also find a place. Indeed it is stated that there are ten artists who cannot be seen elsewhere, and this I can well believe, as their names do not appear in catalogues or ordinary books of reference. In addition to such rare masters and exceptional works there are pictures of value in the history of German and other schools which bear no names at all, but appear only with monograms or initials. These varied treasures have been gathered from the Walpole Gallery, the Crozat Gallery, the Malmaison Collection, the Gallery of the King of Holland, &c. Like other divisions of the Hermitage, the schools of Germany, Flanders, and Holland have been brought together by the Empress Catherine II, and by the Emperors Paul I, Alexander I, Nicholas I, and Alexander II. The total number of works in this division is no less than 948.

The ancient masters of Germany, Flanders, and Holland, dating from 1420 to 1520, are not particularly strong. There is no picture by Albert Durer, and the two portraits assigned to Holbein are doubtful. Beginning with Jan van Eyck, very perfect of its kind is the picture of 'The Salutation' (443). The scene is laid in a marble hall with a mosaic floor; the archangel Gabriel appears richly clad; the jewelled drapery as a piece of painting has scarely been equalled, and never surpassed. Of good quality too is 'St. Luke' (445), assigned to Memling. Both these pictures, which come from the collection of the King of Holland, have, I am sorry to say, undergone, since their arrival at the Hermitage, the perilous operation of transfer from panel to canvas.

Dr. Waagen adds some interesting data relative to the last picture which I may quote with advantage :—

'This (445) is a contemporary copy of a picture in the Munich Pina-kothek by Roger van der Weyden, which contains, opposite the St. Luke, a Mary enthroned with the Child. Although the colour of this beautiful copy is more tender than the broken tones of the original, it lacks the same depth. Doubtless a Madonna and Child belonged to it formerly; apparently this portion must have been separated from the picture on the sacking of the convents in Spain, where it remained up to the year 1813. The original in Munich must have been a great favourite in its own day, as another, also a contemporary, copy exists, which in the year 1860 was in the possession of the sculptor Hans Gasser in Vienna.'

By Quentin Matsys, the Blacksmith of Antwerp, is a large and important work, also from the King of Holland's collection, 'La Vierge Triomphante' (449). I am sorry to report that in the ateliers of the Hermitage this picture has been flayed alive: I would rather see a ruined panel than a span new canvas: in imperial galleries there is often a fatal passion for making everything look smart. Fortunately Matsys is vigorous enough to stand a good deal of bad usage; hence, notwithstanding picture cleaners, the heads remain strong in drawing and in character, and solid realism still marks the jewels and the draperies. The composition is one of the fullest by Matsys with which I am acquainted; it comprises, besides the Madonna and the infant Christ, God the Father, two prophets, two Sibyls, King David, and the emperor Augustus. This picture was found walled up in the Cathedral of St. Donation at Bruges, where doubtless it had been immured to preserve it from the iconoclasts of the sixteenth century. By Matsys the younger are two replicas of the oft-repeated 'Misers,' of which the best known version is in Windsor Castle. It is interesting to trace the fraternities which spring up

in the picture galleries of Europe; art is a universal
bond of union, and pictures have been so itinerant,
and painters so peripatetic, that the Hermitage holds
historic or personal relations with almost every great
or national collection. Gerhard David is present in
St. Petersburg by a work of rare art merit, finished as
a miniature, 'The Dead Christ in the Arms of the
Virgin' (458). I have not marked for merit any one
of the six pictures assigned to Lucas Cranach. 'The
Portrait of Erasmus' (465), ascribed to Holbein, is one
of the many uncertain repetitions scattered over Europe.
Dr. Waagen considers 'A Portrait' (466) to be a genuine
Holbein, and says it resembles in colour and architectural treatment of background the likeness of Johann
Herbster, in the Baring Collection, London. Mr.
Wornum does not record the existence of a single
work by Holbein throughout the extent of the Russian
empire, yet possibly for the best possible reason, that
he does not know Russia. The only remaining picture
it can be needful to mention is an amazing example
of that great but somewhat grotesque painter, Lucas
van Leyden. 'Christ Healing the Blind Man' (468)
has been named by Dr. Waagen as the artist's masterpiece. The treatment accords in spirit with Leyden's
etchings and engravings : character prevails over concord, dramatic story over symmetry, the lines are
singularly angular, the composition studiously irregular.
The spirit of Christianity seems foreign to this original
and eccentric painter, whose merit is that he speaks
out his thoughts plainly and forcibly, without affectation or any assumption of what he does not feel.
In this remarkable product of an artist but too seldom
seen, the numerous personages are dressed in the
costume of the period at which the picture was painted,

an anachronism that has an interest and value of its own.

The next division of this Teutonic school extends from 1520 to 1600, comprises 38 works, and includes painters who for the most part fell under Italian influence. The first master I have marked is Schoreel, who was the earliest painter to introduce the Italian style into Holland, his native country. Two portraits (478–479) are of rare merit; but it would be rash to assert that Schoreel is actually the painter, as few artists are more difficult to identify. Next follow two heads which ought never to have left England, the portraits of Sir Thomas Gresham (480) and of Lady Gresham (481) by Antonio More. The first, a noble work, Dr. Waagen ranks among More's masterpieces: another likeness of Sir Thomas was among National Portraits at Kensington in 1866. The reader will at once guess that the Hermitage possessed itself of these works when it acquired the Walpole collection. There seems nothing special to say of Orley, Coxie, Porbus, Heemskerk, Frans Floris, Goltzius, Jordaens, Elzheimer, and Rottenhammer. Of most of these painters I know better examples elsewhere. A word however must be afforded to Susterman, by whom I never remember to have seen a more satisfactory work than 'The Adoration of the Magi' (491). This artist accompanied Cardinal Pole to Italy, and fortified his tendings to Italian art in the school of Andrea del Sarto.

We need not be detained from at once reaching the 'Epoque Florissante' of the Flemish school (1600 to 1690). Foremost we encounter Rubens, who is here jocund and jubilant amid 60 of his most triumphant works, to which are assigned in the catalogue over five and twenty pages. A large number are from the Walpole Gallery, and some come from the Crozat Collection. I will deal with this astounding display of genius as briefly as practicable ; indeed the style of Rubens has become so familiar even to the least travelled of our people, that the reader's imagination will go far to fill up any blanks in a written description. Some of these works however claim attention as exceptional. In England, for example, we have a right to feel special interest in two sketches for the famous painted ceiling in the palace of Whitehall. A sketch for the same ceiling was exhibited at the Art Treasures, Manchester. Abounding in spirit and full of liquid colour is the composition (572), which, in the printed catalogue of the Hermitage, receives the following amusing description :—

'572. The glory of James I. The King of Great Britain, seated on the throne, extends the sceptre towards the young Prince Charles, who is supported by two women representing Scotland and Ireland, whilst Great Britain raises above his head the crowns of the three kingdoms. In the upper part of the composition are two genii with the King's armorial shield, and at the left the genius of peace burns the weapons of war.'

Another rampant sketch, by no means one of the best, comes from the collection of Gotfried Kneller, the portrait painter. Rubens composed nine sketches for Whitehall ; the date of the two in the Hermitage is 1630. The following description of the second may serve to relieve the tedium attendant on an epitome of the contents of a huge picture gallery ; such 'word-painting' tends to bring allegorical art into contempt.

'573. The apotheosis of James I. The King seated on a cloud, and clad in armour, with a mantle of purple, the sceptre in his right hand, his feet on a globe, is sustained in the air by an eagle that has thunderbolts in its claws, and conducts the monarch towards Olympus, where await him Pallas, Religion and Fame, surrounded by numerous Genii bearing the crown, the globe, palm branches, trumpets, &c.'

The world contains more large and elaborate pictures by Rubens than most people care to look at, but of small and rapid, brilliant and masterly sketches, we cannot have too many.   Of such the Hermitage boasts examples which prove a fertility of invention, a wealth of resource, a fire of imagination, a facility of hand, an affluence of colour, which show Rubens the greatest improvisatore with the brush that ever lived.   Yet these extempore effusions cost too little thought ; they rely on common-places, and abound in repetitions ; they may be compared to clap-trap harangues, composed to catch applause.   Six designs, arches of triumph (561 to 566), from the Walpole Collection, were composed by Rubens in 1635 for the solemn entry of the Cardinal-Infant Ferdinand into Antwerp.   The architecture is well put together ; Rubens evidently was most ready in construction—indeed he might have been an architect.   One of these hasty productions, ' Les Victoires du Cardinal-Infant ' (562), I have annotated thus :—' this slight sketch gives more pleasure than most finished pictures : the richest harmonies of colour are gained by a mere rubbing in.'   Here are also other oil sketches for several of the series in the Louvre.   Rubens was summoned to Paris in 1620 by Marie de Medicis, and within five years were finished the one and twenty pictures for which he prepared, as may be here seen, preliminary studies.   These sketches, for my own pleasure, I much prefer to the large pictures ; they are at any rate not quite so obnoxious. Marvellous also is ' The Adoration of the Magi ' (537).   In the catalogue I have made the remark, ' in character and in handling this brilliant sketch is not unlike the drawings of Sir John Gilbert.'   Also among these impromptus are, ' The Feast of Herod ' (542), ' The Last Supper ' (544), ' Ecce Homo ' (545), ' The Coronation of the Virgin ' (547),

'The Lipithes and the Centaurs' (553), 'The Triumphal Return of a Roman General' (556), 'The Virgin giving a Cloak to Saint Ildefonso' (557), 'Five statues of Emperors and of Kings of the House of Hapsburg' (558), 'A Lion Hunt' (590), 'The Statue of Ceres' (593). In all there are more than 20 sketches: I know not of a parallel collection elsewhere.

Among the finished pictures by Rubens special attention may be directed to the following; 'Abraham dismissing Hagar' (535), 'a veritable jewel,' says Waagen, of which a repetition is in the Grosvenor Gallery; 'Jesus at the House of Simon' (543), from the Walpole Collection; a repetition (546), with considerable variations, of 'The Descent from the Cross' in Antwerp; 'a Bacchanal (551), supreme in colour, more than commonly diabolical —a favourite composition of Rubens; 'Perseus and Andromeda' (552), most brilliant, a subject which has been repeated four times; and 'The Rape of the Sabines' (555), smaller than, and vastly inferior to, the same subject in our National Gallery. Among fifteen portraits the two wives of Rubens are included almost as a matter of course. 'Helena Fourment' (576), the second wife, bears the palm as usual. She is here depicted not in 'chapeau de paille,' the name given to an analogous portrait in the Peel Collection, but in a 'chapeau noir;' her satin dress is equally black, relieved however by ribbons, lace, and jewels. The lady is in *grande toilette*, and her husband has spared no pains, especially in the painting of the hands and sleeves. Dr. Waagen prefers this masterwork to the 'Chapeau de paille,' now in our National Gallery. I scarcely think the picture in St. Petersburg has a right to this supreme position, at least in its present degenerate state; the black dress has lost its relieving lights, and the black sky throws out of tone

the face and neck, now too white. Yet I am disposed
to rank this prize from the Walpole Collection as one of
the very best known versions of a face which is multiplied more freely in the galleries of Europe than any
other, with perhaps the exception of Erasmus.

Also in the Hermitage are examples of the mastery of
Rubens as a painter of animals. The galleries of Europe
bear witness to the unrivalled power and spirit which
the artist threw into the chase and the combat between
wild beasts. 'Lions' (592), and 'the Lion hunt' (590),
are works of this character ; the first of these pictures is
bold in handling, each stroke of the brush is decisive ; the
monarch of the forest is delineated to the very life.
Rubens, like Sir Edwin Landseer, was a student of lions :
'Daniel in the Lion's Den,' contributed by the Duke of
Hamilton to the last Exhibition of the Old Masters in
Burlington House, has a decision, force and action foreign
to Landseer. Lastly, the universality of Rubens is further
attested by landscapes, which, for largeness of manner
and glory of colour, are only surpassed by Titian. Few
painters have ventured to reflect upon canvas the eva-
nescent hues of 'The Rainbow' (595). Rubens, rejoicing
in endless resource, was ready to challenge difficulties
from which painters of less power are wont to retreat.
Bold effects of atmospheric light and colour are to
the artist's liking ; thus in a striking composition, 'Le
Voiturier,' on the borders of a river surrounded by rocks
and trees (594), Rubens contrasts with telling effect the
conflict of light between the setting sun and the rising
moon. The trees are drawn with a care worthy of
Wynauts, the elements assume a dramatic action and a
phantasm of colour rarely equalled by de Loutherbourg
or by Turner. I think I have said enough to show that
the Hermitage satisfies the most ravenous of appetites

for the highly seasoned viands served up by Rubens. For myself I confess to no feeling of satiety after devouring the whole collection of 60 works.

Next to Rubens naturally follows his pupil Vandyck, liberally represented by 34 pictures. In this exceptional display the Hermitage is only surpassed by Munich, which has 37 examples of the master: next follow Vienna with 26, Madrid with 22, Paris with 20, Dresden with 19, and London with 6. Many of these pictures by Vandyck, gained on the purchase of the Walpole Collection, we can ill afford to spare from England ; portraits of a king, of a queen, of nobles, of men of genius, are of the nature of national property, of historic muniments. Vandyck worked and died in England, and only in England could be painted the pictures now in the Hermitage of 'Charles I' (609), 'Henriette' his Queen (610), 'Archbishop Laud' (612), 'The Herbert Family' (614), 'Earl Danby' (615), 'Lord Wharton' (616), 'Sir Thomas Wharton' (617), 'Elizabeth and Philadelphia Wharton' (618), 'Lady Jane Goodwin' (619), 'Sir Thomas Chaloner' (620), 'Lord Wandesford' (621), 'Inigo Jones' (626). To these may be added the portraits of four English ladies (633 and 634), supposed to be of the Herbert family. We almost imagine ourselves at home in England while walking among these familiar faces: the sad story of the sale of these heirlooms may recall Sheridan's famous scene wherein Charles Surface knocks down by auction the portraits of his ancestors. It is but a poor consolation to find that portraits acquired by the Hermitage are scarcely in Vandyck's best manner. Charles I, with the exception of his armour, is inferior to other transcripts of the same melancholy but high-born countenance. ' The Herbert Family' is very sketchy, though study has been thrown into the heads, and care taken of the attitudes ; this sketch was the prelude to the great picture now at Wilton. I have marked as among the best in the collection the half-figure of Sir Thomas Chaloner, also the head of Inigo Jones—a head so broadly chiselled, and so animated in expression, is bound to come out effectively on canvas. This portrait fortunately exists elsewhere ; a replica, certainly not inferior, was exhibited among National Portraits at Kensington in 1866, as well as a very fine half-length miniature in monochrome. Thus England, in bartering away the Walpole Gallery, happily did not lose all record of her great men.

But we in England have also to deplore the loss of other and even more important works, which prove the greatness of Vandyck in the high sphere of religious art. Scarcely short of the first rank is 'La Vierge aux Perdrix' (603), once in the gallery of Charles I, and subsequently in the collection of Lord Walpole. This, like other famous works, has been repeated more than once ; another example, with alterations, is in the Pitti Palace ; also in Lord Ashburton's collection is a much smaller yet beautiful replica, with the addition of four angels in the clouds, formerly in the gallery of Prince Talleyrand. We are at home so much wanting in com-positions which carry Vandyck into an ideal and imagi-native sphere that I well remember how, accustomed as I had been to mere portraits, I had not realized till I reached Antwerp that the greatest of portrait painters imported from the Continent since the time of Holbein had descended from the high rank of sacred and historic art. 'The Christ on the Cross' (605), a mere sketch, is a superb indication : indeed I here seemed to recognise more of absolute genius than in any other creation of the master with which I am acquainted. So also in the

full and imposing composition above mentioned, 'La
Vierge aux Perdrix,' with landscape and clouds, including
the accessories of partridges, fruits, trees and sunflowers,
there is a care and a minuteness to which we are wholly
unaccustomed, at least after the time when Vandyck fell
into the profitable trade of generalising and beautifying
his fashionable sitters. Yet none of the works in the
Hermitage have gift of imagination, or glory of colour ;
just at the very point when genius appeared ready to
assert itself, the artist became frigid, circumscribed, and
fetter-bound. After all it would seem that Vandyck's
true vocation lay in portraiture, hence I am happy to
close this slight notice with two of the best portrait-
pictures in the Hermitage. 'Snyders with his Family'
(627), free, firm, bold, and in colour approaching Rubens ;
also 'A Mother and Daughter' (635), superbly painted in
the heads and draperies.

Very characteristic of the showy tastes and of the
flaunting styles which obtain in the Hermitage, is the
alarming fact that no fewer than 14 works, many
doubly obnoxious by enormity in size, are conspicuous
by that most vulgar of painters, Jordaens. This choice
gathering ranges from 'St. Peter' (646) to 'Mercury'
(648), and from 'St. Paul' (647) to 'Diana' (649). I
scarcely regret that space fails me to mention mediocre
works by Vos, Faes, Quellin, and Oost.

But the compositions of David Teniers, father and
son, assume numbers and dimensions which cannot be
ignored even by the least sympathising of critics.
The pictures by Teniers the younger run up to 40,
a total only surpassed at Madrid. Other European
galleries come in the following order :—Munich has
24 examples, Dresden 23, London 13. To revert
to the father, two landscapes in the neighbourhood

of Antwerp may be named as showing a pronounced family manner, though evidently the father had a more prosaic idea of nature than even the son. It is said, as I can well believe, that the earlier and weaker works of the celebrated son are attributed to the more obscure father. Of all that Teniers the younger was capable here is abundant proof: this great, if not greatest of genre painters, I have never seen elsewhere so nearly at a point surpassing himself. Indeed ' The Arquebusiers of Antwerp ' (672) almost rises to the import and dignity of historic art. This truly national work is comparable to the 'Night Watch' bý Rembrandt, and to the 'Banquet of the Civic Guard' by Van der Helst, severally in Amsterdam. Though smaller in scale, the treatment of the heads and the figures with the accessories of the costumes is similar. The artist reaches picturesque dignity. Black dresses, red sashes, white collars, &c., give decisive and individual character. It is a striking instance of how completely the Hermitage has been a sealed book to writers on art, that Dr. Waagen does not even name this *chef d'œuvre* in the exhaustive Hand-book of the German, Flemish, and Dutch Schools published by Murray in 1860. This conscientious critic, however, makes amends for the omission when he gets to St. Petersburg; there he passes a high eulogy on the work, which he says has been valued at 2000 guineas. The picture is historic; many of the heads are veritable portraits; Teniers himself, as a leading man of his time, is as a matter of right present; the costumes are true to the period, the local surroundings comprise the Hotel de Ville and the former residence of Charles V, which exists to this daý. The whole scene is a living representation of one of those stirring half-civic and half-military ceremonies which were common among the city guilds of the Netherlands. A literal unimaginative painter like Teniers makes a trustworthy chronicler. Another marked work, more too in the painter's line than the genre of history, is 'The Interior of a Kitchen' (698). According to the catalogue of the Houghton Hall Gallery, Teniers has inserted himself as the master of the house, and the kitchen is supposed to be painted from his own pleasant country retreat at Perck. The goodly 'Chateau of Teniers at Perck, a turreted house among trees,' with the painter, his wife, and son in the spacious garden, forms part of the Peel Collection in the National Gallery.

It may be remembered that Rubens also fondly painted his own chateau ; artists with an eye to business as well as to an æsthetic and epicurean life are apt to lay their lines in pleasant places ; in our own days, Mr. Birket Foster has planted his house in the midst of capital sketching ground, likewise Mr. John Linnell is known to use as studies for his pictures, woods which lie around his country dwelling. Teniers in like manner bought himself a seat at Perck, a small village between Antwerp and Mechlin ; here he assumed the air of a grandee, he received the nobles of Spain and of Flanders, he gave lessons in painting to Don Juan of Austria. The kitchen of this mansion which we see in the Hermitage picture bears all the signs of good living. On the left stands David Teniers himself, in a grey doublet with a fur cap on his head, on his wrist perches a falcon, beside him are his dogs. An old blind fisherman, led by the cook, drags along a great fish ; and a second fisherman, bearing the last catch under his arm, advances towards the master of the house. On the right and in the background appear men-cooks and a servant girl, the foreground is crowded with vegetables, provisions, pails and other kitchen utensils. It would appear that Teniers furnished his table from his own estate, for in the picture in the National Gallery, he depicts six men dragging a net in the moat before his chateau, while the gardener is seen bearing away a pike. The kitchen at St. Petersburg bears the signature 'David Teniers 1646 ;' the execution is unequal, only in parts is this large canvas of the fine quality habitual to smaller panels. Next comes one of the painter's comic scenes, 'A Kitchen invaded by Monkeys' (699). It seems natural that Dutch art, which often deals with the lowest forms of humanity, should descend one step further and include apes. Even the great French painter Decamps could not resist the temptation of assigning to monkeys human attributes, and Teniers we may be sure makes himself quite at home among these grotesque parodies on man. Thus in the Munich Gallery 'A Drinking Party of ten persons' is immediately followed by 'A Dinner of Monkeys' and 'A Monkey and Cat Concert.' It must be admitted that the composition in the Hermitage is the best of its kind both for character and execution. Also equally good are 'Le Corps de Garde' (673), 'Leṣ Fumeurs' (694), 'Le fumeur Villageois' (695), and 'Les joueurs de Cartes' (688). As a matter of course the oft-repeated 'Temptation of St. Anthony' (671) forms part of the series. I need not trouble the reader with further examples of a style neither recondite nor unfamiliar.

I may mention that there is a work (713) by Abraham Teniers, son and pupil of David Teniers the younger. Thus the Hermitage displays a phenomenon which, as far as I remember, is without precedent, a grandfather, a father, and a son,—three generations of painters standing in the relation, moreover, of masters and pupils. Two generations are not uncommon, thus there have been Filippo Lippi the father and Filippino Lippi the son,

Holbein the elder and Holbein the younger, Titian the father and Titian the son, Giovanni Santi the father and Raphael the son, Veronese the father and Veronese the son. But the inheritance of talent in these instances stopped short of the third generation. And yet the exception in the Teniers family almost proves the rule that art genius is not hereditary, inasmuch as Teniers the grandson was practically a nonentity. Indeed never has been known more than one art genius in a family. There is no analogous case to that of Chatham and Pitt. The father always eclipses the son, or the converse. Talent in art is not of a stamina for procreation : it is as a spark, as a fire which burns fitfully for a short season, and then expires. This generalized sketch of the Hermitage it is not necessary to encumber with four-and-twenty pictures distributed among Tilborgh, Miel, Coques, Meulen, Uden, Huysmans, Millet, and Bloemen. I may just mention that no fewer than eleven pictures in the usual style belong to 'Velvet Breughel.'

The next great name, specially great, if not the greatest in the Hermitage, is Rembrandt. This supremacy counts for all the more when it is remembered in what force this most forcible of artists appears in the galleries of the Hague, of Amsterdam, Dresden, Munich, Cassel, Paris, London, and Vienna. I had studied Rembrandt in all these cities, and yet was astounded on getting to St. Petersburg to find forty-one .pictures, which by their grave import could not be forgotten in the artist's biography without doing injustice to his grand life-labour. Rembrandt is represented in the leading European galleries in the following numerical proportions: the Hermitage numbers 41 pictures, Dresden 19, Munich 15, Paris 15, London 13, Vienna 10,

Berlin 8, Florence 2, Brussels and Madrid, severally, 1. This unparalleled assemblage in the Hermitage is derived from various collections, viz., the Crozat, the Walpole, the Malmaison, the Choiseul, the Brühl and the Saint Leu, while some twenty works, that is, one half of the total, appear without any pedigree. But it does not follow that these unaccredited pictures are dubious; on the contrary, some whose ubiquity over the period of two centuries is without published record, I have specially marked for merit. In a collection so extended and miscellaneous, gathered from all accessible sources, and scarcely casting off as unworthy the sweepings found in odd corners of Europe, much inequality necessarily subsists. Such tolerance of works, good, bad, and indifferent, may be taken as peculiarly significant of the Hermitage. This startling inequality is, in fact, correspondent with the strong contrast found throughout Russia, wherein refinement and vulgarity, riches and squalor, education and ignorance, go hand in hand.

The picture which seems to me the finest in quality is a 'Holy Family' (796); indeed this composition, simple enough in its component parts, and consisting of nothing more than a mother, an open book, a cradle and an infant, leaves nothing to be desired, in light, shade, colour, or texture. The spectator is here impressed not with the mannerism, but with the consummate merit of the master. It is true enough that purity of form, elevation of religious sentiment, cannot be looked for, yet the general expression has much tenderness, homishness, and simplicity. In fact, this 'Holy Family' in Dutch costume is nothing more than a humble group within a cottage: the cherubs come tumbling in without ceremony, like bats or cockchafers. The picture, which is from the Crozat Collection, was painted at the age of thirty-seven, in the artist's prime. Hanging in the same neighbourhood are several biblical compositions, which more or less confirm the general conviction that Rembrandt had no vocation for religious art. Possibly Mr. Spurgeon, judging from his recent invective against Italian art, might find in Rembrandt a spiritual brother. But Rembrandt is grand not grotesque in his plebeianism. He is in fact the greatest genius which has appeared in the arts of northern Europe : even his vices lie on virtue's side. His characters though vulgar are not vicious, his women though homely are honest, his men though rarely handsome have dignity befitting burgomasters and free citizens. Thus much I read in the faces to which I am introduced by Rembrandt in the Hermitage. The entire collection may be accepted as an exhaustive exposition of the painter's successive manners. 'The Return of the Prodigal Son' (797) is a characteristic composition, the handling is broad, coarse, and sketchy. 'The Descent from the Cross' (800), which came from the Cassel Gallery, is one of several renderings of this subject, and certainly not the best. Other religious compositions tend to the coarseness of the unregenerate and the unwashed multitudes who appear to have served as the painter's ideals : such works do little justice to the every-day religion of the shepherd, the wayfarer, and the mechanic ; and they are wholly antagonistic to the heavenly beatitude of beings who have conquered the body and purified the fleshly clay. But the Hermitage gives no shelter to any art allied to the spiritual Fra Angelico. The religion of Pre-Raphaelite days receives no countenance within its walls. And yet I should be sorry to speak of these pictures of Rembrandt as if they were hostile to religion. As a rule they are more in the spirit of the Old Testament than of the New; thus while the type of Christ is uniformly low, the heads of patriarchs, such as 'The Father of the Faithful,' are noble. Rembrandt favours the Jews : his Jewish Rabbis are magnificent.   In 'The Sacrifice of Isaac' (792) the head of Abraham is a fine study.   Another important composition hanging close at hand, 'Abraham at Table with the Angels' (791), is too naturalistic to be religious; it is always a bad sign when the wings of angels are taken from large birds of prey.   In the best times of spiritual art, wings were treated ideally and etherially, in colours they were prismatic, as if the flight of angels was by the path of the rainbow.   Even Rembrandt has not missed the opportunity of illuminating the plumes of these heavenly visitants, with rich and varied hues; indeed the whole composition is a fine study of tones and textures; no man better knew how to enhance the dignity of age, or to suggest a remote period of time by rugged surface or profound shadow.   The mystery that dwells in impenetrable darkness becomes sometimes well-nigh religious, and one reason why Rembrandt deals best with the Old Testament may be, that prevailing shadow comports well with a dispensation wherein the ways of providence were seen, as in a glass, darkly.   In the New Testament this art is best in keeping with tragic scenes, such as 'The Passion;' the veil of night shrouds 'The Descent from the Cross' (800), grandeur and terror reside in this awful shade.   No painter has ever gained so much impressiveness by the mere trick of the brush, or play of the pallet knife.   'Abraham and the Angels' (791) would scarcely have the power to hold attention long, were it not that the eye is curiously attracted by the marvellous skill shown in the management of the surface textures.   In parts the colours are loaded on

solidly and then glazed into, and sometimes the top
lights are got by rubbing away this surface glaze. The
mottled, marbled effect has been heightened by dragging the brush over the surface, while the under colour
remained tacky: in short the dodges are many, almost
endless. Indeed, the analysis of the Rembrandt process
is quite as interesting and instructive in its way as the
elucidation of the Titian method. Each means was
perfect after its kind; each painter, though in opposite
directions, made the material of his art the medium of
his thought. No two artists have given such divers
embodiment to 'Danae.' The version (802) in the
Hermitage proves that Rembrandt was as far removed
from classic as from religious art. Habitually coarse
was his idea of the female form, and yet by play of light,
shade, and colour, the eye is made to dwell with pleasure
on a form which otherwise had been repellant. Rembrandt, it must be admitted, was not over nice; thus—
he paints on full life scale 'A Young Jewess' (812), in
state of advanced expectancy; yet here again he obtains an absolute triumph by richness of broken colour,
transparence in shadow, and facility yet firmness in
touch. The headdress of flowers reaches the realism
of a flower painter. This canvas, which is dated 1634,
proves that Rembrandt at the age of twenty-six had
already matured a thoroughly individual style. Three
years later is 'The Portrait of a Man' (811), in the artist's
finest and least mannered manner, yet the brush has
been used slashingly. 'The Portrait of an Old Jew' (810)
is apparently of the time when Rembrandt was himself
old; the paint is daubed on clumsily.

The Hermitage contains four-and-twenty portraits by
Rembrandt, many of which need no mention. The
following may be enumerated: 'The Portrait of the

caligrapher, Lieven van Copenol' (808), other likenesses, also an etching of the same head exist ; ' The Portrait of a Young Warrior' (809), the type ideal, some have conjectured that Alexander the Great is intended ; ' Portrait of an Old Military Man' (814), an early work, careful, detailed, timid ; ' Portrait of an Old Man' (818), ' Portrait of an Old Jew' (815), and ' Portrait of an Aged Woman' (823). Rembrandt I think is the most literal transcriber of a face when dilapidated by time which the world has yet seen. Denner's stereoscopic reproductions of the age of three score and ten (1284 &c.) often degenerate into caricatures. A gallery furnished by Denner is only inferior to Madame Tussaud's waxwork exhibition. But an old man or an old woman by Rembrandt is something more than a mechanical reproduction of wrinkles. Indeed I do not hesitate to say that the head of ' An Old Man' (816) ranks with the greatest portrait pictures in the world. Almost unsurpassed is this face for individuality, and for quiet dignity, for firm yet soft and fleshy modelling, and for handling of brush, which in its play expresses the endless undulation of features, tossed about by time and trial. This portrait, which is famous for the execution of the beard, is another illustration of the dodgy way in which the artist went to work. The end of the brushhandle has been used over the wet paint to incise lines, into which when dry dark colour was glazed. The beard is white, the dress black, an opposition which secures strong contrast. In order further to enhance the effect, colour is thrown into the flesh of a warmth unusual to Rembrandt. The tones indeed are allied to the reds of Rubens, while the modelling is comparable in delicacy to the handling of the so-called ' Gervartius ' in the National Gallery. The oft - repeated head of

Rembrandt's mother is here multiplied four times. The first in the catalogue was not painted until the artist had lost his mother fifteen years. The portrait evidently served as a stock subject in the studio. Another replica, finished only three years after the mother's death, and engraved by Schmidt, is not surpassed by any of the many versions of the face familiar in the National Gallery and elsewhere. Rembrandt as a landscape painter is seen by two examples, the best 'A View on the Rhine' (831); here the sky is very lovely in grey toned clouds, warm browns in boat and figures complete the harmony of this exquisite yet most unpretending composition. Next follows Rembrandt's pupil Eckhout, who in the Hermitage, as in other galleries, is probably responsible for some of the inferior works made to pass under the name of the great master. Of such errors the large composition 'Christ blessing little Children,' purchased for our National Gallery as a Rembrandt, is a signal example; the work is now by general consent transferred from the master to the pupil. No picture by Eckhout in the Hermitage calls for notice.

Other painters of Holland merit some slight attention. Flinck and Bol here naturally follow as the disciples of Rembrandt; by the former are three examples, by the latter no less than twelve. Of these last, 'Le Savant' (847), 'Le Philosophe' (852), and two portraits (850–852) of 'Jeunes Hommes' are among the best of extant examples of the Rembrandt school. Bol I have never seen in better estate, in no gallery is he so well represented. Hals and Van der Helst are also present : by the latter is a noteworthy picture of 'The Family of Paul Potter' (778), from the Saint Leu Collection. Portraits of artists by fellow artists never fail of interest. Honthorst, known in Italy from his night-like shadows illumined with light, as 'Girardo della Notte,' also present in England as a portrait painter in the time of Charles I, and especially to be remembered by the picture of the Queen of Bohemia as Queen of Hearts, is seen in the Hermitage by nine works. I have usually found in the galleries of Europe much more of this vulgar artist than I could desire, and should not now think it worth while to find space for him or his works, were not 'The Christ before Caiaphas' (746) among the most impressive of his productions. The general conception, almost as a matter of course, is superior to the execution and the colour; the latter struck me as especially poor and disagreeable. Repetitions of this effective composition, which is said to have made the artist's renown, are found in Rome, Vienna, and London. My notes do not enable me to say which of the four examples is the best. Van der Werff, an Italianized Dutchman, I have seldom seen better save in Dresden. Here also must be mentioned Poelemburg, because conspicuous by eleven pictures, of which one ranks as the largest and most ambitious known, otherwise I should willingly have excluded wholly so hybrid an artist. This production, 'The Repose of the Holy Family' (757), is as a matter of course poor in colour and execution: it is the genre of religious art. The picture with others of the kind was acquired for the Hermitage by Catherine II.

The small Dutch masters flock into the Hermitage in crowds. By Gerard Dow, for example, are twelve pictures, a number exceeded only in Dresden, Munich, and Paris. The marvellous finish of these miniature panels may be understood by a simple anecdote: Sandrart relates that on visiting Gerard Dow with Peter de Laar, the pains bestowed on a broomstick

was much commended, whereupon Dow replied that
he had still to give it three days more work. One
of the examples in the Hermitage, 'An Old Rabbi'
(907), is exceptional inasmuch as the manner shows
the largeness of the painter's master, Rembrandt. 'An
Old Woman' (858) by Maas is another instance of how
old women of both sexes were glorified in the school
of Rembrandt. Dow entered the atelier of Rembrandt
at the age of fifteen. An old Rabbi is known to have
been then a favourite model, probably therefore the
above head in the style of the master was painted
during years of pupilage. Dow, like Rembrandt, seems
to have been enamoured with his own face, several
repetitions of his well-known physiognomy are to be
found in the Hermitage, in Dresden, in the National
Gallery, in the Bridgewater Gallery, &c. The pecu-
liarity of the version in St. Petersburg is that it bears
a date which would bring the painter to the fifty-second
year of his age, while the features retain the younger
aspect of thirty. It is naturally supposed that this
and other like portraits are repetitions from an earlier
picture. We may imagine Dow's head, by no means
ugly, set up perpetually on an easel in his studio, and
just as an Italian painter might multiply the figure
of a favourite saint, so would a Dutchman serve cus-
tomers with a portrait of his own person in the act
of playing a violin or smoking a pipe, as the case
might be. When sacred art was secularized, a tobacco-
pipe might fitly take the place of a palm-branch, and
a besom or a kettle become as precious as the offerings
of the Three Kings. 'Two Young Girls at a Bath'
(910–912), also a youth undraped (911), show better
drawing of the figure than could have been expected.
These three small companion pictures have been called

'les perles de Gerard Dow.' 'The Doctor' (903) is more in the painter's usual line; of the many renderings of this subject I know of none better : replicas are found in the Belvedere, Vienna, and in the Leuchtenberg Gallery, St. Petersburg. Also of first-rate quality are two versions of 'The Herring Merchant' (904, 905), both formerly in the Cassel Gallery ; likewise equally fine are 'The Thread-winder' (909) and 'The Reader' (913).

Of Frans Mieris, called by Dow the prince among his pupils, there is not much to say, yet I have marked for superlative praise three masterpieces : two of these are engraved, indeed I may here observe that the majority of the works in the Hermitage have been reproduced in some form, mostly as might be expected before they reached St. Petersburg. Metzu, another follower of Dow, has one picture without merit, three of medium merit, and one, 'The Breakfast' (880), from Malmaison, of first-class merit. Tol and Schalcken, also followers of Dow, are likewise seen in this exhaustive collection. Terburg, who belongs to the same time and school, asserts his presence by three of his most brilliant specimens of white satin, nothing could be more perfect of the kind. Caspar Netscher, the pupil of Terburg, paints somewhat in the manner of Sir Peter Lely a portrait of interest to us in England—'Marie Stuart' (882), daughter of James II, and afterwards consort of William III. De Hooghe, the greatest master of bright sunlight and quiet shade, is supreme in 'The Aged Lacemaker' (862). This was one of the many acquisitions made by Catherine II.

Jan Steen, notwithstanding his vulgarity, calls for prominent notice. Here are eight of his compositions, a larger number than is met with in any one of the

ten principal galleries in Europe: the Hague boasting
of only six. This jolly tavern-keeper was certainly
more at home in card-playing, love-making, and drink-
ing-bouts than in such subjects as 'Esther before
Ahasuerus' (895). The composition is little short of a
burlesque, though the artist goes out of his way to
approach high life and gain decorative details. Steen
is quite himself again among Topers in a rustic room
(898); also scarcely to be surpassed in the vulgar
line is a peasants' marriage (901). The artist, as was
his liking, introduces himself among the company:
Steen is seen in the character of a peasant playing on
the tymbal to a crowd of drinking and riotous boors.
This too is in the taste of Brower, of whom unfortunately there are five examples; one, a low scene of
peasants smoking and carousing, has not often been
surpassed. Two Ostades are present, Adrian the most
famous, and Isaak his brother and pupil: by the former
are sixteen specimens after the usual manner: specially
may be mentioned as small conceits 'Touch' (956),
'Sight' (957), and 'Taste' (958), being part of a highly
wrought series known as 'The Five Senses.' The idea
is poor and tends to vulgarity. Bega, a pupil of Adrian
Ostade, and as far as I have observed a scarce artist,
is seen to much advantage in two characteristic subjects
taken from low life.

I fear the reader may be weary of this interminable
catalogue of Dutchmen who are bound to be much
alike all the world over. But to omit Paul Potter is
impossible. I have been twice to the Hague to see
the great bull, and yet I had still to travel to St.
Petersburg to appreciate Potter fully. I am thankful
to say that in the Hermitage there is nothing in size
approaching to the much overrated bull, which, save

in the head, is painted in a heavy and mechanical fashion. Not so the cow, here ruminating in a beautiful landscape (1051): with reason this highly-finished panel has been regarded by many as the artist's master-piece. The pedigree is interesting and complete. It is amusing enough to read that the picture was in the first place refused, though painted on commission, because the cow was not liked. The changing fortunes of this chef-d'œuvre are as follows. In the year 1750 it became the property of the King of Sweden; in 1806 it fell into the hands of Napoleon I, who presented it to Josephine; thence from the Gallery of Malmaison it was purchased for the Hermitage at the large yet moderate sum of 190,000 francs, the estimated value having been 250,000 francs. The enthusiasm awakened in me when I first came upon this mere cow picture may seem ridiculous to those who do not know the delight given by supreme art quality irrespective of subject matter; great is the pleasure of seeing a simple piece of nature transcribed truthfully and lovingly. Here cows are enjoying the sunshine, and men and women are quietly working as if labour was its own reward; the whole scene is as a page taken from nature or as a story written in a book. Turning to the execution, I would say that the handling is simply the perfect medium by which nature speaks through art. Next in importance comes a simple landscape (1056), the most elaborate tree study I know by Potter. Then there is 'The life of the Hunter' (1052), a composition which I look upon chiefly as a curiosity. Here in successive scenes incidents of the chase are depicted graphically, even comically. It cannot say much for the art discrimination of either Goethe or Waagen that this late and inferior product obtains from these critics the warmest eulogy. Infinitely finer is a wolf-dog the size of nature (1055), indeed for mastery, for sketchy, offhand, yet complete realism, I do not scruple to say that this life-size dog is superior to the full-size bull of the Hague. Again we have a pedigree long and reliable as the family-tree of an old house. After many vicissitudes the picture was acquired for the Malmaison Collection, and thence of course the transit to St. Petersburg is easily understood. It may seem too much to say that I felt repaid for my trouble in taking this long journey to Russia when I discovered these masterpieces in the Hermitage. An animal painter can scarcely justify sublime emotions, no one should pretend to feel quite the same for a sheep or a cow as for humanity. Yet a saint or an angel ill painted is in art inferior to an animal well painted. The works I have quoted prove once more Paul Potter to be among the very greatest of the masters who have striven for simple and literal truth in the delineation either of inanimate nature or of creatures domesticated by man. Quietude and simplicity, drawing firm yet undulating, and a touch plastic and liquid yet crisp and sparkling, constitute a technique which leaves little to be desired. Few are the masters and rare the works which merit this praise.

I cannot affect equal enthusiasm for Wouverman, though nowhere except in Dresden is he seen so profusely. Only Rubens with 60 works outnumbers him in the Hermitage. Wouverman's contributions to European galleries are numerically as follows: in Dresden are 62 examples, in the Hermitage 50, in Vienna 13, in Munich also 13, in Madrid 10, in London none, till the purchase of the Peel Collection, and now 5. It has been estimated that Wouverman found time in a short life to turn out of hand eight hundred pictures, most of which are supposed to contain at least one white horse, but such haste necessarily implies inequality, accordingly the half hundred works now before me are of very varied merit. In art quality, as in numerical strength, I incline to think them rather inferior to the unexampled display in Dresden. Many were acquired in the time of Catherine: others are from the Crozat and the Brühl Collections. 'The Halt of Travellers' (1017) and 'The Dunes of Holland' (1043) are of great beauty in the tender greys of the silvery landscape; the execution is crisp yet liquid, facile, and dexterous. Often the trees are most delicate and detailed in pencilling of stems and in finish of foliage; and in tone and execution exquisite are the 'The Young Bird Catchers' (1037), and 'The Harvest Gatherers' (1041). 'The Stag Hunt' (1034), which is regarded as a cap' opera, was it is stated purchased for the Hermitage at the price of 20,700 livres. Peter van Laar, to whom Wouverman was much indebted, is represented by only one product. Jan le Ducq, somewhat in a like line, has here his largest canvas, 'The Halt of Troops in a Grange' (933). In quality however this picture is inferior to a smaller panel, a 'Guard Room' (934). Not even in Munich do I recall a more characteristic product of this scarce and choice master.

Italianized Dutchmen, more popular formerly than now, naturally abound in the Hermitage, where, as already said, late styles are dominant. Thus Berchem has 16 works, a number only exceeded in Munich, where are 18. Dresden follows with 13, Paris with 11, Turin with 7, and London with 2. No painters have fagged away so untiringly as Dutchmen; their art was so much a mechanism, that they needed to tax

the mind only occasionally for a thought. Berchem
was one of the most industrious of these painters, and
when at the height of his fame he is said to have sold
his labour from early morning till four in the afternoon
for ten florins a day. Such grinding drudgery will
account for much servile repetition. And yet it must
be admitted that during his lifetime he tried varied
manners; specially to be admired are his Italian landscapes with shepherds, shepherdesses, ruins, and cattle,
all pleasantly lighted by the warm glow of the setting
sun; the aerial perspective is fine, the poetic feeling,
though common-place, is agreeable. Yet compared
with Turner, Berchem is a teaboard painter. From
Malmaison comes an unaccustomed subject, large though
mediocre, 'The Angels announcing to the Shepherds the
Birth of the Messiah' (1070); the picture cost the Hermitage 7000 francs. 'The Rape of Europa' (1072), to
which Dr. Waagen pays tribute as holding the first
place among Berchem's life-size pictures, is also beyond
the painter's power. In 'Autumn' (1073) Berchem also
comes out in an unaccustomed line; here is a medley of
nudes, goats, and angels. 'The Halt of the Hunters'
(1076) brings the artist to his senses; though now black,
some have taken the picture to be the artist's masterpiece, and I know no better. It is needful only to
add one more example, 'Italy' (1081), in the artist's
popular and most romantic manner, very choice of its
kind. That it should still remain in doubt whether
Berchem ever entered Italy at all is a sad satire on
these Italian compositions. In the sister art of poetry
Lalla Rookh affords an analogous case. Tom Moore
had never been to the East when this Oriental romance
was penned. Karel du Jardin, the pupil of Berchem,
and the emulator of Paul Potter, happened to die in

Venice, therefore a legitimate Italian parentage to his pictorial offspring cannot be questioned. Indeed Du Jardin at an early age was already in Rome, where he formed his style. I scarcely know of a more delightful painter; Italians are apt to idealize too much, but this Italianized Dutchman struck the happy mean. 'Cattle' (1086), and a river scene in the Roman Campagna, with a young girl of the country who has just passed the stream with cows and sheep following (1090), are both in the best manner of this exquisite artist. A more circumscribed style distinguishes Jan van Goyen, a painter born at Leyden, and who died at the Hague; there is no suspicion that his native art was infected by the idealism of Italy, hence to the last it remained true to the sand-hills, the watery meadows, and the ruminating cattle, with a grey and rainy sky above, which continue to this day the characteristics of his native land. 'The Dunes near Scheveningen' (1127), 'A Winter Landscape' (1129), and 'The Meuse near Dordrecht' (1126), have each the habitual charm of this simple student of nature. The last Dr. Waagen names as the chef-d'œuvre of the master, from which judgment I differ; the work is only chief in size. Of this winning artist we have unfortunately no example in the National Gallery.

Landscape painting—only the Dutch naturalism, not the grander Italian ideal—comes out capitally in the Hermitage. Ruysdael, for example, is remarkably well represented, indeed I was astounded to find no less than fourteen pictures by this painter. In Dresden I know him to be strong, but he there numbers one work less, and the average merit is lower. Next follows Munich with ten Ruysdaels, and afterwards driblets lie scattered throughout Europe, six fair specimens falling to the lot of our National

Gallery. 'The Marsh,' in the midst of oak trees, including a lovely study of water-lilies, resembling a picture lent by W. Wells, Esq. in 1871 to the Exhibition of the Old Masters in the Royal Academy, has with reason been designated as the painter's masterpiece. 'Paysage' (1145) is, I incline to think, the finest of the many waterfalls assigned to this painter *par excellence* of waterfalls. The relative distances have varied tone, in other words, less sacrifice has been made to the force which resides in blackness. 'Paysage montueux' (1147), an engraved work, I mention as quite exceptional in the art of Holland, a country unconscious of anything approaching to a mountain or even a hill. Ruysdael here attains the grand gloom of mountain lands. The picture is imposing and imaginative. This picture would seem to fortify the conjecture that Ruysdael gathered his materials in Norway. Hobbema, the usual companion of Ruysdael, is, strange to say, all but absent, yet nothing can be accounted strange among the miraculous draught of fishes caught for the Hermitage; in fact, to use a vulgar expression, anything that comes here to the net is fish. Wynants, whose genuine love for nature gives him a place in English and foreign collections side by side with Ruysdael and Hobbema, has landscapes which would in Christie's sale-rooms attract the spectacles of all the old gentlemen about Town; artists too would be impressed by their truth, and yet in the Hermitage I was much struck with the absence of artists. But that is an old story; in our National Gallery Royal Academicians are seldom seen, not because they have nothing to learn intellectually, but nothing to gain commercially. So in St. Petersburg the many artists who live or starve on public patronage do not find their market along the the strait and narrow way trod by the old masters.

These Dutch masters I confess bored me in the Hermitage, there was no end to them. Thus no sooner was Teniers ended than I had to take to all his disciples, and then followed landscape artists, and now a word must be given to the painters of interiors. This duty is positively incumbent, because if the Hermitage is to be described, fair play must be dealt all round. By Steenwyck, father and son, both being present, are some conscientious transcripts of Gothic and Italian architecture (1195–1197); and by Peter Neefs, the pupil of the elder man, are various interiors (1198–1201) which anywhere but in the Hermitage would have long ago acquired European reputations. Really here one reputation kills another, there is no room for all even in the most capacious of memories. Italian pictures may each obtain in the mind a separate niche, but as for these Dutch duodecimos of the smallest thoughts, even pigeon-holes are wanting in the most voluminous of intellects. Jan van der Heyden, who has sometimes been called the Gerard Dow of architecture, and whose works in English collections have told with excellent effect among the Old Masters in the Royal Academy, is uncommonly well represented in the Hermitage. Here are eight pictures, which is double the number found in Dresden and more than the total in eleven of the principal galleries of Europe. It has been justly said, that this painter knew how to reconcile an infinite detail with a keeping and a collective effect, which accorded precisely with nature as seen through a diminishing glass. Of such mechanical merit yet indescribable charm are 'Un Chateau' (1200), and 'La rue interieur de la ville de Cologne' (1207). The landscape painter Both is poorly represented, but Pynacker, who also studied in Italy, appears, as ever, brilliant in atmosphere after the manner of southern schools.

Snyders has fourteen pictures in the Hermitage, a total vastly in excess of the number in any other gallery except Madrid. In the numerical representation of this master, the Museums of Europe stand in the following order : Madrid has twenty-two works, St. Petersburg fourteen, Paris and Dresden each eight, Berlin seven, Turin six, London none. Snyders though coarse had great power : his friend Rubens scarcely surpassed him in force or action. Snyders, Rubens, Vandyck, and Jardaens were close friends, they painted much together, their several styles assimilated ; Rubens put figures into the animal pictures of Snyders, and in turn Snyders painted animals for Rubens, though Rubens was the greater animal painter of the two. Four large compositions which display Snyders in his most repulsive aspects, were purchased by Lord Walpole from the celebrated connoisseur Triest, bishop of Bruges, who had given the commission to the painter. The pedigree therefore is direct and undoubted. I cannot say that the quality of these famous works is commensurate with their size. 'The Fruiterer's Shop' (1312) could have been painted better by the late George Lance. 'The Greengrocer's Establishment' (1313) commends itself by cabbages larger than life. 'The Fishmonger's Stalls'(1314–1320) is not particularly savoury, and yet perhaps of four large scenes, one devoted to Fruit, another to Vegetables, a third to Game, and a fourth to Fish, this last is the best. It is evident that these four shops carried on as roaring a trade as Snyders himself, the artist painted wholesale and traded wholesale. I shall never forget the astounding effect produced by these sign-board pictures. as they hang in the large handsome hall known as the Snyders Gallery. The smaller pictures are the best : thus, amazingly clever is the study of the heads of

four cats mewing (1323), also 'The Concert of the Birds'
(1324). The last has been rightly regarded as one of the
most remarkable efforts of this artist, who, as a rule, had
but a dim insight into the finer instincts of birds or
beasts: he painted the carcase, the hide, the fur, the
plumage, but not the intelligence. Herein Snyders falls
far short of Landseer. This Bird Concert was fitly in
the collection of the sculptor Gibbons, himself a lover of
birds, trees, and flowers; it then passed into the Walpole
Gallery. This fanciful composition, like many of its companions, has been engraved, a tribute to the artist's
popularity. Vos, the imitator of Snyders, has several
pictures, which might easily pass for the master's. Fyt is
another painter in the provision line; 'Fruit' (1334), and
'Trophies of the Chase' (1336), are good examples of
this dead-alive art. Weenix is also capital in his way,
his hares, partridges, and peacocks (1347, 1348) are
certainly very superior commodities. Still-life, including
flowers, fruits &c., are painted to perfection by Huysum
(1378, 1379); there are also good examples in the same
line by Heem, Mignon, and Os. In fact the Hermitage
is well stocked with what may be called conservatory
or market-garden wares. The Russians are known
to have a passion for flowers; when snow is on the
ground, and ice upon the river—halls, staircases, and reception rooms are gay as gardens. The Russians too
are fond of the chase; the present Emperor is a bold
huntsman. Thus Rubens, Snyders, Weenix, Huysum,
and Heem, fittingly find prominent place within the
Hermitage.

The German School in the time of the decadence in
the seventeenth and eighteenth centuries, is seen by
accustomed works. Thus there are a couple of large
landscapes with animals (1280, 1281) by Rosa di Tivoli;

then comes Denner with the familiar head of an old woman, probably a stock model (1286); Dietrich, another painter of last century, is seen to succeed indifferently well with high art and low art alike; 'The Repose in Egypt' (1291), and 'A Roman landscape with cows' (1295), are equally within his sphere; his pictures are sometimes pretty, a 'Mother and Child' in Dresden is an agreeable genre treatment of a sacred theme. Raphael Mengs took a loftier flight; 'St. John preaching in the Desert' (1298) is at once effective and vulgar: there are other weak and pretentious efforts of this mistaken painter, who seems to prove by his egregious failures the impotence of grand theories in the studio. But I was not displeased to find here, in the remote region of Russia, the finished sketch for the fresco of Parnassus, called in the catalogue 'The Apotheosis of a Poetess' (1300). This work got into the collection of Lebrun the expert, whence it was purchased for the Hermitage at the sum of 1000 francs. I have often in the Villa Albani gone to the fresco, of which this is the study, in order to judge what Mengs at his best could do; the art is effete, a compilation and a compromise not to be tolerated in these days, when sincerity of purpose and direct appeal to nature are tests of truth, taste, and talent. This composition, as far as I have been able to observe, is the masterpiece of Mengs. The Hermitage, it may be added, possesses more works by Mengs than any other gallery. Angelica Kaufmann fitly brings this classic eclecticism to extinction. This elegant lady has obtained a wide geographic distribution. I recently found in Dublin that she had decorated mansions. Then in the Dresden Gallery she is known by a graceful sympathetic composition of Ariadne. In Vienna also are pictures which have struck me as among her best, they only want the touch of nature, the fire of genius. In the Hermitage are three pictures by this artist of feminine grace, and feminine weakness.

It has been often said that among Continental galleries the Hermitage alone admits the English school : ' Ecole Anglaise' appears in the catalogue, and obtains space on the printed plan of the gallery. Yet what appearance does it make ? Dawes, a second-rate portrait painter, worked in Russia, was appointed artist to the Court, became member of the Academy at St. Petersburg, and several of his portraits are present. There are also portraits by Walker, Dobson, and Kneller, and historic landscapes by Jones. The victory gained, if victory it be, is that three pictures by Reynolds, of more than usual ambition, are still hanging in the Hermitage. Reynolds received in the year 1785 a commission from Catherine. We are told by Northcote, ' that he debated long with himself on what subject to fix which might be complimentary to the Empress, and at first was heard to say that he would paint the procession of our great Queen Elizabeth, when she visited her camp at Tilbury, in the time of the threatened Spanish invasion.' But at last he made choice of 'The Infant Hercules overcoming the Serpents when in the cradle,' as the most fit, in allusion to the great difficulties which the Empress had to encounter in the civilisation of her empire, arising from the rude state in which she found it. Walpole had suggested as a suitable subject, ' Peter the Great at Deptford, exchanging his own dress for a ship-carpenter's suit, before he went to work in the dockyard.' Perhaps in the preference given to Hercules, Reynolds was fired once more with the ambition to enact Michael Angelo. Leslie says, 'the attitude of the little Hercules was suggested by an old German woodcut, in a book now in my possession, but which formerly belonged to Sir Joshua. All that is finest in the figure, however, is quite his own.' Many children sat for the Hercules. Mr. Tom Taylor speaks of the progress of the picture as follows :

'1787. During the whole of this year Sir Joshua was hard at work on the Hercules. He was assiduous in his use of the model; but his want of methodic skill and assured knowledge told heavily in a work of this scale and character. As he used to say himself of the picture, " there are ten under it, some better, some worse." The plain truth is, that Reynolds was not qualified for such a work; but there was no painter of his time of whom the same thing might not be said.'

Fortunately Russia had then no living painter who could do better. Brullof, who deservedly won European renown by the grand composition now in the Hermitage, 'The last day of Pompeii,' did not come till a generation later. 'The Infant Hercules' was placed over the chimney-piece in the exhibition of the Royal Academy in 1788, and notwithstanding its shortcomings, now painfully felt when brought into competition with the great historic works in the Hermitage, Northcote was able to declare that 'it had the most splendid effect of any picture he ever saw.' Barry also says, 'nothing can exceed the brilliancy of its light or the force of its effect.' The picture was engraved in mezzotint before it left for Russia, and the artist received in recompense fifteen hundred guineas. On reaching St. Petersburg the story goes that when the packing-case was unscrewed, none present could determine which side of the picture it was intended should be hung uppermost; however the Empress fortunately was well satisfied. Two copies of Sir Joshua's Discourses, one in English, the other in French, she had received with the picture at her request.

Shortly afterwards the Russian Ambassador in London waited on Sir Joshua and presented him with a gold snuff-box, on which was the portrait of the Empress enriched with very large diamonds. The portrait is described as a basso-rilievo : Catherine herself writes, 'It is of a composition made at my Hermitage.' The great interest taken by Catherine in the formation of her collections, as well as the desire she felt to add to her knowledge of art, is further attested by the gratifying communication made by the ambassador. The letter, signed by the Empress, contains the following passage, one proof among many that the Sovereigns of Russia have taken the trouble to make themselves acquainted with the art literature of Europe :

'I have read, and I may say with the greatest avidity, those Discourses pronounced at the Royal Academy of London by Sir Joshua Reynolds, which that illustrious artist sent me with his picture : in both productions one may easily trace a most elevated genius. I recommend to you to give my thanks to Sir Joshua, and to remit him the box I send as a testimony of the great satisfaction which the perusal of his Discourses has given me, and which I look upon as perhaps the best work that ever was written on the subject.'

(signed) CATHERINE.

St. Petersburg, March 5, 1790.

The Czarina also purchased 'The Continence of Scipio;' the Hermitage likewise contains a reclining Venus, half hiding her face with her right hand, and Cupid at her side ; this last is a replica of ' The Snake in the Grass.' These three pictures belong to the closing years of the artist's life ; indeed it was the painter's executors who received the purchase money for ' The Infant Hercules.' These performances have made very opposite impressions on various travellers and critics : thus the amiable, easy-going Dr. Waagen says, that 'The Hercules' need not fear comparison with the magnificent pictures by Rembrandt. Mr. Walter Thornbury, on the contrary, received a most unfavourable impression from the works of Reynolds, when brought into competition with the great Venetian and Dutch colourists. I think, however, it may be pleaded that no other modern painter would suffer less cruelly from this severe ordeal. Yet, I feel it to be unfortunate that Reynolds should be tested by the standard of historic composition : portraits would have done him more justice : indeed Reynolds is known to have influenced the art of portrait painting in Russia. A picture by D. Lavitski in the palace of Tsarskoè Sélo is in fact worthy of the school of Reynolds.

The French Gallery is situated in the old part of the Hermitage: the rooms, which command a lovely panorama of the Neva, were occupied by the Prince of Wales at the time of the coronation. Some of these apartments are rich in jasper, mosaic-work, &c. The collection, numbering 171 pictures, is only second to the Louvre : the chief masters, Nicolas Poussin and Claude, are represented by twenty-two ' and eleven pictures respectively, hardly any master of importance is wanting, and there are even some names present which cannot be found in the Louvre. A principal picture by Poussin is 'The Triumph of Neptune and Amphitrite' (1400). 'No finer work of the master,' says Dr. Waagen, 'is to be found in the Louvre.' 'Moses striking the Rock' (1394), from the Walpole collection, and engraved thrice, is the best of four renderings of the same subject. By Gaspar Poussin appear several landscapes, all from the Walpole Gallery. The eleven pictures by Claude are naturally unequal, of some I thought slightingly : the most noted are four, of 'Morning' (1429), 'Noon' (1428), 'Evening' (1430), and 'Night' (1431) ; each composition consists of

a general landscape, with a special scriptural incident, such
as 'The Flight into Egypt.' The figures are by Filippo
Lauri. Of Lesueur no gallery excepting the Louvre
boasts of so many examples as the Hermitage. The
Walpole and Crozat collections chiefly furnish the specimens, among which are conspicuous 'The Martyrdom
of St. Stephen' (1449), 'Moses in the Bullrushes' (1444),
and 'Darius Hystaspes at the Sepulchre of Nitocris,'
(1450). Lesueur, extravagantly extolled as scarcely inferior to Raphael by Victor Cousin in his Philosophy of
the True, the Beautiful, and the Good, never fails to
show himself weak and pretentious. Le Brun, although
much thought of in Russia, is not fairly represented in
the Hermitage. By Mignard no gallery excepting the
Louvre displays such important compositions as 'Jeph-
thah and his Daughter' (1455), and 'Alexander in the
Tent of Darius' (1456); the latter once belonged to the
notorious Duchess of Kingston. Examples are found
of Boucher, Valentin, the brothers Le Nain, Francois de
Troy, and Nattier. In a smaller apartment are fittingly-
disposed cabinet-pictures by Watteau, Lancret, and
Chardin. In an adjoining room may be seen 'The
Death of the Paralytic' (1520), one of the most celebrated compositions by Greuze ; also a group of children
round a cask used as a table (1516), one of the most
telling compositions by Fragonard. By Courtois, called
Le Bourguignon, the greatest French battle-painter of
the seventeenth century, are several characteristic compositions. The Hermitage possesses more numerous
and better works by Joseph Vernet than any other
gallery excepting the Louvre; 'Sea Coast,' 'View of
Palermo,' 'Sea Storm,' are titles which sufficiently suggest the agreeable mannerism and the dramatic plati-
tudes of this over-rated artist. Here in conclusion may

be mentioned Hubert Robert, a capital architectural painter greatly employed by Catherine. The works executed for the empress are among his best efforts. Among the number are ' The Ruins of the Temple of Concord at Girgenti' (1564).

CHAPTER V.

ST. PETERSBURG: THE KERTCH ANTIQUITIES AND THE MISCELLANEOUS COLLECTIONS IN THE HERMITAGE.

A COLLECTION of Artists' Drawings was naturally deemed essential to the Hermitage. The great Catherine made a commencement by the purchase of the cabinet of designs from the Comte de Brühl, at the time she acquired the Brühl pictures. This cabinet was composed of about 600 drawings of divers schools, which are now contained in twelve portfolios. Catherine made additions, and then followed purchases under Paul I. The collection has since reached a total of 11,880 drawings, of which 547 of the most interesting are shown in frames and cases. The rest, which are kept in portfolios, are accessible to amateurs on application to the keeper. The French masters dominate: thus Callot alone is represented by 1067 designs. Important also are 132 historic portraits in crayons, executed by Daniel Dumoustier and his pupils. They include Francis I, Charles IX and Queen Eleonore, Claude, Catherine and Marie de Medicis, Marie Stuart, Marguerite de Valois, &c. The collection further comprises views of towns, historic scenes, architectural projects, &c., many of which are of value to the archæologist and the historian. Among the number are 112 views of Finland, the Crimea, and Esthonia, by the painter C. F. de Kügelgen, who died at Revel in 1832; also seventy-eight views of the Crimea, Turkey, and Switzerland, by M. M. Iwanow, professor of painting in the Academy of St. Petersburg; likewise fifty-eight views of the city of Moscow and its environs, by the Russian painter F. Y. Alexeiew. Among Italian masters there are drawings put down to Mantegna, Da Vinci, Raphael, Michael Angelo, Titian, &c. For the most part these examples are unimportant if not problematical.

The Collection of Gems, one of the very largest in existence, is arranged in glass cases, in a spacious and handsome room. Unfortunately there is neither guide book nor catalogue, and the classification being according to subject-matter, and not by dates or styles, the student finds himself bewildered in a medley of antique, cinque-cento, and modern works. This immense collection—in 1794 Koehner rated the number at 10,000—has been made up from many sources at various times. Among the most important acquisitions was the renowned cabinet of the Duke of Orleans. More recently the collections of General Hitroff and the banker Doeppler have been added. The arrangement is, as I have said, based exclusively on subjects, among which are conspicuous, Roman emperors, Hercules, Socrates, Venus, Silenus, Fauns, Bacchanals, Leda, Diana, Queen Elizabeth, and Cromwell. Some of these characters are in great number. I regret that I have neither space nor knowledge to attempt a lengthened criticism. Days and weeks were needed for an examination and a volume for a description of the collection. I am disappointed to find that Mr. King, in his work on 'gems,' makes no mention of St. Petersburg; apparently he has not seen the Hermitage.

The Collection of Coins is quite as extensive and

remarkable as that of gems. And here again the stranger is struck with the ample space at command. In St. Petersburg, as in Munich, the city and its public edifices are planned for vast developments. The Hermitage in its wide-stretching territories may be said to symbolise the interminable empire of all the Russias. And the proverbial love of ostentation in Tsars and nobles has the salutary effect of preventing the light of science and of art from being hid under a bushel. Thus, while in the British Museum and some of the collections of the continent coins are packed away out of sight in drawers and locked-up cases, the whole numismatic treasures in the Hermitage are exposed to view under glass. I can never forget my amazement on first entering the apartments where were upwards of 200,000 specimens, all classified and labelled. The great Catherine, almost as a matter of course, made the commencement. And the first nucleus has since been increased by purchases and gifts, principally from Baron de Chaudoir, M. Reichel, Count Peroffsky, and M. Beulé. From M. Beulé, the well-known writer on the Acropolis of Athens, was purchased a fine collection of Athenian coins, containing more than 400 specimens of tetradrachms. A stranger, however, will have most to learn from the truly national series of the Russian coinage, here exemplified by 7000 specimens. These historic examples date back to a period when the art of coining was unknown. Before the use of a die was thought of, the practice obtained of chopping off from a larger mass half pounds or quarter pounds of silver, called respectively ' Poltinas ' and ' Roubles.' Pieces without stamp are naturally the most ancient. The modern ' rouble ' takes its name from these rough pieces of unwrought metal. The numismatic products of provinces now subject to Russia, but once independent, are naturally in unexampled number and magnificence. The coins and medals of Poland, downwards from the tenth century, occupy seven cases. The Slavonic races, Bulgarian, Servian, &c., furnish a fine and exceptional series. The Greek colonies of Chersonesus, Olbia, Phanagoria, Panticapæum, &c., show themselves strongly. The kings of Pontus and Bosporus are remarkably well represented. Thus it will be seen that Russia has not lost the opportunity afforded by her geographic position or military power of making these numismatic galleries illustrative of races, civilizations, and nationalities. She shows herself here, as in other departments, ready to aggrandise to herself the treasures of adjacent. and outlying states. From her position she is not only Northern but Oriental. When we here see that gold coins bearing the portrait of Peter the Great were worn as orders of merit, or as personal decorations, we are reminded of the Byzantine practice prevailing in Constantinople down to the present day of using coins as ornaments to the person. Neither in this cosmopolitan collection is England left out. Three cases are assigned to Britain. Of special interest are coins found on Russian soil of the time of Etheldred II, Canute, and Hardicanute. It may be gratifying to an excusable national vanity to know that Anglo-Saxon coins have been discovered throughout Russia from north to south. They seem to have obtained currency by means of the commerce in skins, &c., which subsisted even from Saxon times between England and the territories of the Baltic. We learn, too, that the early coinage of Russia was indebted for its design to Anglo-Saxon models. I have already remarked on the bushels of Anglo-Saxon coins dug up in Scandinavia. It is evident that the numismatic art, as indeed all other arts, came late to the Northern nations of Europe.

The ground - floor of the Hermitage, devoted to sculpture, &c., as I have elsewhere remarked, bears the same relation to the picture galleries above that the Glyptothek in Munich does to the old Pinakothek. But in Munich the sculpture and picture museums are divided, while in St. Petersburg they are under one roof. Hence it is that the Hermitage, compared with other European galleries and museums, is exceptional: sculptures, pictures, drawings, coins, gems, &c., being all brought together. The Hermitage, designed, as already said, by Klenze, the famous Bavarian architect, has naturally borrowed much from the Pinakothek and the Glyptothek ; yet the vast scale and the opulent enrichments are national, because in keeping with the wealth and the extent of the Russian empire. Solid, sombre, almost sepulchral, is this basement story ; and yet if the light be shadowy it is sufficient. The floors are here and there covered with old Roman mosaics, and the stone pavements, where more recent, are brought into accord with the general historic contents. Also the exhaustless supply of Finnish and other Northern stones and marbles gives unusual magnificence to these classic galleries. When native materials fall short, the gaps in the wall-spaces or otherwise are filled up by fitly-designed scagliola. The juxtaposition of colours may not always be under the control of any paramount or prevailing principle, and yet the general effect is that of a grand suite of marble halls. Certainly the whole interior is so skilfully arranged that it becomes difficult to distinguish between rich marbles, solid stones, and their imita-

tions. With this exhaustless resource, the backgrounds
to the antique marbles, though not always the best,
are very varied and generally agreeable. The simple
fact is that the classic statues are seldom first-rate in art
—very often scarcely, in fact, second-rate—therefore all
the more thankful ought they to be to the architect
and decorator for the aid afforded. Strangers in walking through these spacious halls, sustained by stately
monoliths, scarcely know to what regions they have
been transported. They find themselves in vaults of
silence and shadow, shut off from the sunshine or the
snow of the outer city. They are admitted, without
cost or credential, to a magnificence of structure and
of decoration which appears less in keeping with a
simple educational museum than with the ostentation
of some Oriental prince. The objects set up, as I have
before indicated, do not always demand by their art-
merit this imperial display. The Russians fall into a
braggadocio even in museums. Their wealth is usually
in excess of their knowledge and taste; they make
much cry over a little wool. Moreover they have a
propensity towards quantity rather than quality; students who have worked in the Vatican, in the Museum
of Naples, in the Louvre, or the British Museum, feel
that classic art within the Hermitage seldom reaches
the highest standards.

But exception must be made in favour of the hall
which ends these sepulchral chambers. Room seven,
devoted to the antiquities from the Cimmerian Bosphorus, is supported by twenty monoliths of grey
granite. This gallery, though sombre, being lighted only
from one side, is specially imposing by reason of this
double row of columns, which reminds the traveller of
the old Roman basilicas, or of the more recent Munich

counterfeits. And yet here again I have to say that the art effect gained is scarcely commensurate with the lavish outlay: indeed the one impression left on my mind is that Russian Governments never count cost or economise material; that when they do not screw they squander; that where they do not starve they supply to satiety. Hence the violent extremes between the squalor of the hut and the splendour of the palace. Hence, also, it may seem to follow that in the Hermitage a cost which has not been counted, and which probably will never be made publicly known, sometimes stands but as empty parade. And yet I am bound to confess that after having visited every museum in Europe worth visiting, the magnificent room on the basement of the Hermitage, set apart to the Kertch antiquities, is unrivalled in its structure, its decoration, and its contents. I had been told beforehand that a summer trip to St. Petersburg was easy and pleasant, and that in the Hermitage I should see a collection of gold ornaments, &c., not surpassed, if indeed equalled, in the Vatican. I found the tour both easy and pleasant, though I am bound to add not cheap, and in the promised Kertch antiquities I certainly was not disappointed.

The Galleries of antique sculpture consist of odds and ends variously collected, with a small percentage of works approaching first class merit. Peter the Great, Catherine II, Paul I, Nicholas I, Alexander II, each in turn made purchases or presented donations; one of the latest additions being forty-three statues from the Campana Collection. The figures of highest merit come from Kertch. I regret to say that a wholesale system of bold and unscrupulous restorations, more reckless than the many modern transformations

which disfigure European galleries generally, materially detract from the value of the antique sculpture
in the Hermitage. The primary motive evidently has
been to produce an imposing effect, and with this end
archæologic truth is sacrificed. 'A Mercury' has
been made up thus: the torso is fine and the head
is antique, but the one does not belong to the other;
again, 'A Bacchus' is half ancient and half modern,
the right hand, the left arm, and a great part of the
legs are restorations. I am glad however to be able
to say that the official catalogue confesses the whole
truth. 'The Venus of the Hermitage,' which has a
claim to pass for a good contemporary copy, though
scarcely by a first-rate hand, of the 'Venus de Medicis,'
has received the following additions:—the end of the
nose, part of the upper lip, the right hand, and the
whole of the fingers on the left hand. Yet such restorations, compared with others, are of minor importance.
Among the very few works which deserve to be known
beyond St. Petersburg are, 'Bacchus' (156), 'Antinous'
(60), 'Augustus' (193), 'Demosthenes' (197), 'A Sarcophagus' (191); all except the first are from the Campana Collection. The Egyptian and Assyrian antiquities are of minor importance.

The famed Kertch Collection is contained, as already
said, in a magnificent room supported by twenty monolith columns of grey granite. The antiquities here
united were all found in the Cimmerian Bosphorus, on
the eastern side of the Crimea, occupied from about the
year 500 B.C. for several centuries by a Greek colony,
governed by dynasties of kings. The district around
the modern town of Kertch, which gives its name to
this memorable collection, has been long known as the
site of ancient sepulchres, and since the year 1825

excavations have been carried on, latterly by the Government, which have brought to light no less than fifty-eight tombs, some found to have been already opened and pillaged, as were the sepulchres of Egypt and Etruria, but many others remaining intact. These discoveries have an import for art and archæology comparable to the excavations at Pompeii and Nimroud; indeed in some departments, such as gold ornaments, the remains at Kertch, Theodosia, and other neighbouring localities, are wholly without rival. Two exceptional discoveries have specially contributed to enrich the Hermitage; the one was of the necropolis, with its royal tomb of Koul-Oba in 1831, the other, made in 1858, consisted of the Tumulus called 'Paul' (Pavlovskoi Kourgan). A large portion of these remains were naturally first deposited in the local Museum of Kertch; they became however of such imperial, not to say European, importance, that their removal to St. Petersburg was a politic if not an inevitable step in state policy.

In a tomb near Kertch were found the two finest statues in the Hermitage; a husband and wife who were therein buried. The period is not earlier than the first century of the Christian era, but the style is so pure and noble, the attitude so individual, and the head so portrait-like, that at once the comparison is suggested with the figure of Aristides or Æschines in Naples and the companion figure of Sophocles in the Museum of the Lateran. Hence it is scarcely too much to say that this husband and wife rank among the finest portrait statues that have come down from classic times. The draperies are broad and finely cast, and the general treatment is charmingly simple: the presence of writing materials has led to the conjecture that the man was erudite;

such accessories in other works indicate some intellectual calling. I would give much to have seen these figures presiding in calm dignity over their own graves.

The collection of funereal gold crowns is not equalled in the Vatican or elsewhere; of these thirteen are laurel, seven parsley, one olive. The number of crowns found on the heads of the dead in the tumuli of Kertch is in accordance with the law and the custom among the Greeks, which permitted that any person who in life had acquired a crown of merit might wear it when carried in funeral procession. These crowns and headdresses show play of fancy, and a fine adaptation of forms beautiful in nature to decorative ends; that they are so naturalistic in treatment may arise from the fact that crowns of honour were often woven out of living leaves gathered on the soil of victory. One of the most exquisite of these head ornaments is a composition of ears of wheat, assigned either to the fourth or to the third century before Christ. The workmanship, it will be readily imagined by all who are acquainted with classic gold, is equally perfect as the design.

The finest collection of classic jewelry in the world the Hermitage owes to the Cimmerian Bosphorus; neither the Castellani Collection in the British Museum, nor the riches of the Vatican, approach the treasures exhumed from the tombs at Koul-Oba, Theodosia, and other Crimean sepulchres. The specimens consist of necklaces, head-bands, bracelets, brooches, filigree-buttons, earrings, &c.; the last are varied by every possible motive, such as winged cupids, winged victories, winged horses, &c. These small articles being easy of transport were not of necessity made on the spot, indeed it is sometimes difficult to determine, especially where local character is wanting, whether the crowns, vases,

jewelry, &c., found in the tombs were wrought by
artists living in the colony, or whether they were
brought in the course of commerce from Greece or
Asia Minor. Either hypothesis is consistent with the
facts of the case. The collection of gold necklaces,
no less than forty in number, for design, workmanship,
and rich variety of material, puts to shame the work
of the most skilled modern jewellers. The enrichments
are of filigree, enamel, and precious stones, with pen-
dants of Victories, Medusa heads, bulls' heads, &c.
Again, I was struck, not only with the wide geographic
distribution of art types through the south of Europe,
but also with the persistent permanency of certain art
manufactures in given nations. It seemed to me
evident that the skilled gold-workers of Russia in the
present day are the lineal descendants from the Greek
colonists in the Crimea, the designs now used are
often analogous to, and sometimes identical with, Greek
work of the third century before Christ ; thus for more
than two thousand years has there been a succession
of skilled artisans, and just as in the art of painting
the Byzantine type is handed down from generation to
generation, so in the art of working in gold and silver
the traditions of the craft have been carefully conserved.
Yet the art degenerated in the course of its descent
through times of barbarism. I do not remember to
have seen among modern Russian gold-work chains as
delicate as their prototypes ; indeed some of the chains
found in the Crimean tombs are almost more like a
silk ribbon than a piece of metal work.

The tombs have preserved, in addition to the treasures already enumerated, collars of pearl, ornaments
in amber, cornelian, and agate, amulets in chalcedony,
rings plain and engraved, &c. In the queen's tomb of

Koul-Oba, one of the richest yet discovered, was a magnificent gold head of Minerva, with a grand head-gear composed of sphinx, griffin, winged horse, and owl. This precious design is supposed to preserve the type of the Minerva of the Parthenon, and partial critics have been found who assign this very work to the age of Phidias. In the neighbourhood of Kertch have also been discovered objects in glass of varied forms and enrichments; the so-called 'Tear Bottles' are of exquisite beauty. This part of the collection shows to what rare perfection the art of fusing varied coloured glass had reached—a method borrowed by the Venetians from the East at a later period. The universal tendency to polychrome is here once more apparent; the Crimea, indeed, would seem to be the spot where Grecian form met and mingled with Oriental colour.

Also these sepulchres—which proved as rich as if they were art museums—contained works in silver, bronze, and iron. There are now in the Hermitage helmets, pieces of armour, poignards, swords, &c.; the warrior was buried with his weapons, just as by the side of a lady were placed her jewels. The collection of silver vases and drinking vessels is unrivalled. The designs, consisting of figures and animals in low relief, are sometimes in the purest style of Greek art—nothing better exists in the analogous painted designs on the fictile vases found in Magna Græcia. The British Museum is fortunate in the possession of a few like examples of this silver *repoussé* work. The metal-work from Kertch, however, displays a mixture of styles pure and impure, a mingling of manners civilized and barbarous, which, as will be seen in the sequel, are peculiar to the locality. Here is a vase, for example, in electrum, wherein the figures and costumes are Scythian, the bas-reliefs resemble certain of the designs on the Column of Trajan, wherein appear the peoples who dwelt on the shores of the Danube.

Next must obtain mention some unique plaques of box-wood and of mammoth ivory, whereon in outline are engraved human figures, horses, &c., equal to the purest designs on classic mirrors. No outlines on Greek vases are more faultless. The date of the finest may be 300 years before Christ, but chronology I hold to be here again uncertain; some authorities actually fix the fourth or fifth century B.C. as the epoch. I do not think these very exceptional works are generally known, especially as they do not obtain mention in Mr. Maskell's volume on ivories. The compositions include the ' Judgment of Paris,' also ' Horses and Chariot,' scarcely inferior to the bigas in the Elgin Frieze. These plaques are fragments, probably from caskets now destroyed. Flaxman and Stothard would have rejoiced over designs which embody the ideal which they strove for and attained. There is also in this matchless hall devoted to the Crimean antiquities a coffin in cypress-wood finely chiselled with Greek ornaments, likewise a Juno in bas-relief on wood, the figure and drapery are grand. I should doubt if there be more valuable wood-work in the world, whether for antiquity or for art. The wood-work in Westminster Abbey is comparatively of but yesterday. The climate, as also the geologic strata of the Crimea, must be less than usually destructive. Here colour is again present; this sarcophagus retains the remains of vivid pigments. The arrangement of harmony is apparently not peculiar to the colony, but characteristic of Greek proper. It is evident that the well-conserved antiquities from Kertch furnish important data towards determining much-debated points in classic polychrome.

The collection of vases in the Hermitage is numerous rather than choice. Of 1800 specimens, the best are either from the Crimea or from the Campana Collection. From the latter is the remarkable 'Vase of Cumæ,' supposed to be an Athenian work of the fourth century before Christ. The form is of exquisite beauty; the greater part of the surface is black, upon which two bands of figures in relief, and coloured with gold, blue, red, and creamy white, tell out with superb decorative effect. Time has changed the original colours. The figures in design and modelling, though of a high order, and of a good time, are scarcely up to the perfect type or execution of the best Greek or Roman sculpture. This vase might be cited as collateral evidence in the much disputed question as to whether the Greeks coloured their marble statues, at any rate it would seem to prove that the artists of Athens were as supreme in colour as in form. Of the 400 vases which have been found near Kertch, some two or more correspond in the painted reliefs to the 'Vase of Cumæ.' One which represents the combat of griffins and the Arimaspi, is supposed to be the work of an Athenian artist living in the Chersonesus, the subject being local, and the generic style being also modified by treatments peculiar to the spot. The manner falls short of the best standards; for example, the transition between low relief and high relief is not understood; the modelling, too, is in parts clumsy. These faults teach a truth often forgotten, that even the Greeks are imperfect, save in their choicest works. To me this vase was of supreme interest as an example of polychrome applied to surfaces in relief; here are two magnificent griffins tinted with blue, ochre, and gold—the decoration is superb. Numerous terra cottas also prove that Kertch was the region of colour, yet the design and workmanship are rude. Among a multitude of subjects I noticed a replica of a favourite group in the Vatican, often repeated, a child struggling with a swan. The ancients were as much addicted to the repetition of a favourite idea as the moderns.

A room in the Hermitage is devoted to the antiquities from Scythia, Siberia, and Sarmatia, which last corresponds in part to European Russia. We have seen in the remains from Kertch that Greek art preponderates, here, on the contrary, it is in the minority. One case, devoted to the objects found in the tomb of a Scythian king on the banks of the Dnieper, is of supreme interest, as showing how divers styles were in these regions brought together. Here the gold ornaments are mostly barbaric in design and execution : Greek works were evidently importations and luxuries. Northern types prevail, even Scandinavian forms are present, and the lowest art, or rather the absence of all art, is reached in works assigned to the Finnish race. In this rich tomb of the Scythian king were treasured a large vase and dish, silver-gilt, which serve to illustrate how Greek art became modified by locality. The silver vase, which is more than two feet high and belongs to the best period of Greek art, is decorated with figures in relief, representing Scythians taming horses, also griffins attacking stags. The prevalence of griffins throughout all these remains, whether Grecian or barbaric, is accounted for by a tradition that this fabulous animal was born and bred in these parts.

Before finally quitting these remains, a few more illustrations may with advantage be quoted of the

manner in which arts of various periods and nationalities are brought together in the sepulchres of Kertch.
The Crimea, in fact, offers to the archæologist problems
analogous to those which arise in Cyprus. Recently
we have seen in London a collection from that island
which proved that the local art fell successively under
the control of Egypt, Greece, and Rome. A like combination of distinctive nationalities is discovered in the
Crimea. For instance, in the tumuli are found the blue
vitreous figures which abound in the tombs of Egypt,
also is present the scarabæus, which if not necessarily
Egyptian, is probably of Egyptian descent. There
also occur gold ornaments in form of fantastic monsters
after the type common in Scandinavia; for instance,
'The Gold Collar of the King of Koul-Oba' is supposed
to be Scythian. But it is interesting to observe, in
elucidation of comparative national archæologies, the
resemblance between this Scythian work and the Scandinavian collars in the Stockholm Museum. Yet to
conjecture that at some distant period Scythia and
Scandinavia were identical would be to jump too boldly
at a broad conclusion. But at all events such collars
do not belong to classic art : thus the collar round the
neck of 'The Dying Gladiator' is taken as a proof of
a barbaric race, and yet these collars, though Northern
in design, are in point of execution up to the standard
of the best classic metal-work. Then again in this
tomb of Koul-Oba are gold ornaments, the figures
Phrygian in costume, and similar to the personages
who appear in the cylinders of Babylon and Persepolis.
Also are found Assyrian lions and Scythian horsemen.
Other treasures are said to resemble certain remains in
Etruscan tombs ; there are works too which come down
to the Roman period. These several specimens, foreign

to the Crimea, are planted in the midst of rude products which sprang up indigenous to the soil. Thus it will be seen that the analysis of these remains brings out a close correspondence between the arts and the local conditions. The Crimea was a half-way-house, where the arts of the East and of the West found a home, where the perfect form of Greece and the glorious colour of Persia joined in close compact. The Crimea by the fertility of its soil and the beauty of its climate attracted to its shores peoples from Athens and the Greek colonies in Asia Minor. The emigrants brought with them the styles which belonged to high civilization, while the aboriginal inhabitants retained their native forms, which, if semi-savage, were vigorous and naturalistic. Such may be considered the simple analysis of the somewhat complex art-products found in the ancient tombs of the Cimmerian Bosphorus.

CHAPTER VI.

RUSSIAN ARTISTS. THEIR LIVES AND WORKS.

RUSSIA encountered an exceptional difficulty when she determined to create a school of modern art which should accord with the modern civilisation she had resolved to assume. Unlike other nations, she had no historic basis whereon safely to build. Throughout the empire the art of Byzantium held tyrannic sway— an art which, in Constantinople, having settled into stiff and solemn inanity, has been handed down, century after century, as a sacred petrifaction which could not be changed without fear of sacrilege. And so it happened, that when the time came for political regeneration, this art, which refused to move on, had simply to be set aside. In other words, the vital elements for the or- dained revival not being extant within the empire, modern art and living artists had to be imported or created for the occasion; just, in fact, as shipbuilding and other industries had to be learnt in Western Europe, or the needful mechanics brought already trained to St. Petersburg. The consequences of these exceptional conditions may be readily conjectured; instead of an unbroken chain of historic development, stretching as in Italy over a period of many hundred years, there occurs in the pedigree of Russian art a sudden break, a broad chasm, accompanied by strange and contradictory manifestations. The misfortune is that the old art is too old, the new art too new; and the intermingling of both is like that of new wine in old bottles. It may be pleaded that the new product is at all events cosmopolitan; certainly the constituent materials, as will be seen in the sequel, have been collected from all the capitals of Europe, and for this reason the art which obtains currency is but too often a confused compilation, a jargon of many tongues, a chaos wanting the order of nature, the unity of creation. And yet it is hard to see how Russia could have acted otherwise; like England she imported what she needed, and at the same time took efficient measures to make the arts grow and thrive in soil within the confines of her territory,

Under an absolute monarchy the arts spring into life by Imperial decree; hence in Russia a sudden and amazing birth. Mosaics are manufactured which weigh ten tons a-piece; domes and ceilings are covered with pictorial designs life-size; churches are enriched with devotional and decorative art; and galleries and palaces hung with historic compositions, genre pictures and landscapes. The origin of this remarkable movement does not date further back than the eighteenth century. St. Petersburg itself—the youngest if not the grandest of capitals—was founded as recently as 1704. And Peter the Great, whose name the city bears, fearing that the new-born civilisation might prove a little bald and plain without the aid of the arts, sent Russian youths to Italy, Holland, and other countries, to learn architecture, sculpture, and painting. This goodly practice has, to my knowledge, been kept up to the present time; for over a period of nearly a quarter of a century I have met in Italy and other Continental states with art-students, pensioners from St. Petersburg—a class of men well selected, well trained, and altogether well appointed and provided for. Russia has, like most other nations, with the exception of England, established a branch Academy in Rome: she grants to each student a pension of £160 per annum; £40 is allowed for the journey out, and the same sum for the return. Six years is the time allotted for this foreign apprenticeship. We shall see in the sequel that it is not unusual for Russian artists to take up a permanent residence abroad. I remember to have visited in Rome the studio of Piceno Orloff, a historic genre and portrait painter; also the studio of M. Ivanoff, at the time when he had completed the great work of twenty years, 'Christ appearing at the Baptism of John.' It may here be observed, that comparatively few of the most famous pictures of the Russian school have been painted within the Russian frontier: even in St. Petersburg is yet wanting that atmosphere of art, that fellowship of artists, which in Düsseldorf, Munich, Florence, and Rome, sustain and animate the painter in his work. Artists in St. Petersburg live in comparative isolation: they are as a colony planted on the utmost verge of civilisation; they are as exiles or exotics, far away from the commonwealth of art, left to pine or starve in a cold and sterile soil.

The rapid and all but unprecedented rise of Russian art may be ascribed to a twofold cause: first, a national art was needed for national ends; second, the nation— in other words, the Imperial Government—took all requisite measures for meeting the want. By means of the usual high-pressure appliances the supply soon became equal to the demand. As long ago as 1757 —that is, eleven years before the existence of the Royal Academy of London—the Academy of St. Petersburg was established and endowed. Catherine II, following the example of Peter the Great, patronised art and pensioned artists: but the difficulty was to disengage the affection of the painter and of the people from the old sacerdotal style—identified with the stagnation school of Byzantium. Yet the Academy once established has, down to the present time, done good service. Backed by the talent, industry, and creditable work of its pupils, members, and professors, this noble institution compares not unfavourably with sister associations in Western and Southern Europe. The spacious and stately building wherein the Academy is housed forms one of the series of imposing classic façades on the banks of the Neva. The structure has a frontage of 400 feet; columns, pilasters, a central cupola, and a colossal Minerva, make a composition after the usual grandiose pattern in this showy capital. The interior, too, in the manner of these Imperial establishments, is lofty and large in vestibule, staircase, halls, schools, and galleries; and the whole establishment is well ordered and liberally equipped. Thus an extensive and judiciously chosen collection of casts informs the pupils of the history of sculpture. In like manner, by copies from the chief works in the Vatican, some executed under command of the Government by students during their pensionate in Rome, the art of painting is brought to the knowledge of the future Raphaels and Michael Angelos of Russia. The ample though not always choice products of this Imperial munificence are gathered together in picture-galleries, which contain a fair epitome of the Russian school since its rise, little more than a century ago. The chief works here exhibited will fall under notice in the sequel. The Academy is so richly endowed that it educates, and in some degree maintains, 300 pupils. The handsome edifice serves also as the residence of professors, academicians, and others who merit favour or can confer honour or advantage. Within the circuit is comprised the Imperial establishment of mosaics, and so ample is the provision afforded that the total number of persons accommodated under the roof has been estimated at not less than 1000. Assuredly there is something grandly wholesale in this way of going to work.

The artists of Russia in their up-hill career have also been greatly helped by the 'Society for the Encouragement of the Fine Arts.' I have not been able to learn very much of this Association, but during my stay in St. Petersburg I visited a permanent exhibition in the Newski Prospekt which appeared to be identified with the Society. A director, who said his ambition had been to tread in the footsteps of King Cole of Kensington, handed me a pamphlet, which set forth the aspirations and efforts of Imperial administrators. This Society has been in existence many years : thus Count Raczynski, in 1841, says that he cannot close his epitome of the Russian school without homage to its services. Established in 1820, it has been protected and sustained by three successive monarchs, Alexander I, Nicholas I, and the reigning sovereign, Alexander II. It supports students at the Academy, it sends on foreign travel young artists of talent, it gives to painters commissions, besides laying out sometimes in a single year as much as £1000 in the purchase of pictures. Brulloff and Ivanoff were among its pensioners, and without such timely succour the ability of these and other painters, who have cast lustre on the land of their birth, could not have found adequate development. Possibly in the course of another century painters may no longer need a fostering hand, but for the present Russian art is pretty much in the position of literature in England at the time when Dr. Johnson had to seek a patron in the ante-room of Lord Chesterfield.

The Russian school, though in comparative infancy, has been prolific: pictures to be numbered, not by tens or hundreds but by thousands, and occasionally attaining to dimensions of full five-and-twenty feet in length, are in St. Petersburg distributed between the Hermitage, the Winter Palace, the Academy, the Cathedrals of St. Isaac and of the Kazan, the Permanent Exhibition, the Historic Portrait Gallery, and the Palaces of Peterhof and Tsarskoé Sélo. Moscow also comes in for her fair share of national products, scattered among palaces, museums, and galleries. The difficulty of gaining an accurate knowledge ˉof art and artists in Russia is greatly enhanced by the absence or the inefficiency of catalogues.

In Russia, as in England, the national school had its origin in portrait-painting—an art which, lying near to necessity and responding closely to the affections and vanities of mankind, is among the foremost to find birth in all nations. But Russia has been, in more ways than one, less fortunate than England. In the first place, her national portraiture wants antiquity: we search in vain for heads coeval with England's historic portraits of Richard II, John Wycliffe, Geoffrey Chaucer, &c.; and noble families are wanting like the house of Derby, which boasts of a lineage of family portraits from the first Earl in the fifteenth century. Then again, Russia, in point of art-merit, finds herself at a long interval from England; not so much, however, by reason of inferiority in her native painters, as because she has never been able to press into her service men comparable to Holbein, Antonio More, and Vandyck. The Russian Historic Portrait Gallery had been recently opened at the time of my visit to St. Petersburg. The collection was gathered from Imperial and private galleries in St. Petersburg, Moscow, and other places. Of the 800 pictures thus brought together, the major part naturally belonged to the eighteenth century, though some dozen or more were of the seventeenth or sixteenth centuries. In walking through the rooms, it was curious to observe how loyalty had led to the multiplication of certain Imperial heads : not even Henry VIII is known to posterity by as many replicas as Peter the Great and Catherine II. Of the former were collected twenty-three portraits ; of the latter, no less than fifty-six. The entire collection, I am sorry to say, proved in how low a state the art remained down to the middle of last century. Still there is cause for regret that so little has been known of a Gallery which, in the way of historic records, could scarcely be overrated. With the exception of a short paragraph in the ' Pall Mall Gazette,' I have seen no notice of the assembled monarchs and their illustrious contemporaries. The best portraits I have met with in Russia are in the palace of Tsarskoé Sélo : the painter Demetrius Lavitski is said to have formed his style in England, under the influence of Reynolds. Russia, in fact, owes much to England. Catherine II purchased, in 1779, the Walpole Collection ; and thus Vandyck's portraits of Charles I, of Henrietta, of Laud archbishop of Canterbury, of Inigo Jones, of ' Two English Ladies,' &c., all of which we covet for our National Gallery, now enrich the Hermitage. The importation of these and other master-works from the Walpole and Houghton Collections was well timed : by contact with foreign schools the formless art of Russia was fashioned anew. The connexion with England became still closer when the Empress gave to Reynolds a commission to paint, without limitation of price, the large picture now conspicuous in '*l'école anglaise*' of the Hermitage. It may thus be readily understood how the style of the aforesaid Lavitski was all but identical with that which prevailed in England in the time of Reynolds and Gainsborough. Nevertheless some surprise was naturally felt when there appeared at the International Exhibition of 1862 that capital portrait of ' Glaphyra Ilymof' (date 1776), a full-length figure of a well-dressed lady, gracefully handling her harp. The picture, which in quality I deem to be one of the very best products of the Russian school, was only inferior to Reynolds in colour and felicity of touch. I will not trouble the reader with a transcript of my notes on a dozen or more fairly good portraits by Brulloff, Kiprensky (called the Russian Vandyck), Tutrumof, Varneck, Keller, Pleschanoff, and Zarianko. Portrait-painting is the common resource of Russian and English Academicians alike: thus the figure-painters of St. Petersburg I find described, with prevailing uniformity, as 'historical genre and portrait-painters.' Hence · a century of portrait-painting in Russia naturally responds to the changing styles in other departments : consequently it is not needful further to treat of the art separately.

The reputed father of the Russian revival is Iwan Lossenko, one of the many artists engaged by Catherine to decorate her palaces. This painter had a career which is typical of the whole school. He first served a pupilage in the Academy of St. Petersburg ; he then received a pension to pursue his studies in Paris and

Rome; at length he matured that high and historic style which entitled him to assume a professorship and directorate in the Academy which he had first entered as a student. In matters of art Russians seem ever to be arguing in a circle : they commence with a foregone conclusion, they end where they begin; hence each painter does little else than tread in the footsteps of his predecessors, and progress becomes difficult, if not impossible. The nascent style, though new in Russia, was old in Europe: certain artists at the outset took to fresco-painting, and palaces in and about St. Petersburg show in ceiling decorations the influence of Watteau and Boucher. Pictures in the Hermitage, however, indicate more of Italian than of French influence. Thus 'The Miraculous Draught of Fishes,' by the above - named Lossenko, emulates Raphael, and is not much inferior to the Carracci : the style is directly academic and eclectic, and yet, though there is a parade of learning, first principles are imperfectly understood. One thing is certainly but too apparent in the performances of this period,—the determination at any cost, whether of time or of money, to achieve for the Russian empire an art ambitious and imposing. Ugrumoff, pupil of Lossenko, and in due course appointed Professor and Rector of the Academy, followed in the footsteps of his master. A couple of pictures by this well-reputed painter, placed permanently in the Hermitage as a pledge of individual and national genius, the one 'The Capture of Kazan by John the Terrible in 1552,' the other 'The Election of Michael Romanoff to the Throne of Russia,' find mention in my Journal in the following unflattering terms :—' These two pictures are very large, very feeble, very pretentious. It is evident that the first reformers and innovators were not strong enough to deliver themselves from the conventional, smooth, and debilitate manner of their Byzantine progenitors. The colour, as usual, is bad, though Oriental splendour has been attempted.'

The best way to understand the revival of painting in Russia is to accept the movement as a constituent part of a greater whole. First came a newly-ordered empire, a newly-constituted civilisation. Contemporaneously arose the arts of utility. Then were superadded beauty and decoration, the arts of refinement and of luxury. And in this new birth, architecture of course, as the connecting link between utility and beauty, necessity and superfluity, led the way, and imposed the conditions. Hence the stranger, when he walks through the squares and streets of St. Petersburg, and beholds the parade of classic columns, pediments, and cupolas, can tell at a glance what must be the pictorial arts which reside within academies and palaces. As I have before stated, Russian painters, in breaking loose from historic moorings, plunged headlong into the Italian Renaissance; they had wrenched themselves with such violence from the old prescriptive art of the empire, that at one rebound they leaped to the furthest extreme, and had neither time nor inclination to stop among the early pre-Raphaelites, or to tarry with the mediæval Gothic arts which might have offered them a half-way resting-place. Thus these Russian revivalists, at one fell leap, landed themselves in the midst of European decadence. In the review of the works produced, I do not wish wholly to condemn manifestations which in older nations might savour of the tyro or the schoolboy. Russia, considering the difficulties of the position, has done well: perhaps, under the circumstances, she could scarcely have done better. She has, at all events, brought to bear upon the arts which adorn her chief cities, strong resolve, definite system, and vast wealth.

Russia is no exception to the law that the grandest art has always been the issue of a united Church and State. The world owes its great Cathedrals to the combined religious and temporal power. By such power, centred in the Tsar of all the Russias, has the Cathedral Church of St. Isaac been reared. What St. Peter's is to Rome, what St. Paul's would become for London if fitly decorated, the Cathedral of St. Isaac is to St. Petersburg. It is the embodiment of a great idea, a sacrifice to God, an offering up of what is most precious in the nation's substance. I will not stop to inquire whether the wiser course would not have been to have adopted the Byzantine architecture of St. Sophia for the design of the grandest temple yet raised to the Greek ritual. What chiefly concerns the present argument is, that when once the forms of the Eastern Empire as found in Constantinople, Ravenna, and Venice, were rejected in favour of the Italian Renaissance, as exemplified by St. Peter's in Rome, the treatment of all the accessory arts, the style of all subsidiary sculptures, mosaics, pictures, and other mural decorations, followed in logical sequence. Thus the external statues and bas-reliefs, even when Russians have been employed, partake of the French or modern Italian manner; the mosaics also, instead of being severe or archaic, belong to the mode known as the pictorial; while the paintings, though here and there bearing trace of the Greek school, pertain substantially to the Italian decadence. This surrender of all claim to nationality was of course to be expected, as soon as a French architect, M. de Montferrand by name, was called upon to make the design and carry out the work. But, at all events, the pictures are in great part by Russian artists ; the mosaics, too, are directly national, if not always in design at any rate in execution. Likewise the structural and decorative materials — the richest ever brought to the service of the Church—consisting of malachite, lapis lazuli, polished porphyry, and many-coloured marbles—are all the produce of the Russian dominions. The collective effect, though far from satisfactory when tested by strict standards, is most assuredly not devoid of Oriental splendour or barbaric grandeur. Yet it must be confessed that the pictures in oil suffer in competition with the sumptuous materials wherewith they are surrounded. Mosaics must inevitably make merely painted designs look weak and poor. And frescoes, which would have been a more equal match to richly encrusted decorations, were forbidden, as incapable of sustaining the severe vicissitudes of the northern climate. Perhaps the wiser course had been to exclude, as in St. Peter's in Rome, oil-pictures altogether, and so to trust for pictorial embellishment to mosaics exclusively. But mosaic—the art for eternity—cannot be carried out in a hurry. In the meanwhile, recourse was had to oil-painting on canvas. But the architect, foreseeing the difficulties involved, gave strict injunctions that all pictorial compositions should be treated with breadth, simplicity, and decision—instructions all the more needed because these are the last qualities we look for in Russian art. It may be fortunate for the painters concerned that their shortcomings are shrouded by the sacred shadow of a gloomy interior.

St. Isaac's suffers, in common with the interiors of all Greek Churches, from the strict interpretation of the commandment, 'Thou shalt not make unto thee any graven image.' Thus even Thorwaldsen's statues of Christ and the Twelve Apostles, as set up in the Protestant Church at Copenhagen, would be deemed in Russia of the nature of idolatry. An architect is in fact precluded from using, either for the purposes of decoration or devotion, any figure in the round : only are permitted pictures, mosaics, bas-reliefs, and other designs on a flat surface. It were foreign to my purpose to point out how illogical is this distinction ; all that is here needful to say is, that it will always be hard for the arts in Russia to stand against this obloquy thrown on the noble art of sculpture. In St. Isaac's the pictorial decorations were apportioned between Frenchmen, Italians, Germans, and Russians. The following names of the artists employed declare tolerably well the several nationalities engaged : — Pluchart, Chamchine, Mussini, Steuben, Riess, Markoff, Schebouief, Moldavsky, Zavialoff, Brulloff, Neff, and Bruni. Only the last three have executed works in St. Isaac's, the Church of the Kazan, or elsewhere, which call for individual mention.

Karl Brulloff (born 1800, died 1852), known as a historic portrait and genre painter, professor in the Academy, Knight of the Order of Wladimir, &c., was the first Russian artist to acquire a European reputation. This distinction is rightly due to one of the most remarkable pictures in modern times, 'The Last Day of Pompeii,' conspicuous for something better than size among the works which constitute the Russian school in the Gallery of the Hermitage. Karl Brulloff the painter was brother to Alexander Brulloff the architect; the latter can scarcely be forgiven for having disfigured the Kremlin in Moscow, perhaps the most picturesque position in Europe, with a palace which in art-design is surpassed by some of the Manchester factories and warehouses. Each brother, as a matter of course, studied in Italy, and thence, as the custom is, imported into Russia corrupt and hybrid styles. 'The Last Day of Pompeii' is allied to the school of the Carracci; indeed Russian painters half-a-century ago, conforming to the tendency of the times, thought with Reynolds that too much study could not be given to the masters of Bologna. Yet this great work also shows the influence of David, Lebrun, and Girodet. Brulloff studied in Rome while Girodet was Director of the French Academy on the Pincian: the Frenchman and the Russian met, and their styles evidently intermingled. 'The Last Day of Pompeii,' which was painted in Rome just about forty years ago, is engraved in the work of Count Raczynski, and has been known throughout Europe as the most memorable achievement of the Russian school. Over a canvas five-and-twenty feet long the city is in flames, the inhabitants are flying, the ashes are falling. The picture is well conceived for situation and dramatic action. The heads, the general anatomies and the draperies, prove study and persistent labour; but the manipulation, as usual in Russia, is mechanical; the surface is smooth, even to weakness; texture there is none. The work as a whole is perplexed by anomalies and contradictions. It is formal and yet extravagant, it is academic yet spasmodic, it leaves the spectator cold because, instead of issuing from the heat of imagination, it comes piecemeal by a process of slow elaboration. When a Russian painter deems that his

subject wants more heat he throws in a little fire and
brimstone, just as a cook adds pepper or curry-powder
to a hash. In Moscow I recall a dozen or more
studies and pictures which prove Brulloff to have been
a man of no ordinary power and resource. He died
full of work : yet the designs made for the decoration
of St. Isaac's, carried out by inferior hands, are far
from satisfactory. 'The Triumph of the Madonna,'
in the dome, is a confused extravaganza, which might
have been compiled in competition with the same
subject by Correggio, known as the 'Hash of Fogs.'
Yet Brulloff has rightly been held in high esteem,
and how favourable was the impression made by his
master-work will be seen by the following interesting
entry in the journal of the late David Scott:—

'21*st January*, 1833.—Meet Gibson, Macdonald, and Severn, and go
in a body to visit Overbeck. . . . . Out into the open air again,
we pass along to the studio of Brulloff, a Russian, who has nearly finished
a large composition, 'The Last Day of Pompeii.' He has made a grand
work, with good painting on the surface, good drawing and design, and
great unity of invention; upon the whole, one of the best of that class of
pictures I have seen. But there is awanting something to stir the mind
strongly and awake thought. All is expressed and lain open. A whole sheet
is spread before you, written from beginning to end, and you tire of what is
so fully and often told. The costume is very exactly attended to. This
historical accuracy the French have the merit of introducing; it has since
spread over all the Continent, but is resisted by some of the Germans.
My companions praised both the Russian and the German, but Gibson
afterwards began to criticise.'

F. Antonowitsch Bruni, a family name found more
than half-a-dozen times in the annals of European art,
is a painter who merits to have his biography written.
First a pupil in the Imperial Academy, then a resident
for years in Rome, he returned to St. Petersburg in
1844, became professor and director, and entered on
colossal undertakings. The manner he brought back

with him was naturally that of the late Italians.
'The Brazen Serpent,' scarcely less famous that its
companion picture in the Hermitage, 'The Last Day
of Pompeii,' is five-and-twenty feet long; it comprises
thirty groups and as many dramas; the drawing is
good, the expression and action are intense. But the
manner, as might be expected, tells of the painter's
foreign studies. Battoni and Benvenuti are present;
David is not far distant; and yet to a prevailing
eclecticism are added the vigour and impetuosity which
occasionally enter into these northern schools. Moses
and the surrounding priests are noble; still I fail to
distinguish in this crowning achievement any distinctive nationality, anything amounting to a new element
in the way of art-creation. Bruni fell into a fault but
too common among these Russian painters: inconstant
ever, they pass from style to style, from subject to
subject; at one moment they paint Venus and the
next they compose 'The Last Judgment.' As an almost inevitable consequence, individuality is lost and
sincerity and conviction are surrendered. Thus in the
Hermitage the same artist produces a coarse and
voluptuous 'Bacchante,' and 'The Agony in the Garden.'
The last widely-diffused composition may have suggested to Joseph Meyer one of the most impressive
scenes in the Passion Play at Ammergau. It is the
misfortune of these Russian painters that they serve
two masters—they are by turns sacred and profane.
Still allowance must be made for the tentative efforts
of an infant school, which not unnaturally tries everything in order to prove wherein its power may lie.
Bruni's life has been crowded with work; he painted
for a church in Constantinople, for the Kazan Cathedral
in St. Petersburg; and his arduous undertakings in St.

Isaac's have for scale and wide range of thought been compared with the labours of Michael Angelo in the Sistine. The compositions extend from the transept to the door; they comprise a grand Biblical series, including 'The Deluge,' 'The Sacrifice of Noah,' 'The Vision of Ezekiel,' and 'The Judgment Universal.' The colossal Christ, standing with upraised arms in the midst of quick and dead, is two or three times the size of the surrounding figures—a treatment consonant with Byzantine practice, size being here put as the outward sign of Divine power. On the one side the overthrow of the wicked is a grand, impetuous passage, which recalls the compositions of Signorelli; on the other, beings who enter on life eternal have a beatitude and beauty akin to Fra Angelico. Thus the reader will already have surmised that Bruni owes somewhat to Raphael, Michael Angelo, and Il Beato; something also to Overbeck, Cornelius,. and Kaulbach. In thus attempting to assign the exact whereabouts of the artists of St. Petersburg, it may not be wholly fanciful to indicate points of analogy between Russia and America. Each country has vast territory, occupied and unoccupied; each nation is comparatively new to art and to civilization; each is alike fired by ambition in excess of knowledge, by zeal beyond discretion. And thus the painters of Russia and America 'rush in where angels fear to tread;' as adventurous settlers who overrun a thousand or more miles, they engage to cover two or three hundred square feet of canvas, and if they lack capacity or creative thought they borrow and annex what is most to the purpose or nearest to hand. They appropriate too, on slightest pretence, not only foreign art but the foreign artist: thus Bierstadt is claimed as an American, though born and educated in Germany; and in like manner Bruni is deemed the head of the Russian school, though his birth-place was Milan, and his name, and in great part his education, were Italian.

Timothee Andréewitsch Neff, judged by his naked nymphs, which are more often copied than any other figures in the Hermitage, can have no very decided vocation for religious art. But Neff and his brethren in St. Petersburg, like Cornelius and Kaulbach among the Germans, treat all themes and all creeds, if not with absolute indifference, with perfect impartiality; and thus Mount Parnassus, Mount Olympus, and the Mount of Transfiguration, have equal claim on their time and talents. Neff, when most true to himself, most nearly approaches Riedell, Winterhalter, or Leopold Robert; but, like other artists in the Russian revival, nothing contents him till he reaches that last infirmity of feeble minds, the perpetration of high art. He has painted for the chapel of the Winter Palace 'Greek Saints' and 'The Last Supper.' His works have obtained place in St. Isaac's, and his designs are translated into mosaics in the Imperial manufactory. Neff was born in 1805 in Esthland, on the Gulph of Finland : as the province is chiefly held and cultivated by Danes and Germans, the question here again arises as to whether the painter's nationality is strictly Russian. But the Imperial patronage which brings from the north and from the south, from the east and from the west, all outlying talent, attracted Neff to St. Petersburg. In the year 1837 he is painting portraits for the Royal Family, in 1844 he is in Rome, in 1851 he is again in St. Petersburg, patronised by the Court. Such, in brief, is the life and the labour of the leading artists in Russia.

Russian painters, it is said, are short-lived, and subject to sudden overthrow. Brulloff died while yet strength and work should have remained to him ; some report through passion for his art, others surmise from passion of another sort. I have understood, and can well believe, that self-indulgence is an infirmity to which art-genius in the northern states of Europe is peculiarly prone. The poet and improvisatore Bellman, the Burns of Sweden, died, it is not precisely known how or why. Popular writers, who turn plainest facts into thrilling romance, would have us believe that Bellman expired, as the fabled swan, in the act of singing. Others assert, as a literal truth, that the poet's soul was sighed out in a fit of drunkenness. I have been informed, that in these northern climates the art temperament is singularly subject to catastrophe. At any rate, as to the general population of St. Petersburg, I can testify that in no other European capital is drunkenness seen so openly in the public streets. Within the space of a short walk from my hotel in St. Michael's Square I have counted, about the hour of twilight, more than a dozen men and women reeling between the wall and the gutter. The cause of this popular habit it is not hard to divine. Provisions are dear, while spirits, hot as wildfire, are so cheap, that the luxury of getting drunk can be purchased for twopence. Moreover, in climates humid and cold, stimulants may seem the natural resource.

It might be interesting to carry the argument some steps further, and to show the relation which subsists in these northern zones between the arts and insanity. Yet, judging from the internal evidence afforded by the many thousand pictures painted within a hundred years—which is about the limit of the art-period in northern Europe — I should say that the painters are not insane enough. With comparatively few exceptions the works have been done to order in cold blood; they lack afflatus; they are too prosy and heavy to be touched by madness. M. Zichy of St. Petersburg, however, has an imagination by turns exalted and debased by a species of demoniacal power. And Malmström, the Swede, enters fairyland with a kind of hobgoblin fancy, which seems to tread on the confines of artistic inspiration and high artistic phases of insanity. I find myself led insensibly towards questions of utmost interest, difficult as they are delicate. It is well known that the dark nights, the long dreary winters of Norway, engender brooding melancholy verging on madness. In the arts of Scandinavia I see dark shadow and dismay. In the wood-carved doors and pulpits of churches, in the tables and chairs of domestic dwellings belonging to a barbarous age, I find the serpent and the dragon devouring their prey. The gall of bitterness, the tooth of poison, the tongue of flame, have from time out of mind entered into the arts of these moodily-imaginative races. The relation between race, climate, religion, government, on the one hand, and the arts on the other, lies at the root of national art growth. In Russia, however, a problem always difficult to solve becomes further complicated. The icy cold of the north is thawed, as it were, by contact with the sunny waters of the balmy Mediterranean. And this conflict and fusion of antagonistic elements may serve to explain the statement above made, that the artists of the north are frail and short-lived. If we imagine a plant taken before its prime from its first habitat in St. Petersburg, then plunged in the Roman Campagna, and, after there growing in summer sunshine side by side with the acanthus, removed from the banks of the Tiber to the shores of the Neva, we picture to ourselves the severe experience of Russian artists. Few constitutions are strong enough to withstand the trial. If again we imagine a mind naturally lethargic, engulfed in the gay dissipation of Paris, or strung up to a high pitch of tension and sensitiveness by mingled study and pleasure in Italy, if we suppose such a nature taken back in the conflict of hope and fear to St. Petersburg, a capital termed for its dissipation the Babylon of modern Europe, we can well understand how men prematurely break down.

The art evolved is just what might be expected. It has a groundwork heavy and dense as a clay subsoil : plodding stolidity lies as its substratum, and then on the surface come a play of hectic light, a pulse of fever, an electric flash, as when a galvanic wire convulses the stiffened limbs of a creature whose life is gone. Such is the penalty when the order of nature has been defied ; when the arts which have affinity for the Equator are dragged within sight of the North Pole. But possible escape may come. In the streets of St. Petersburg are sold delicious melons, ripest grapes, and figs ; they are grown on the sunny shores of the Black Sea, in the fertile fields of the Crimea. Even so, when Russia shall have planted or conquered a southern capital, may spring into life the arts which of yore flourished in the soil of Greece or under the sun of Italy.

There are certain outlying capitals wherein painters of genius may labour for life with little chance of achieving European reputations. Vienna hardly lies within the commonwealth of art, and the more distant cities of Moscow and St. Petersburg are all but severed from the great centres of contemporary schools. Otherwise it might appear astonishing how little is known beyond the Russian frontier of artists who, if they belonged to Paris or London, to Berlin or Munich, would have been made familiar as household words. At all events, almost unheard of in Western Europe are three painters, Professor Gay, M. Flavitsky, and M. Ivanoff, who, if somewhat inferior to Delaroche, are about on a par with E. M. Ward, R.A. when at his best, or with J. R. Herbert, R.A. when most academic. Yet of these three distinguished men Ivanoff was a close student in Rome for twenty years, and Flavitsky and Gay have contributed large historic and sacred works to International Exhibitions in Paris and London. The chief work by Professor Gay with which I am acquainted is 'The Last Supper,' a large imposing picture that serves in its place within the Academy on the Neva to pronounce the ambition, the power, and even the originality of the Russian school. The conception and composition are new and bold; the Supper is not arranged at a long straight table as by Giotto, Leonardo, and others, but more after the manner of a triclinium, as by Poussin. Unwonted prominence is given to Judas, a grandly dramatic figure in deep unbroken shadow cast with startling contrast against a surprise of light. The situation is tragic, even melo-dramatic; and to gain all possible force, even surface-texture is not neglected, a quality in which Russian artists are usually deficient. I would point to another work by Professor Gay, 'Christ's Agony in the Garden,' a conception of rare originality and power. The figure is in grand isolation, the disciples are away, and the Saviour kneels alone in prayer and agony. The olive trees around are true as if painted on the spot. I have myself walked and sketched within the inclosure half-way up the Mount of Olives, which still bears the name of Gethsemane, and the trees that yet survive are said to have witnessed the Agony. The artist gains reality by his fidelity; fancy could not have filled in so fitting a back-ground.

I may here add that one of my objects in making a tour to Russia was to observe how the head of Christ had been treated by the Greek Church from the early Byzantine times down to the present day. The space at my command does not permit me to enter on so large a topic. I will therefore only observe that Professor Gay has introduced into Christian art, almost for the first time, the Slavonian race. The type differs from the head of Christ in da Vinci's 'Last Supper.' The brow is less serene; the eyes are small and sunken, the cheek-bone is high, altogether the head is more individual than ideal, at least in our Caucasian sense. Yet the artist evidently strives after an ideal—the divine in the human—only his basis or starting-point is not Caucasian, but Slavonic. I may further add that the growth of the hair, divided in the middle of the forehead and falling in long lank ringlets down to the shoulders, is after the style adopted by the priests of the Greek Church. Professor Gay agrees with the masters of Italy in giving to the head of Christ a lofty coronal development; on the contrary, Tilbruni, who finds a place in the Hermitage, as well as some other Russian painters, fall into the fatal mistake of a low sloping forehead, with a flat unelevated crown. Russian artists need to be informed of the laws of cerebral development. I would here remark that I have never seen in Italy or in the East finer models for prophets or apostles than the priests who officiate in the Kremlin, Moscow, or in the cathedrals at St. Petersburg. An English photographer, Mr. Carrick, residing in St. Petersburg, has

made valuable studies of the head and robes of venerable ecclesiastics ; the series, if published, as originally
intended, would be prized not only by artists, but by
persons of various religious denominations interested
in the faith and the ritual of the Greek Church.

Constantin Dmietriewitsch Flavitsky (born 1829, died
1866), successively pupil, pensioner, and professor of the
Imperial Academy, is one of the many Russian painters
who has been carried off in his prime. His large picture,
' Christ on the Cross,' gained him a pension ; his composition in the Academy, ' Early Christians about to
be given up to Wild Beasts in the Coliseum,' though
florid and extravagant, does credit to his training ; his
third and last work, ' The Legendary Death of the
Princess Taraknoff,' the most memorable among the
Russian contributions to the Great Paris Exhibition of
1867, gave him a place by the side of Delaroche among
the illustrious dead. The drawing and modelling of the
figure were true and firm, altogether the work displayed
a well-trained maturity which took Western· Europe by
surprise, full credit not having been given to Russia for
the strenuous and noble efforts made to rear and to
sustain a school of high art. Yet Flavitsky's imagination was fevered ; instead of a mind like that of
Delaroche, preserved in the calm balance and the ab-
stracted contemplation which befit the student of history,
this artist, in common with his contemporaries, fell into
sensation and melodrama. This lady of the legend is
seen calmly awaiting her watery grave as the flood
sweeps upwards to her point of refuge ; rats driven
from their holes and hiding-places gather round her.
It has been thought that a rat is too ignoble a creature to find admission into high or imaginative art ;
Mr. Millais, in his picture of drowning Ophelia, at first

introduced a water-rat, but on reconsideration, the artist
determined that the low-bred animal should be painted
out. Flavitsky suffered like other over-wrought men,
he was borne down under stress of work at the early
age when Raphael died ; he permitted himself no
respite or recreation ; he was literally worn out in his
thirty-seventh year from want of rest. At the time of
his death he was busy on designs of saints for one of
the churches at Wilna. Of like Church patronage it
is hard to see the limit or the end ; for example, in
Moscow is a vast church, the pictorial decorations
whereof will occupy years, and throughout the empire
new edifices will from time to time be raised, or old
places for worship restored, the walls of which will
give employment to artists yet unborn. A future for
the Russian school is thus secured, and that future
presents points of analogy with past epochs in Italy
when the Church was the munificent patron of art.

Yet, in the meanwhile, the life of the Russian artist
is chequered, shadows darken the sunlight, the heart
grows sick through hope deferred. Such was the lot
of Alexander Andréewitsch Ivanoff, whose master-work,
' Christ appearing to the people at the Baptism of John,'
is by far the most important example of the national
school in the public gallery of Moscow. Thirty years
ago, Count Raczynski, judging from studies then made,
predicted that the picture would constitute an epoch
in Russian art. The conception is fine. The multitude,
draped and undraped, are gathered on the banks of the
Jordan awaiting baptism. The Saviour comes. St.
John, a grandly conceived figure, exclaims with upraised arms, ' Behold the Lamb of God.' Some deride,
others look with mingled wonder and worship. The
Saviour, still in the distance, slowly bends His steps

to the place of baptism, but as yet He is alone; the solitude of the figure is most impressive. The figures, life-size, and five-and-thirty in number, have been justly extolled for accurate drawing and forcible expression, yet it has been objected that the forms are monotonous, as if the models had not been sufficiently varied, and undoubtedly the colour is crude and exaggerated. I remember the time, now nearly fifteen years ago, when the picture just finished was the talk of Rome. The artists in the Café Greco were unanimous in its praise, but the colour was known to be so outrageous that an English photographer, who had been commissioned to take a plate for transmission to Russia, declared the task impracticable. Yet I fancy that a cheap print which I purchased under an archway in Moscow must have been indebted to a photograph for the accuracy of its outlines. The picture in this popular reproduction may be said now to form part of the pictorial Bible of the people. The Russian peasant has a craving for prints, made the more popular by hot stimulating colour, and during fairs, and at places of pilgrimage, the sale of Madonnas and Saints, and pictures of miracles performed expressly in honour of Russia, becomes quite a flourishing trade. But poor Ivanoff did not live to enjoy the popularity which awaited his picture. In my mind's eye, I see him now, silent and sad, careworn and broken in health, as he stood beneath the immense canvas which embodied the anxious toil of twenty years. He had borne up against poverty, he had struggled manfully through obscurity, and then as the goal was reached he died. The sad tidings, when they reached England, moved me deeply; even in the proverbial calamities of genius few stories are more touching. Russian artists overtax their powers, and imperial patronage has been known to come as a death-warrant. Brulloff, as we have seen, died in harness; Flavitsky broke down from want of rest; Ivanoff barely lived to see his life's work accomplished.

The number of artists in Russia who can execute a fairly good historic picture is much greater than could well be imagined. England, at least since the dissolution of the Fine Arts Commission, must yield to Russia in the way of high art. The surprise that a semi-barbarous nation should take the lead in what is deemed the most advanced walk in the profession, may be lessened by the consideration that mediocre historic pictures are of all works the most easy. Vasari boasted that even in his time art had made such astounding advance that it was possible in a few days or hours to carry out designs which in previous centuries had called for years. Even in the same proud position has the Imperial Academy placed the artists of St. Petersburg. The number of painters who can execute respectable academic works almost exceeds the bounds of belief. Among the best of their kind I have noted the following:—MM. Müller, Egoroff, Reutern, Bassine, Tilbruni, Simmler, Bronnikoff, Jacoby, Ravolof, Chumakof, Sheremetef, and Kiprensky. These, and other painters with careers well defined at home, are in Western Europe as absolutely undistinguished as if they lived and laboured in the Chinese Empire. For instance, Theodore Müller, who deserves to be remembered for a rapturous and Raphaelesque composition, 'The Preaching of St. John in Patmos,' finds no place in biographical dictionaries, though more than forty artists of the name of Müller are studiously recorded. Five out of the above dozen painters, however, figure in Dr. Waagen's work on the Hermitage. Kiprensky has been called the Russian

Vandyck; his portrait of Thorwaldsen has character and power. Egoroff's composition, 'Christ Bound,' is at all events not without ambition. Bassine's 'Socrates defending Alcibiades in Battle' may be received as a standard work by reason of the place accorded to it in the Hermitage. The Academy cherishes a large number of prize pictures rewarded, with gold medals: the fault of these pretentious performances is that they but too closely resemble the inflated essays of school-boys. Altogether, it must be admitted that the Russian pictures in the Hermitage and the Academy suffer in comparison with the works of French artists—Le Brun, David, Gericault, Robert, Vernet, Ingres, Flandrin and others in the galleries of the Louvre and of the Luxemburg. But for Russia the future is hopeful: Russian art is in progress while the French school is now in decline.

Russia affords interesting illustration of the well-known affinity between national arts and generic races, between pictorial styles and conditions of physical geography. Sometimes, however, the art product comes as an anomaly and a surprise. For example, in Perm, an outlying town on the Ural mountains which a traveller might reach from Moscow in the space of a week or ten days, is born a man, Theodore Bronnikoff by name, who paints nothing more cognate with his native land than 'Horace reading Satires in the presence of Augustus and Mæcenas,' a work which, notwithstanding some flagrant faults, found a place in the Great Paris Exhibition of 1867. The explanation of the apparent anomaly is easily given: Bronnikoff has resided much in Rome. When I come to speak of genre painting it will be found that the shores of the Caspian and the wilds of Siberia have paid tribute to art; in other departments, too, painters have been gathered from Finland and the borders of the White Sea in the north, and from Poland and the Crimea in the south. Thus the geographic distribution of the arts is already widely extended. Poland indeed, as may readily be imagined, is more fertile in art than Russia proper. Joseph Simmler was a Pole of whom Russia, pursuing even in the arts a grasping policy, may be said to have possessed herself by right of conquest. Simmler, born in Warsaw and educated in Munich, received tardy recognition when, two years before his death, he was elected Honorary Member of the Academy of St. Petersburg. The love of his native land showed itself strong in his art,—'The Death of Barbe Radziville, wife of Sigismond August, King of Poland,' is an able and powerful composition. Art genius among the oppressed people of Poland is not exceptional. It may be remembered that Madame Jerichau of Copenhagen is a Pole, and travellers who tarry at Cracow, or other cities in Austrian or Russian Poland, do not fail to recognise in the peasantry and townspeople the presence of an artistic race, manly and graceful in bearing, and eminently picturesque in costume. Great indeed is the contrast between Poland and Russia. In the south of Russia I have travelled post two hundred miles, at the rate of ten miles an hour, but the carriage was an open cart filled with straw and without springs, and the roads could scarcely be distinguished from open arable and pasture land. On reaching the Polish frontier at Czernowitz all was changed, instead of wild interminable steppes, desertlike, was a country tilled as a garden; in place of barbarism were the outward signs of civilization; in lieu of a peasantry unconscious of art as the Bedouin

Arab or the native of Australia, were a people who walked the earth proudly as dethroned kings or dispossessed nobles, who carried themselves with histrionic command as if they had once played important parts in the drama of history. Never have I seen finer models or more effective subjects for pictures, than in and around the city of Cracow: it was market-day, and the Poles were dressed gaily, as if they intended to make of each street and square a picture.

Russia, an empire not only of undeveloped resources but of unascertained talents, is not, like other countries, worn out. At any moment genius may break forth brilliantly in unexpected places. When in St. Petersburg, I met with a student, Henry Scemiradsky, of whom, if I mistake not, Europe will take notice. Having gained the gold medal, he was occupied when I saw him on a historic composition of usual gigantic proportions which bids fair to win for him the prize of Rome. In the heat of youth the artist had already thrown off wild fantasies such as 'The Destruction of Sodom and Gomorrah' and 'The Descent into Limbo.' The Russian Government kindly provides a remedy for such youthful indiscretions,—the student is sent away on his travels with a pension, and in six years may return the Raphael or the Kaulbach of Russia. Every master is simulated save Titian,—the colour of Venice has hitherto been denied to St. Petersburg.

Russia labours under disadvantage in not having struck out either new styles or new subjects. It was easier no doubt to fall into routine, to copy than to create, but Russia will fail of that work which is reserved to her by right of race and religion, of geographic position and political power, if she do not bring into the field of art new ideas. It is the peculiar

province of the painter and of the sculptor to embody
in visible forms the thoughts which find utterance in
a nation's literature, the sentiments which obtain voice
in a people's songs, the traditions which haunt historic
monuments, the poesy which animates and personifies
the woods and the streams, the elements of earth, air,
and water. It is strange as it is lamentable that the
folk-lore of Russia has hitherto done little or nothing
to enrich the national art, and yet when I turn to such
a volume as Mr. Ralston's 'Songs of the Russian
People' I find in every page a picture. Nature, in
the people's literature, lies on the confines of the
supernatural, sylvan nymphs and demons, water sprites
and shadowy beings of the upper air dwell in the solitary places. The traditions are all the more pictorial
because the powers of Nature are personified, — the
aspects and phenomena of Nature assume human significance. The rainbow is recognised as a road which
leads from this world to the other world ; the milky-
way is a station where stand four mowers who guard
the sacred road and cut to pieces all who attempt to
traverse it. The subject here shadowed forth is scarcely
less grand than the four riders of the Apocalypse as
depicted by Cornelius. Then we come upon word-
pictures which tell how passionate is the longing of a
people immured in snow and ice for blissful realms
where no cold winds ever blow, where no winter ever
enters. The 'Midsummer Night's Dream,' which gave
to Sir Edwin Landseer a fairy-like theme, is not more
suggestive to the painter than are these northern sagas.
Sometimes the myth is clothed in beauty, more often in
grandeur. Kaulbach's weird personation of 'Tradition'
with a black raven at either ear, is in the spirit of
these northern imaginings. We read of mighty forms,

of the spring-tide of storms; of the snake older than all snakes; of the prophetic raven—elder brother of all ravens; and the bird, the largest and oldest of all birds, with iron beak and copper claws,—'The Lightning Snake,' 'The Tempest Bird.' Russian artists are guilty of a dereliction of duty in not endowing with pictorial form the bold and beauteous images which hold in strong possession the minds of the people. Now is the time or never; in yet a little while the barbarism which permits wild growth to imagination must make way for an unpoetic and unpictorial civilisation. Russian artists are right to go to Paris for manipulation, but not for inspiration; imagination, if true to race and traditions, must burn as the Northern Lights which illumine the skies of the Russian winter.

Russia has need of military painters, but the time has scarcely arrived for the celebration of naval victories. With one fleet sunk in the Black Sea before Sebastopol, and another fleet said to be too antiquated or rotten to venture out of sight of Cronstadt, naval painters can find little or nothing to do. Indeed, England as monarch of the seas is almost the only nation that has reared an able body of marine painters; and assuredly no other country in Europe can show works comparable to Stanfield's 'Victory towed into Gibraltar,' or sundry storms at sea and naval battles by Turner, such as 'Trafalgar' in Greenwich Hospital. French pictures of this class are as disastrous as the defeats which the French navy has usually suffered. Baron Gudin, who was for years ready to signalise any sea victories which might fall to the good fortune of Napoleon III, knows so little of the ocean that he cannot draw a wave. It is then scarcely to be wondered at that Russia can

boast of but few marine painters. Jean Ayvasowsky
has indeed rushed headlong into ' The Deluge,' a furious
and formless extravaganza, which wins a place in
the Hermitage, more by its ardent imagination than
by its knowledge of art or of nature. Perhaps the
only Russian who has proved himself equal to a naval
combat is Alexis Bogoluboff. Like the no less famous
Kotzebue, who was a soldier before he became a battle
painter, like our Clarkson Stanfield, who had been a
sailor before he was a marine painter, Bogoluboff
served as an officer in the navy before he painted a
sea combat. Born in 1824, this seaman carried off the
grand prize in the Academy of St. Petersburg at the
age of twenty - seven, six years later he was made
Academician, and in 1861 was appointed professor.
Yet in common with most of his contemporaries he
is far from being wholly a home product; Bogoluboff
in fact owes much to having studied in Düsseldorf,
under the great coast painter, Andreas Achenbach.
Among the many works I have seen by this artist,
fortunate in Imperial patronage, may be noted for more
than common excellence, ' The Debarkation of Russian
Troops in the Gulph of Agrakhan, under the command
of Peter the Great,' ' A Naval Combat at Irengham,'
and ' A Seaport in Normandy.' The manner is down-
right and manly, the artist is without ostentation, he
knows what he is about, the conduct of his pictures is
sailor-like and soldier-like. This enterprising painter
has travelled far and wide, his subjects range from
Constantinople to Normandy, from the Crimea to
Kamschatka ; the artist and his works are alike cosmopolitan. Two pictures in the International Exhibition, Kensington, sustained a well-earned reputation.

Russia has struggled through campaigns which she

can scarcely wish to see recounted upon canvas. The
Crimea is at least for the present a territory closed to
her battle painters, and the internecine wars with the
Circassians are not conspicuous in her picture galleries.
The overthrow of the first Napoleon, and the retreat
from Moscow, furnish dramatic scenes which have been
committed to the French painter Yvon. The Winter
Palace on the Neva shows a large panorama of troops
struggling through interminable snow tracks, but the
scene might just as well have been laid in Siberia as
on the road from Moscow; Yvon never visited the one
region or the other. Like objection is said to hold to
the numerous military manœuvres of Kotzebue, the
only Russian battle painter known beyond the frontier
of the empire; the only artist rewarded in the great
Paris Exhibition with a prize. And though the medal
was but a third class, it is to be observed that Adam,
the highly reputed battle painter in Munich, took no
higher rank. Alexander von Kotzebue has for some
time also resided in the Bavarian capital, where I have
seen his pictures and learnt of his mode of work. It
may be he is spoilt by success; in fact, he seems to
have been borne down by the weight of Imperial
commissions. The Emperor Nicholas conceived that
the career of Suwarrow in Switzerland and Upper Italy
would yield pictorial incidents which might redound
to the national honour; accordingly Kotzebue was
engaged to depict twelve large scenes, the best known
of which is 'The Passage of the Devil's Bridge by the
Russian Army in 1799.' The painter formed his style
as usual by contact with contemporary art in the chief
capitals of Europe. Having won the gold medal in
St. Petersburg, he entered on the accustomed course
of travel; he visited Holland, Belgium, and Italy, he

also studied in Paris at the time when Horace Vernet may be said to have established the laws of battle-painting for the century; finally, he settled down to hard work in Munich, at the period when Kaulbach, Piloty, Adam, Horschelt, and others, had reduced historic painting, whether civil or military, to a set system, a grand routine, a stately march, answering, as it were, to beat of drums and sound of trumpet. Kotzebue, however, has one exceptional advantage, he brings to the battle-field the knowledge of a soldier; he commenced life in the cadet corps at St. Petersburg, and up to the age of two-and-twenty he served in the imperial guard. This training enables the painter to lay out his battle-field as a tactician; the foreground is planned for military movements, the whole action is brought before the eye vividly and intelligibly; the surrounding landscape is pleasing as a picture and useful as a chart. Among painters of Russian campaigns should not be forgotten M. Grouzinski, who exhibited at South Kensington in 1872 that brave battle-piece, 'The Assault of Gounib.'

It may be here observed that in Russia military men show aptitude and affection for the arts. An officer who lost his right arm in the battle of Leipzig took then to the brush. We have seen that Kotzebue, while studying tactics, dabbled in paint, and that Bogoluboff served on board ship before he tried his hand in depicting a naval engagement. And certainly an officer in regions lying on the boundary line of savage life, thrown among tribes nomadic as the Bedouin, picturesque in costume and manners as the wandering gipsies, must have many temptations to the use of the pencil. In no part of the globe have I ever seen a military pageant so resplendent as the fête of

the Empress at Tsarskoé Sélo; neither in Egypt, Syria,
or Turkey, have I seen mendicants or pilgrims so apt
for the sketch-book as in the sacred city of Kief.
Amateurism in Russia, it may be supposed, is further
favoured by an unusual amount of leisure: in few
other countries does time lie so heavily on the hands.
The practice of art, at all events, is said to have crept
into the higher classes; even statesmen are known to
have gained a proficiency almost professional. M.
Théophile Gautier relates that when in St. Petersburg he was introduced to a sketching club at which
amateurs and artists met on equal footing; a subject
was given, and in the course of the evening the
members and visitors threw off in illustration an im-
promptu drawing. In Russia the arts will gain by
more wide diffusion: sketching clubs and drawing
schools may tend to mitigate the intolerable sublimity,
the supreme isolation, of high art as set up by the
Imperial Academy.

The renowned Zichy was a member of this sketching
club—an artist rapid and reckless — the Gustave Doré
or Fortuni of Russia; picturesque as Cattermole, versatile as Decamps, rowdy as Gavarni. To a man of
this astounding talent all things, even the highest, had
been possible, if only power were tempered by modera-
tion. Zichy is not over-scrupulous; photographs are
made from certain of his drawings and sold in St.
Petersburg, which in Holywell Street would be seized
by the police. Morals in Russia are lax, as travellers
who have visited the foundling hospitals of St. Petersburg and Moscow well know; but rarely does licen-
tiousness creep into art. Zichy is rapid and versatile;
he is the '*fa presto*' of Russia; by turns he will paint
a boar-hunt and decorate a fan. His brilliant talents

have made him a favourite of fortune, the friend of emperors and princes. He accompanies the Tsar to the chase, and sketches deeds of valour which may redound to his master's glory; he receives at his studio the Prince of Wales; he sends drawings to London which are purchased by members of the Royal Family for birthday presents. And yet, though thus highly favoured, it seems doubtful whether he will win a place among the first artists of the age. He paints too much for the immediate occasion to stand the test of all time. A design now before me, 'Monks at Vespers,' savours more of the police court than of the church or the cloister. Zichy caricatures the nature he depicts; he emphasises accidents; he magnifies deformities; his draperies are either tinsel robes from the stage or beggar's rags from the street. We stand aghast at genius thus given to riot and erratic phantasy.

It may be questioned whether the true sphere of the Russian artist does not lie in domestic life and in genre generally. The Russian people are kindly and peace-loving; they like to live at home at ease; and when they walk abroad, in town or in country, they show themselves less warlike than picturesque. Few countries offer to the simple naturalistic artist such paintable materials; the bazaars of Constantinople, Damascus, and Cairo do not present to the sketcher more tempting subjects than the Gostinnoi Dvor in St. Petersburg and Moscow. Russians, if not imaginative or creative, are able to imitate whatever they see, and painters having been permitted to follow their innate promptings, have of late years been tending to naturalism and realism. In fact, some twenty or more men might be named who, eschewing high art, and resisting the temptation to Italian costumes and

Italianised styles, give a fair share of their time and talent to expressly national themes. Thus Andrew Popoff, born and resident in Toula, the Birmingham of Russia, is conspicuous in the Imperial Academy by a well-painted scene, 'The Fair of Nijny Novgorod.' I have seen this picture in St. Petersburg and Paris, and on each occasion I was persuaded that the hope of the Russian school does not lie in the direction of the ideal, but in the true and literal transcript of nature. I have also met with graphic sketches of character by John Sokoloff and Peter Sokoloff. To the former attaches a personal history which might sound exceptional save in semi-civilised regions, where talent crops up when least expected. John Sokoloff was born at Astrachan, on the far-off shores of the Caspian, and after studying at the Academy of St. Petersburg, became a professor at Sudscha, a small town four hundred miles south of Moscow. His studies in Little Russia and the Caucasus have made Western Europe acquainted with regions and peoples which lie far beyond the beat of the ordinary sketcher. That Russia has a goodly array of students, more or less faithful to nature, will be indicated by the following names :— Swertshkoff, Strashinsky, Branski, Wereshtshagin, Schurawlew, Clodt, Morozof, Jacoby, Miassoyedoff, Poukireff, Philipoff, Schwartz, and Riemers.

Some of these genre painters I have met with in international galleries, others can only be seen in St. Petersburg. A list so extensive excites astonishment as to where all these painters can come from, and what they can find to do. Labourers in a land where pictures are scarcely recognised as a want are apt to languish in neglect and penury. A calling which is more inviting than remunerative has been over-crowded, by reason

partly of the paucity of professions to which youths
of good ability can betake themselves. What makes
the matter worse commercially, is that the commodity
produced must be consumed, at least for the present,
at home. I could scarcely name half-a-dozen pictures
which a dealer would care to bring into the London
market ; not that Russian paintings are worse than the
average run of works which command a fair price, but
the standard and the aim ·are far removed from the
accepted routine of Western nations. This will have
become apparent to any one who may have examined
last year in the International Galleries, Kensington,
a large and remarkable composition, 'The Butter Week
(Carnival) at the Admiralty Place, St. Petersburg,' by
C. Makowski. That this picture is a fair and indeed
a favourable specimen of what a Russian painter can
do, is attested by the fact that it taxed the artist's
energies for two years, and then was purchased by the
Emperor for £1200—a handsome sum in Russia. The
picture was much talked of in St. Petersburg, it is
engraved in one of the illustrated papers of the capital,
and it naturally was one of the works selected for exhibition when Russia determined to prove to England
what her art was worth. Judged by our home
standards the colour is singularly crude, the yellows
and reds are glaring, the blacks assert themselves offen-
sively, the pigments too are opaque, and the execution is heavy and coarse. Thus the reader may easily
understand how widely different, as already said, is
the aspiration of a Russian painter from the aim of an
English or of a French artist. But due allowance
having been once made for this diversity, the mastery
of the work will be readily admitted. The Russians
seldom fail in a story. This winter fair is crowded

with booths, peep-shows, itinerant mountebanks, small merchants, vendors of drinks, idlers, and merrymakers of all sorts; the incidents and characters are worthy of Hogarth. The figures bespeak a motley race; the costumes — the snow-boots, fur coats, fur caps, sheepskins — consort with the northern clime; the snow is on the ground, the air is icy. The painting may have little delicacy or subtlety, but it is real; the forms have substance and solidity, the characters live upon the canvas. Such is the power which pertains to these northern schools when true to their nationalities.

Some years since I discovered, not without surprise, that certain earnest realistic scenes exhibited in Paris came from a Russian artist, born beyond the Ural Mountains, in the wood-built town of Tobolsk. The painter, Basil Peroff, having made his way to the Academies of Moscow and St. Petersburg, obtained the usual honours, and fortunately his original talent was not ground down to conventional standards. 'The Village Interment,' a touching incident, mourners bearing in a sledge a coffin through the snow, has a pathos Edouard Frère never reached. Death in these wintry solitudes comes with ghastly terror, yet emotions kindle into fire under a covering of snow. In the peasant - pictures which come from St. Petersburg, Moscow, and Siberia, we detect unaccustomed lineaments; the features are sternly set as with suffering, the hands are pinched with cold; the fight for life is hard, body and soul are kept together as in a struggle with death. Verily Russia has much to reveal to the world of the shadow and sorrow side of life. Each race, each latitude furnishes new materials for dramatic composition, yet sometimes nature is too wild to submit to art treatment, sometimes the tragedy of humanity is too terrible for pictorial transcript.

My knowledge of the Russian school of painting was extended by the truly representative works sent to the International Exhibition at South Kensington in 1872. In previous exhibitions in London and Paris Russia proved what she could do in the way of high art, but last year, for the first time, was England made acquainted with the recent movement in the direction of the literal study of nature. Landscapes, domestic scenes, and genre generally, were in the ascendant. A novelty in material was present — a wax - painting on coarse - grained canvas ; the woven fabric was sufficiently visible through the pigments to give to the surface of the picture a texture approaching fresco or mosaic. It must be confessed that the result was far from satisfactory. The ancient process of wax-painting has been revived with more success in Paris, Munich, and London. Yet this bold example of the vigorous naturalism which now more and more takes hold of the North of Europe is one among many proofs that in Russia no method or expedient, historic or otherwise, is neglected which can exalt or extend the national art.

The narrative already given of the modern school of painting in Russia is all but exhaustive. Yet the account would remain incomplete did I not include Basil Wereshtshagin, whose pictures have created a sensation both at Kensington and the Crystal Palace. This painter, a Russian by birth, combines in his own person the enterprise of a pioneer, the valour of a soldier, and the skill of an artist. He traversed during the years 1868, 1869 and 1870, pencil and sword in hand, the vast and wild territories which range east of the Ural Mountains and stretch onwards between Siberia, India, and China. The adventurous painter, having been first educated in the Naval School of St. Petersburg, was qualified to join the Russian military corps, the exploits of which he witnessed and portrayed. M. Basil Wereshtshagin is qualified by nature as by education to record and even to exaggerate the sensational incidents which fell in his way. First a pupil in the Academy of St. Petersburg, he next fell under the influence of M. Gérôme in Paris, then he took a studio in Munich, where many of his works were matured. By the time he made his appearance in London he was able to. challenge his master Gérôme by creations unsurpassed for callous cynicism and cold-blooded cruelty. The artist pleads that it was his duty to paint the horrors he saw. I am bound to say that I do not place implicit confidence in his pictorial narratives. He tells on canvas travellers' tales — he shoots with the long bow. For example :—' The Apotheosis of War,' dedicated 'to all great conquerors—past, present and future,' consists of a pyramid of about 8,000 skulls; this incredible scene was paraded at the Crystal Palace, with an official announcement as follows :—

'This picture is historically true; Tamerlane, who drenched the whole of Asia and part of Europe with blood, erected everywhere such. monuments of his greatness. In comparatively recent times the head of a learned German traveller (Schlagintweit) found its way into a similar heap.'

A Russian painter must indeed have been in luck's way to find 'erected everywhere such monuments,' especially in a region where inhabitants are scanty, and where in consequence heads must be scarce. A pyramid of 8,000 skulls occurring constantly may possibly be beyond the credence of Western Europe. But

having made this protest, I willingly note such data
as the painter added to our general stock of knowledge concerning Russia in Central Asia.

Guerilla war, whether conducted by the French in
Algeria or by the Russians on the confines of Siberia,
and whether chronicled by Horace Vernet or by M.
Wareshtshagin, cannot fail to be eminently picturesque.
'The Unexpected Attack,' 'Surrounded and Pursued,'
and 'The Presentation,' are terrific scenes of hot
slaughter and of cold-blooded brutality. Across a
wide plane, without boundary save a circuit of wild
hills, a savage horde of 'barbarians rushes onward as
a fierce wind bearing a storm cloud.' Attila, 'the curse
of God,' led such fiends to plunder and to slaughter.
A firm front is made and a compact square formed,
but in vain, the men fall thickly and heavily, the
foreground of the picture is strewn with the dead,
weltering in blood. 'Within' is on the confines of a
walled town ; turbaned soldiers, dressed, as in mockery,
in gay costumes of green, red and blue, lie scattered
on the ground in the agony of death ; the living carry
away the dead on stretchers, and range the corpses
with military precision in one long row beneath the
shadowy wall of a lofty fort. Gérôme never painted
a scene more ghastly. Again, in 'Victory,' the dead
lie in blood outside the ramparts, a comrade standing
by lights his pipe in cool unconcern. With equal
mastery is depicted 'A Bleeding Head,' cut off from a
lifeless trunk and held up Medusa-like by a Muscovite soldier exulting in his prize. Important to the
ethnologist are the studies of all the strange people
whom the artist encountered. Here are 'Kalmuck
Women,' a perfect picture of ugliness, stupidity, and
dirt ; then there are 'Dervishes,' an order of beggar

monks, bundles of rags and yet gay in Oriental colour; also 'Solone Men and Women,' savage, stern, indolent; and 'Kalmuck Lamas,' cunning knaves, degraded monsters, 'but also, with God's help, consulting physicians.' The painter's strength lies in the delineation of character. Take as an instance 'Opium Eaters at Tash Kent,' these are 'Tartars,' a people who dwell in perpetual misrule and misery; mark well their haggard physiognomies, their broken-down frames clothed in rags, see how they squat on the ground in stupor or slumber, in reverie or delirium, as the drug clouds the sense or thrills the nerves with intermingling pain and pleasure. The scene is all the more terrible because unflinchingly true; the drawing is accurate, the execution firm, the touch keen and unrelenting. Such studies from the life prove that Russian painters can walk in untrodden paths. The landscape sketches by the same artist will be noticed in the sequel.

Count Raczynski, writing in 1841, found fifty-eight Russian artists worthy of mention, after the lapse of thirty years the number has at least doubled. The pictorial phenomena it has been my privilege to pass under review have naturally been somewhat abnormal; yet the art revival I have endeavoured to trace commands respect, not to say admiration. The talent brought into play does not proclaim a barren land. Genius in the high significance of the term may be rare, but fair average power competent to do good art work is certainly not denied to the Russian people. The future of the school will of course be determined by the fortunes of the empire; a land proverbial for undeveloped resources would seem to promise to the arts expansion. Railroads are opening up new territory not only to trade but for art; wealth in its accumulation, as well as in its more wide diffusion, adds to the number of patrons ; a middle class improved in position, a peasantry endowed with freedom, will swell the ranks of skilled artisans, artists, and art consumers. Russia has a work to accomplish ; like England she may carry the arts round an empire on which the sun never sets.

CHAPTER VII.

THE IMPERIAL MANUFACTORY OF MOSAICS AT ST. PETERSBURG.

I FOUND the famous Mosaic Manufactory of the Russian Government in St. Petersburg in full operation. Travellers who have visited the kindred establishments in Rome and in Venice, or Englishmen who have seen the mosaic workers at South Kensington, will be able to picture to themselves the *ateliers* in St. Petersburg. The premises, though not large, are sufficient for the works in hand; they stand in the rear of that spacious Academy of Arts, which, with other like imposing structures, gives imperial state to the banks of the Neva. In the ante-room are ranged on easels minor works wrought in emulation of the Roman and Florentine mosaicists; in a raised gallery range ample stores of enamels distributed in pigeon-holes, and classified according to colour; while in adjacent apartments may be seen manufacturing appliances, such as lathes and blowpipes, for the fusion and the abrasion of the enamels. Into one large workshop are concentrated the resources and energies of the establishment: the artisans, or perhaps, more properly speaking, the artists, are not divided off into separate studios, but group themselves under one roof around the several mosaic slabs in process of making. This picturesque scene recalled the workshops, which I had visited a twelvemonth before, of Messrs. Salviati, on the Grand Canal in Venice. On the walls were hung cartoons of finished works; such, for example, as the grand picture-mosaic sent to the

Paris Exhibition, and now in the church of St. Isaac; and upon the ground stood drawings of works still in progress, among which I specially noted an 'Entomb-ment' 12 feet long, and a 'Last Supper' 18 feet long, the figures life-size; both for the enrichment of the same cathedral. The pictorial manipulations were carried forward with timorous care and tentative de-liberation. The silence which reigned in the room was broken by little save the occasional chipping of a *tessera* into shape. The process is necessarily slow; no one is in a hurry; not a hand moves with speed— an idle hour will not materially delay a composition which cannot be completed for some years. In im-perial manufactories quality is more thought of than expedition. The director and his staff are handsomely paid by the Government, upon the principle that pro-ducts of a high and exclusive character cannot be sustained on a purely commercial basis. In England, unfortunately, we do not tolerate such subsidies; in Russia, on the contrary, partly because art remains in a state of precarious infancy, requiring fostering care, the State extends munificent patronage. In the Russian department of the Paris Exhibition, the most remarkable products were due to imperial factories, such as '*Manufacture Impériale de Porcelaines,*' '*Manu-facture Impériale de Verreries,*' '*Fabrique Impériale de Péterhoff,*' '*Jardin Botanique Impériale de St. Péters-bourg,*' and last, but not least, '*L'Etablissement Impé-riale de Mosaiques à St. Pétersbourg.*' The result of this imperial favour is, that the mosaic manufactory at St. Petersburg is surpassed, if at all, only by that in Rome.

The parent of the imperial establishment in St. Petersburg is the Pope's mosaic manufactory in the

Vatican. It is indeed singular that, for the revival of an art anciently rooted in Byzantium, Russia should have to seek for precedents and practical knowledge so far beyond her frontiers as the Roman States. It might have been supposed that mosaics at least would form an exception to the rule that all art in Russia is imported from abroad. It would naturally have been imagined that the widely-comprehensive system of wall-incrustation, which from Constantinople had extended to Ravenna and Venice, would have found its way northwards to the ancient capitals of Russia. And yet in Moscow I searched in vain among the churches of the Kremlin for a single fragment of mosaic. The only remains of that Art, which is said to be fitted for eternity, is in the cathedral of St. Sophia at Kief— an ancient capital and place of pilgrimage, sometimes called the Jerusalem of Russia. It is interesting to observe the structural points in common between this cathedral and the church of St. Mark, Venice; the mosaics are equally of one school, that is, they are of Byzantine origin. Russia being thus all but destitute of examples dating back to historic times, and the art having fallen into desuetude in Constantinople, the ancient seat of the Eastern Empire, recourse was had to Rome, the centre of Western art, when the moment came for Russia to make mosaics a national manufacture.

Signor Bonafide, an Italian, the favourite pupil of Chevalier Barberi, the celebrated mosaicist of the Vatican, was in 1846 entrusted by the Emperor Nicholas to establish in Rome a provisional institution, which might afterwards serve to introduce the art of mosaic-work into Russia. Four youths were sent from the North to serve their apprenticeship in Rome. I cannot find any statement of what remuneration they received, but the Government is known to support liberally her art-students in foreign lands : ordinary students in the Roman branch of the Russian Academy are 'sent for six years, with a pension of £160 a year each, for the journey £40, and for the return £40.' The Russian Government seems to have been more than once thwarted in its endeavour to procure the enamel-colours needed for the execution of the mosaic picture of St. Nicholas and other works it had put in hand. The enamels produced under contract with the Roman mosaicist, Vincent Raffaelli, had proved unsatisfactory, and in Rome itself it appeared impossible to obtain the needful materials ready-made. Under these difficulties it was resolved that the Russians should commence to manufacture for themselves ; accordingly, a suitable laboratory was taken in Rome, and furnaces were erected. Signor Bonafide, appointed by the emperor chemist to the establishment, reports upon his success as follows :—'Myself and my brother set to work, ourselves directing and watching the smallest details, so that, in the course of a short time, we were enabled to exhibit productions which surpassed in quality all that existed in Rome in the trade, and which perfectly resembled all that could be found in the stores of the Vatican, even *scorzette* and *porporines*, which had not hitherto been produced for a long time. The production of our enamels was hailed with lively satisfaction by all the mosaicists, and gained the full and entire approbation of Prince Volkonski, both for the choice and beauty of the colours which we had obtained, and also for the square form we adopted for the "pizze" (pieces) of enamel, a form the most convenient for use, and at the same time the most economical. During the existence of the Russian establishment at Rome, we produced 45,181 pounds of enamel, divided into 4,700 different shades, including enamels of gold and silver. The cost of rent, installation, wood, apparatus, transport, and *personnel*, amounted to 10,667 *écus Romains* and 93 *baiocchi*, which gives a cost for every pound of enamel of 21⅓ *baiocchi*, or 28 *kopecks* (Russian),' —equal to about 9*d*. English. I may add, that I doubt the correctness of this price in common with other prices from the Russian establishment. When a manufactory is made imperial, prices if not immaterial are often untrustworthy.

In the year 1851, Signor Bonafide, since deceased, received from the Emperor Nicholas, through Prince Volkonski, instructions to leave Rome and proceed to St. Petersburg, 'there to assist in establishing the art of mosaic-making in Russia; and to overcome, as far as might be, the inconvenience of the unsatisfactory quality of the enamels produced by the Roman mosaicist Vincent Raffaelli, who was then engaged in St. Petersburg, under contract, to supply the necessary materials for the work' in hand. There seems to have been naturally some delay in the organisation of the school of mosaicists and in the establishment of the workshops. Ultimately it was settled that the enamel colours should be made in one place, the '*Manufacture Impériale de Verreries*,' while the mosaics were to be set up in another *locale*, a portion of the Imperial Academy. The staff at the latter manufactory has of late years consisted of about fourteen artists and eight artisans. Painters, such as the late Professor Neff, also another Russian artist, likewise an Italian painter, severally employed on cartoons, are not included. The above facts substantiate the statement

that St. Petersburg first borrowed the art from modern
Rome, and at the same time they account for the
close resemblance between the picture-mosaics made
on the banks of the Neva and those manufactured
on the banks of the Tiber. I think there can be no
doubt that the Russian Government did wisely to go
to Rome. In Venice the art had, until a recent period,
been long neglected ; and even under the revival effected
by Dr. Salviati, works as delicate and elaborate as those
executed in the establishment of the Pope are quite
the exception. I may add that in Ravenna I have
seen a Roman mosaicist employed in the restoration
of 'The Good Shepherd' and the maintenance of other
historic remains. This Italian, working under ancient
traditions, used Roman *tesseræ*, which in Ravenna were
deemed better than Venetian. I see no reason to
call in question the statement that the *tesseræ* now
made in the '*Manufacture Impériale de Verreries à
St. Pétersbourg*' are equal in quality and in variety
of colour to the enamels manufactured in Rome. In
fact a chief end sought to be attained through the
apprenticeship served by the Russians in Rome was
to perfect the material, as a material, in the essential
particulars of colour, substance, and permanence. In
St. Petersburg the designs of the mosaics are poor compilations, ostentatious and empty, as for the most part
is modern art in Russia. And such good care has been
taken to secure excellence of enamel and workmanship, that there is a fair chance that these commonplace compositions in Russia will long survive creations of
genius confided elsewhere to less trustworthy materials.

The *technique* of the Russian manufacture has been
established, as we have seen, on a sound and scientific
basis. Valuable. data of the processes employed may

be gathered from 'Appendix S. to Eleventh Report of Science and Art Department,' incorrectly entered in the margin as 'Mr. Sandham's Description of a Russian Mosaic Establishment,' whereas Mr. Sandham merely acts as translator. The report dwells on 'economy' of manufacture, notwithstanding the proverbial extravagance of all prices in St. Petersburg, whether of luxuries or of bare necessaries, and tells how the consumption of gold may be diminished. 'With us,' states this official document, 'it is a vital object to economise to the utmost the precious metals, and to obtain the same results by metallic oxides less costly. Copper, for example, is well known by chemists to be capable of three different degrees of oxidation. We obtain from this metal not only three primative colours, such as yellow, red, and blue, but also the mixed colours, orange, green, and violet. Besides, with the aid of other materials which we employ, and by means of some modifications in manipulation, we obtain all the compound colours, in an infinity of shade.' Professor Archer was more precise when, in the columns of the 'Art-Journal,' he stated that in St. Petersburg 'the metals chiefly employed are gold, silver, copper, cobalt, manganese, lead, tin, antimony, iron, and chromium : carmine, purple, and rose colours are obtained by gold ; yellow by silver, lead, and antimony ; blue by cobalt ; red by copper ; brown by manganese ; black by iron ; green by copper and chromium, &c. ; orange by lead.' The late director in St. Petersburg lays claim to inventions in mechanism and to chemical discoveries which it is supposed may have improved the products of the furnace. I do not attach to these claims much importance : 'a shovel of a new form,' for example, scarcely implies any great amount of creative genius. The processes seem much the same as those I have witnessed in Murano. The Russians as a people are more imitative than creative; and that they should be able to produce after established precedents a material equal to the best manufacture, whether ancient or modern, is greatly to their credit.

As I write are ranged on the table before me *tesseræ* which I have at various times collected. Among the old materials are remnants from mosaics on the façade of Orvieto Cathedral; also from mosaics in St. Mark's, Venice; likewise from the mosaic of 'The Good Shepherd,' a work in Ravenna. And among the new materials are Salviati's glass *tesseræ*, used in the repair of the old mosaics in St. Mark's, as well as for the modern works at Windsor, and in the Houses of Parliament; to these may be added the ceramic or earthenware squares of Messrs. Minton, employed in certain figures at South Kensington; lastly, the *tesseræ* I brought from St. Petersburg. A comparison of these several examples shows less difference than might have been anticipated. As to relative opacity and transparency, the Minton and the Salviati compositions are opposite extremes; Minton's mixture, which seems little else than baked clay, is opaque and dead in surface as earthenware; while, on the contrary, Salviati's compound is translucent and sparkling as glass. Each material has distinctive advantages. I notice that Sir Digby Wyatt, in a paper read before the Institute of Architects, suggests that the opaque material should be used for the high lights, while the transparent pieces might be reserved for the shadows. Such practice would correspond to the well-known maxim in oil-painting: 'Load on your lights, and keep your shadows transparent.'

The materials from St. Petersburg are intermediate in character: they are not quite so translucent as the Salviati glass, nor are they so opaque as the Minton clay; they may be likened to the consistency of sealing-wax, which, as far as I remember, was the prevailing aspect of the substance used in the Vatican. Accordingly the Russian picture-mosaics when complete, as seen for example in the master-works put up in the church of St. Isaac, throw off light from the surface quite as forcibly as frescoes, and yet on the other hand they do not reflect light as when *tesserae* of burnished surface shine like a multitude of small looking-glasses. This last effect was the unpardonable fault of the Salviati mosaics set up a few years since in the Central Hall, Westminster. At St. Petersburg considerable credit is taken for 'The colour *porporine* —purple.' 'The reproduction of this colour was the object of the researches of many distinguished chemists, but although they arrived at the constituent elements of this enamel, no one was able to produce it. It is to the laboratory of our establishment that the credit belongs of having produced, in 1847, and down to the present day, an enormous quantity of this precious colour.' Also, not without reason, do the Russians claim excellence for perhaps the prettiest of mosaic products, glazed gold *tesserae*, specially needed in a country where, after the example of Byzantium, gold is lavishly used in backgrounds. Mr. Ruskin speaks eloquently of the beauty and utility of this exquisite manufacture as used in St. Mark's. The process by which the gold-leaf is laid on, then placed under the protecting pellicle of glass and so hermetically sealed, has been often described; and the glistening product, whether ancient or modern, whether it come from Venice or St. Petersburg, is nearly identical both as to durability and decorative use. It is interesting to observe with what care, with how much attention to minute circumstance, various mosaic manufactories have devoted themselves to the safe and lucent incrustation of the goldleaf. Even the colour of the vitreous background upon which the gold is mounted has been carefully considered. Salviati lays gold upon red, blue, or green enamel, according to the tone desired : the Russian chemists carry out the same idea, and the factory being imperial, that is, sustained by subsidy and independent of commercial considerations, no pains have been spared to render the substance and surface as nearly perfect as practicable. I have reason to believe that the cost mounts up to that of a luxury ; in other words, the outlay, as in the state factories of France, is so heavy as to close access to the markets of the world. As to permanence, it is almost impossible to speak. We all know what absurd claims for indestructibility have latterly been set up for mosaics ; the fact being that the finished work must perish with its weakest part, viz., the mortar-bedding. But I have before me a fragment from Orvieto, which shows that the *tesseræ* themselves are subject to disintegration, and seeing that even granite crumbles under an Italian winter, it is easy to believe that in St. Petersburg mosaics, unless well protected, must fall to pieces. But in Russia, mosaics are used solely for internal decoration, and the churches being heated by artificial means, there seems reason to believe that the *tesseræ*-picture may last almost as long as the walls will stand.

Reverting to the matter of gold, I may state that in the St. Petersburg *atélier* I made note of raised or embossed gold-grounds somewhat comparable with flock patterns in wall-paper decorations. This is a novelty which may be turned to good account. The unmitigated brilliance of a gilded surface is apt to destroy all colour with which it comes in contact; and I have been interested to observe in Venice how Salviati has striven, by subdued treatment of gold, passing from light yellow to shadowy tones, and even into still more sombre tints of copper, to mitigate excess of lustre. But possibly, in the still barbaric state of Russian art, such delicate modulations may be accounted as loss of power. The multitudinous domes of the Kremlin in Moscow are mostly gilt; and I was surprised to find that no one would join in my admiration of the gold toned by time, oxidised and brought into broken yet rich harmonies with sky and cloud. Everybody deemed the span-new gilt pumpkin of a dome the nearest possible approach to the divine. The analogy between these golden cupolas and the gold of mosaic grounds is close, if not indeed complete. I have noticed, indeed, that gold mosaics gain in tone by time, somewhat as painted glass; crudeness of tone and harsh contrasts are subdued to harmony. I may be excused for thus dwelling at length on a point which in Western art would be deemed of secondary moment. But in Russia gold is a primary means of decoration, a salient feature in a city panorama. Travellers who have approached St. Petersburg from the sea, or seen Moscow illumined by the setting sun, will know how much of imperial magnificence, how much of Eastern splendour is due to the gold which illumines the dome-crested panoramas. I think the government shows a clear intuition of the requirements and capabilities of national art by fostering a school of mosaic manufacture, which yields a decorative appliance in perfect keeping with historic tradition as well as with the present complexion of popular taste.

The notes I have made on the mode of putting the mosaics together accord with the published report of Professor Archer. A coloured cartoon is the mosaicist's guide; a white surface of plaster laid in a strong framework about half an inch deep is his field of action. Upon this smooth surface the composition is sketched piece by piece. It being thus determined with precision where each *tessera* is to lie, the plaster, which yields softly to the knife, is cut carefully away, and just as carefully is each cube squared, ground, filed, and fitted into its prepared cell. Thus by slow degrees does the white plaster give place to the coloured picture—vastly more slowly than canvas yields before the stitches of a worker of tapestry. 'How long,' I inquired, 'will that large mosaic of "The Last Supper" take to complete?' 'Five men could finish it in four years,' was the reply. The weight of such a work is so immense that the enclosing framework requires utmost strength. The mosaic sent to Paris in 1867 weighed no less than seven tons, and to move such a mass in the *atélier* needs cranes and other mechanical appliances. The Russians deem giant scale essential to grandeur; they consider that their public works must be of a magnitude commensurate with their vast empire; and they accustom themselves as we have seen to move blocks of stone which are without historic parallel since the building of the Pyramids by the old Egyptians. We have found that the monolithic columns of the church of St. Isaac were brought all the way from Finland; and, in like manner, the huge granite blocks for the monument to Catherine, now in course of construction, have been dragged through the streets of St. Petersburg. In some four years' time, when the mosaic of 'The Last Supper' shall have attained an accumulative weight of ten tons, the removal from the studio to the church will become a serious operation. In the meantime much remains to be done. When the last of some two or three hundred thousand *tesseræ* shall be in its place, the whole picture will be turned down on its face, and the plaster cut away from the back.. The roots, or fangs, of the cubes being thus laid bare, Roman or Portland cement will be run over the whole surface. A solid back being thus put to the picture, the work is ready for its destination. During its execution it has been of the nature of an easel-picture; on its completion it will be built into an architectural structure, and thus assume, as far as the treatment may permit, a monumental character.

I obtained a special appointment to see the melting of the enamels under the blow-pipe, the mixing of two colours to make an intermediate third, &c. Travellers acquainted with the glass-works at Murano are not likely to be taken by surprise by the dexterous manipulation needed in the making of the enamel colours in St. Petersburg. The marvellous ductility of glass is, of course, the same all the world over. On the whole the imperial glass manufactory, as represented in the Russian Exhibition of 1870, fell short of the Salviati works, as displayed in the Paris Exhibition; and certainly the feats performed in the way of combination and fusing together of colours were not comparable with the Venetian filagree and other well-known products. But in St. Petersburg they show a somewhat novel arrangement of colours one over the other, as in agate; they also imbed colours by placing one round the other in concentric circles. I have several such circular or oval *tesseræ* on the table before

me, each measuring from half an inch to one inch in
diameter, with usually an eye of white at the centre,
and various shades of yellow, red, brown, or grey around.
The process, being once mastered, admits of manifold
combinations. The advantage, however, accruing from
this ingenious arrangement, is not very evident. The
utmost benefit would seem to be that one *tessera* produces the same effect as many, and one may remain
more firmly in the cement than several. The size of
the pieces usually varies with the greater or less minuteness in detail ; and among the specimens before me
some are drawn out to the thinness of a thread or wire,
and thus a mosaic may be as finely elaborated as a
needle-wrought tapestry. It is evident, as before said,
that no cost is spared, no expedient neglected, to approach perfection ; and although, after the manner of
the moderns, enamel colours are mostly relied on, yet,
as with the ancients, the use is not denied of natural
materials, such as *lapis lazuli*, provided that natural substances will answer the end in view better than artificial.
Thus it will be inferred that all the resources of the
mosaic process are called out to the uttermost : the
materials are excellent and well applied. The size of
the *tesseræ* is varied so as to gain what in painting
would be termed boldness or delicacy of touch ; and
the lines in which the *tesseræ* are laid are so disposed
as to represent, as in line-engraving, the curves and
modulations in surface. From the above it will be understood that the Russian mosaicist has at command
unusual realistic power ; he can add to draperies texture,
to robes enrichment ; by the use of high lights and
deep shadows, by the contrast of transparent and opaque
colours, he can give to the human eye sparkling intelligence, and to jewelry or metal - work lustre and

translucence. An art essentially decorative thus gains in brilliance.

Russian mosaics are costly : economy of manufacture, as before remarked, is rarely an object with imperial establishments ; indeed the idea of a state subsidy is to sustain a manufacture which could not commercially pay its way. It is, therefore, not a little surprising to find Signor Bonafide, in his report to the Government, claim cheapness, at least in the cost of the enamels. The only source of economy stated is the substitution of baser metals for the more precious in the production of the colours. It appears that the enamels, including gold as well as other colours, average the rate of 1s. 8d. per pound, before cut into cubes. This is incredibly cheap, as the uncut gold enamels used by Salviati for the restoration of St. Mark's cost 6s. per pound, while varied colours cost 3s. per pound. There must be some fallacy in the Russian official statement. But independently of the cost of the raw material, the expenses at St. Petersburg are excessive. The process, as before described, indicates that speed and simplicity are sacrificed to excellence of workmanship. It is the boast of the authorities that the most skilled labour is employed : an apprenticeship has to be served, and the pupil must show a medal of honour from the school of design in St. Petersburg as a preliminary qualification. Fourteen artists are usually employed, and the most able have been known to earn £300 per annum. Half that sum would be more than a good income for an Italian copyist of pictures in the galleries of Florence or Rome. The total expense of the establishment to the Government is set down so variously that little reliance can be placed on the figures. Monarchs of unlimited and irresponsible powers do not care to confess to the cost of their favourite

hobbies. Fortunately the Government has not to pass
its estimates for science and art before a House of
Commons.

Neither is it at all easy to ascertain the precise
cost of any one mosaic when turned out of hand. The
works are not on sale; and when we consider that a
single picture may be three or four years in the making,
it will readily be understood that an exact account of
the expenditure cannot be got at. I find, however, that
the cost of the most arduous work yet finished, the
composition of saints sent to the Paris Exhibition, is set
down in the Russian catalogue at £11,000; a sum not
impossible when we remember that the decorations around
the altar of the church of St. Isaac, whereof this mosaic
forms part, are stated to have involved the expenditure
of £500,000. In St. Petersburg, as in Rome and Venice,
the cost of a work of course varies with the fineness of
the manipulation and the expense of individual colours.
Of the various works I saw on visiting the factory, there
was a small head of Christ valued at £80 the square
foot; thus a mosaic may in price be after the rate of
a Turner drawing. How exorbitant is this price can
be judged by the fact that Salviati's figure-mosaics, of
a quality suited to the proposed decoration of our own
St. Paul's, would not exceed £3 3s. per English foot.
Mr. Layard, however, has stated that the most highly-
wrought Venetian mosaic would reach £5 per foot; this
is just the rate paid for the Munich windows in St. Paul's.
The frescoes which are perishing in the Houses of Parliament have cost greatly more—scarcely less than £10
per square foot: mosaic is cheaper than painting. It
may, however, be reasonably urged against mosaics,
that so small a proportion of the total cost goes to art
as art, and so large a part to the material and manufac-

ture. This objection especially holds against Russian mosaics, wherein the design is usually all but worthless in an art point of view. The exorbitant outlay is in the mechanism of the art, the laborious character whereof is indicated by the fact that no fewer than 120,000 *tesseræ* were used in the mosaic of St. Nicholas in the Exhibition of 1862. Each of these cubes represents more than the common amount of labour. In coarse cheap mosaics the enamels are chopped speedily, almost at a blow, as might be witnessed at an English stall in the 1862 Exhibition. In St. Petersburg, on the contrary, every cube is most carefully chiselled into form, and then fitted in its place neatly. Again, in the Salviati mosaics interstices are permitted; the cement may show between the chinks in the enamels; the surface is allowed to remain somewhat uneven; and these irregularities are not wholly disadvantages when the work is to be seen only from a distance. On the contrary, in the St. Petersburg mosaics the *tesseræ* are placed so closely as scarcely to show a joint, while the surface is kept level by a flat edge and the use of smoothing tools. This delicacy of manipulation contrasts strongly with Salviati's economic method of gluing the *tesseræ* face downwards on portable pieces of paper. In the *atélier* on the banks of the Neva the artist sees his work; he does not lay down his picture in the dark. Salviati is commercially right: the Russians are artistically right. The number of colours used in Venice, in Rome, and in St. Petersburg, would seem to vary considerably. Mr. Layard states the number of tints employed by Salviati as only 1500. The number of colours formerly credited to the Pope's factory were not less than 10,000, and in St. Petersburg I was assured that I saw around me no fewer than 14,000 different tints *. But as shades are varied in the furnace at discretion by the intermixture of white, it is evident that the colours might be easily multiplied even beyond the point at which the human eye could detect the difference.

Mosaic workers have in past ages taken rank as artists. They have been deemed, like engravers, more than mechanists—they are not allowed to fall into oblivion ; their names, as, for instance, that of Andrea Tafi, who worked in the Baptistery of Florence, are handed down in the history of art. In like manner any work which issues from the St. Petersburg factory is identified with the names of the mosaicists employed thereon. The following extract from the reports on the Paris Exhibition, 1867, 'presented to both houses of Parliament by command of her Majesty,' gives honour where honour is due :—

'As an important offshoot from Rome, we have,' writes Sir D. Wyatt, the reporter, 'next to consider an establishment which, but for its being "Imperial," and therefore *hors concours*, would unquestionably have received the highest honours any jury could have conferred. I allude to the imperial glass-works of St. Petersburg, under the especial patronage of Prince Gazkarin, and presided over by Signor Bonafide, the favourite pupil of the celebrated Chevalier Barberi, the mosaicist, of Rome. What the French would call a splendid *gamme* of coloured *smalti* for the execution of mosaics, exhibited by this establishment in 1862, received the warmest

---

* The discrepancy between these several figures is so extraordinary that I have thought it due to Messrs. Salviati to ask for an explanation. The letter received in reply states that the figures 1500, as above, are 'correct, inasmuch that they are shades actually kept in our manufactory; but thousands more could be made if required—it only requiring different degrees of heat and colour.' It will thus be seen, as above urged, that there are no limits to the number of colours which can be turned out from a furnace. It still remains matter of astonishment that in St. Petersburg are needed nine times as many tints as are said to be sufficient in Venice.

commendation from the jury, of which I was a member on that occasion, and was subsequently presented to the Department of Science and Art by the Emperor of Russia. The present exhibition shows advance, rather than falling off; and unquestionably the best pictorial mosaic of all in the building is a colossal one executed with *smalti*, from this establishment, by F. Bouronkin, M. Mouraviev, and G. Agavanov, from a picture by Professor Neff. It represents a group of saints, and for breadth of effect and simplicity of execution leaves nothing to be desired.'

Russia has been unwise in the art-style she has adopted. The designs her mosaicists work from belong to the florid post-Raphaelite period. Instead of adopting as her model the early mosaics of Torcello, Venice, Ravenna, or Rome, she emulates the showy designs executed by the school of Tintoret and Veronese. The manner adopted is something between the Caracci, Caravaggio, and Delaroche. The drawing for 'The Last Supper,' now in the *atélier*, was made by an artist of Italian descent, and the other works in hand are essentially modern : they are not Byzantine, not mediæval, not monumental, but pictorial. Accordingly Russian mosaics are often wanting in symmetry, simplicity, and solemnity ; they are more of the nature of easel-pictures than of architectonic art. The Russians would do well to work out a more expressly national style, for which, in fact, they possess ample historic materials—a style rooted in Byzantium and taking on rich colouring from the East. But instead of this true policy, painters have sold themselves to France, and bartered their art to Italy. The mosaicists in St. Petersburg work from the compositions of Professor Neff—an artist known in the Hermitage by nude girls bathing. Religious art is not to be made out of such meretricious stuff. The source of the evil which afflicts the pictorial school lies in great degree in the false style of architecture adopted for the churches and public buildings of the capital—a rank growth of the *Renaissance ;* an ostentatious dressing-up of forms which have long served as common-places for Italian masters. The famed church of St. Isaac, for which the mosaicists labour, is as hostile to a good style of wall-decoration as the interior of our St. Paul's is fatal to a pure style of painted glass. The fact is, the religious arts in Russia are in an anomalous and false position; they are divided between the effete Byzantine and the flåunting modern; there is no interval or intermediate resting-place between a Madonna, black as ebony, and a span-new saint decked in costume as for a book of fashion. The art-revival fostered by Russian emperors is not on a par with even that modern mediævalism, the so-called school of Christian art patronised and pampered by King Ludwig in Munich. That the Government is wise in taking to mosaics in some form as a national system of wall-decoration cannot be questioned. It is evident that the exclusion of sculpture from the Russian church leaves a void not easily filled. Frescoes would have been probably incompatible with the climate, and, moreover, must have been overpowered by the richness of adjacent marble, malachite, *lapis lazuli*, &c.; whereas mosaics, being built up of solid materials, comport well with the surrounding structure. The commencement already made in this magnificent decorative process cannot fail to have ample development in the future. Some years may be occupied in supplying the church of St. Isaac with the required enamel-pictures; further years will be needed for the like decoration of the new church in Moscow. In the meanwhile, with the growing wealth of the empire, other churches will arise, which in time must tax the productive powers of the St. Petersburg mosaicists.

CHAPTER VIII.

LANDSCAPE PAINTING IN RUSSIA.

THE rise of landscape art in any nation usually involves interesting problems. The general law, to which Russia is no exception, seems to be that the painting of inanimate nature is secondary and subsequent to the delineation of human nature; thus landscape art seldom comes into being till figure painting has been long established. And Russia having at the time of her art-revival about a century ago pronounced in favour of high and academic styles as best suited to imperial palaces and state churches, landscape painting struggled into existence as an accessory or an accident. Russia, indeed, in creating for herself the several arts, has been subject in more ways than one to the universal laws of development : architecture she needed first, then followed sculpture, and lastly painting. The pictorial arts as usual commenced with a sacred mission, in which of course landscape painting could take little or no part. In St. Petersburg, it is true, the three sister arts sprang into life at the command of Peter the Great and of Catherine II almost at the same moment, yet the direction given to painting was mainly determined by the special style which architecture assumed. The Italian Renaissance being planted on the banks of the Neva, pictorial arts, as reared in the Academy of St. Petersburg, naturally conformed to Italian precedent ; figures, life-size, left little room for landscape, and only by degrees was inanimate nature permitted to creep in and shew herself, usually in backgrounds. But the tendency of the times in Europe generally having more than ever set in the direction of landscape, Russian painters studying in Düsseldorf, Paris or Rome, fell into the not unpleasing practice of outdoor sketching. And it may be said that while the necessities of the state urged to historic art, the instincts of the people prompted to landscape painting : the one is essentially national, the other is more peculiarly personal. And, judging from the pictures which have fallen under my notice, also in remembrance of the manifest talents of not a few artists who have addicted themselves to the study of nature, I should say that the Russian mind is fully sensible to the grandeur and the beauty of high mountains, vast plains, dense forests, rushing rivers, and restless seas. A people emerging from barbarism and just entering on civilisation are peculiarly responsive to the rude forms and the unruly forces of nature.

Before I proceed to enumerate the best known landscape painters, and to describe the actual condition of the art in Russia, I may detain the reader by one more reason why landscape painting has been so long held in the background. Landscape art in the middle ages was born in Western Europe, and seems never to have been transplanted to the shores of the Bosphorus or the lands of the East. Passing to periods long prior, the Greeks, even of the time of Phidias and his followers, appear to have made the beauty and the grandeur of outward nature subordinate to the drama of humanity. Now the Russian races, with their cognate arts, are Eastern and not Western ; they are allied to the Empire of the East seated at Constantinople, and therefore belong to non-landscape painting peoples.

Furthermore, the ecclesiastical styles borrowed by Russia from Byzantium are stamped with finality; they are precluded from progress and are forbidden access to nature. Landscape, almost of necessity, finds no place in the Church; landscape painting in fact did not exist till the arts became secularised. But nature in all lands sooner or later asserts her power, hence even for the Muscovite Empire a landscape epoch was in store.

Landscape art, it is evident, cannot be wholly neglected when more than twenty painters have a claim to notice. I will briefly enumerate some of the chief, adding the few details I have been able to gather in St. Petersburg from biographical dictionaries, or from the examination of the works sent to successive International Exhibitions in London and Paris. Feodar Jakowlewitsch Alexieff, born 1757, and sometimes called the Russian Canaletto, is the earliest student of inanimate nature I have met with. Yet a landscape with figures in the Academy of St. Petersburg by this artist is chiefly remarkable for its size. Russia, in fact, like Sweden, Norway, and Denmark, commenced with an art which was no art: aboriginal arts in the North of Europe are barbaric; the revival on the shores of the Baltic is traced to the time when intercourse became intimate with the coasts of the Mediterranean. Leon Lagorio, whose landscapes I have known in St. Petersburg and London, is a case in point; he has depicted 'Capri' and 'Sorrento' in the sunny poetic style which is essentially Italian. This painter was born in 1827, and commenced his studies in the Academy of St. Petersburg; in 1850 he gained the first great prize for landscape, and he is now professor in the Academy to which he first owed the rudiments of art. It is evident from two views in the Caucasus sent to the last International

Exhibition at Kensington that Lagorio holds a first
position among the living artists of Russia. He is a
pioneer. The art he matured in Italy he uses as a
means to extend our knowledge of the physical geography of regions comparatively unknown. Here in
the Caucasus he paints a mountain valley with a torrent
tearing through the midst, and a snow peak at the top
piercing the sky sharply. The world is evidently much
alike, especially when the conditions of altitude and
of geologic structure are similar. Thus this faithful
transcript of a ravine in the Caucasus does not materially
differ from Swiss valleys. The atmospheric effect has
been well chosen, a shadowy gloom settles over the
rocky defile, the panorama is solemn and grey, though
warm colour from sunset still lingers. Art treatments
are evidently quite as firmly established and widely
diffused as physical conditions; the landscape painter
in the Russian Empire can but follow the laws of
composition, of light, shade, and colour, which for
centuries have been established in the older European
nations. Thus the second subject from the Caucasus
selected by M. Lagorio, though in its golden sunlight
in direct contrast with the grey shadow of the torrent-
worn ravine, equally conforms with the universal laws
of art. People are apt to suppose that art in the remote
regions of Russia must be wholly severed, even in
elementary principles, from the arts established in old
cities, and at historic centres in Western Europe. But
the rise and development of landscape painting in Russia
offer no exception to Western experience : the laws
observed are not abnormal as in China or Japan.
Indeed this second scene in the Caucasus is amazingly
like the Seine in the neighbourhood of Rouen. Here
are hills, poplars, and shining waters. I am sorry that

I cannot exalt M. Lagorio to quite a first-rate position among the landscape painters of Europe. He wears an amateurish aspect. Still he is faithful, his records are true, his transcripts prove the value of outposts where observers may be placed to report on pictorial conditions of sky, on actual geologic strata, with accessories of buildings and costumes.

At the Crystal Palace, as already mentioned, was exhibited during the present year a remarkable series of sketches of Central Asia by the Russian painter M. Basil Wareshtshagin. We have before noticed the figure-pictures. The studies made on the spot are of real value as reliable records of the landscape phases of countries which seldom come within reach of a painter's pencil. The scenery may be summed up under the category of wide plains, high mountains, long and perilous passes. There are four views of the Alatau Mountains which might have been painted in the Alps. A lake at the foot of these mountains is tranquil and grey; and another lake, of which there are three sketches, is environed by snowy mountains. There are also four views of the Pass of Bars-Kaun, directly Alpine in character; a torrent rushes through the midst, and the rocks on either side bristle with fir-trees. The south-east frontiers of Asiatic Russia do not appear in these sketches as a barren land. It is true that here and there appears a ruined fortress, standing on the border of a desert such as often travellers find within Turkish territory; also are met with the picturesque tombs of saints, not unlike the domed sepulchres which people the sandy desert around the city of Cairo. And yet the land here delineated, though wholly left in the hands of nature, shows capacity for culture and consequent sphere for future civilisation. Possibly the spectator may be surprised that these untrodden hills, ravines, and plains do not contrast more strongly with regions which fall within the beaten track of the traveller, but the fact seems to be established that the great divisions of the globe, made somewhat gratuitously by scientific geographers or political governors, offer, so long as they lie within parallel latitudes, pretty much the same pictorial elements to the landscape artist. Yet, at all events, the contrast is decisive between territories cultivated and uncultivated, with the usual concomitants of civilised and stationary, or uncivilised and wandering inhabitants. The regions by this Russian delineated belong almost without exception to the latter category. Nomadic tribes do not so much inhabit as run over these open tracts : the whole continent is without a hedgerow or boundary, save nature's barriers of rivers and mountains; private property appears to have no more basis than when, on the overthrow of the Babel Tower, the sons of men wandered wherever they might find path or provender. These sketches indeed do not reveal an aspect of nature materially different in Asiatic Russia from the condition of things within Asiatic Turkey. The sketcher, in fact, in Siberia would seem to find himself in about the same plight as in Syria. Indeed I can say, after having travelled on horseback in Samaria, along the sea of Galilee, and among the hills of the Lebanon, that pictorially the difference is but slight between Eastern scenery, as epitomised in Palestine, and the vast regions which stretch beyond the Ural Mountains. These studies, in short, prove little else than that Central Asia is much like the centre of European Russia or the desert tracts of the Turkish Empire. In point of art these vigorous and veracious transcripts are quite on a par with the average works brought home by the painter pioneers of Western Europe. M. Wareshtshagin proves himself well trained; the education which the Academy in St. Petersburg commenced was completed in Paris and Munich; this painter's works accordingly are of unusual maturity.

Eugen Gustav Ducker is an example of the hybrid character of modern Russian art. He was born at Riga, a city which bears a German aspect, being indeed inhabited chiefly by Germans: Riga is the capital of the Baltic provinces, which Germany is known to covet as part and parcel of the imperial patrimony. The painter Ducker then, as his name implies, is not Russian but German; he has too resided much in Germany, especially in Düsseldorf. Russia, however, in a certain sense took possession of the young painter by giving him an education in the Academy of St. Petersburg and endowing him with a pension. Herr Ducker's landscapes are powerful, brilliant, and broad. 'The Bed of a River,' sent to the last International Exhibition at Kensington, evidently is a product of the Düsseldorf school, yet the style shares the roughness which pertains to Northern Europe, the manner is unflinching and unflattering, stern and strong. Several painters, who scarcely rise above prevailing mediocrity, merit but cursory mention. Baron Michael Clodt belongs to a family of artists; the most illustrious baron of the name was a sculptor; he is not living. Another Baron Clodt paints figures in vigorous genre fashion, and a third landscapes. The last named, who obtained the grand prize for landscape, and is now professor at St. Petersburg, did not contribute anything worthy of his name to the International Exhibition of 1872. Baron Michael Clodt is best known by views taken in the Government of Orel;

these landscapes have obtained fairly good positions in divers International Exhibitions. Jean Schischkine may also be here named as one of many Russian artists who have matured a landscape style in Düsseldorf. Silvester Schtschedrin, though wholly unknown in Western Europe, is another landscape artist of renown; in common with his contemporaries he received timely aid under the liberal endowments made for art talent wherever it may turn up within the Russian Empire. His works are sketchy and effective, they have colour and atmosphere, but want detail and close study. Ausenius Mestschersky, also deservedly of repute, was born 1834, in the town of Iver, lying north of and not very distant from Moscow. His birthplace in the provinces is one of many indications that the Russian soil is not barren of art. This painter, like others already mentioned, received the great landscape prize of the Academy in St. Petersburg, he subsequently studied under Calame in Switzerland: his pictures also show the influence of Düsseldorf. The style thus matured he carried with him into the remote regions of Finland; a winter evening scene in that country is one of the most true and striking studies we have yet received from Russia. For quality and texture, colour and transparency of snow and ice, this first-class work has seldom been surpassed. Peter Soukhodolsky, who also carried off the first prize in landscape in St. Petersburg, and subsequently resided in Moscow, is another of those painters who merit gratitude for having, in common with his contemporaries, opened up new regions to art: at all events, of topographic, if not of artistic value is 'View of the Village of Jelny in the Government of Kalougha.' Artists in Russia, as in all the world, are of most worth when they tell of what they know best.

The Crimea is the garden of Russia, it is as the land of Goshen, it is the field of the olive and the vine, its sky is as brilliant as that of Italy, its sea as lucent and blue as the waters of the Mediterranean. Indeed the Crimea shares with the East an Oriental splendour. The climate is moreover subject to sudden and striking atmospheric changes which favour the landscape painter. Violent storms are followed by dazzling sunshine, a silvery haze softens the outlines of hills and of cliffs, sunset lights the landscape with a blaze of colour. The atmospheric conditions, in short, are essentially Italian; the effects are those which Turner gained during the period when he deliberately set himself to rival Claude. Accordingly the Russian Turner, for so John Ayvasowsky is called, is a product of the Crimea. Also Orlowsky, who is allowed to have command of a large, masterly, and intelligent manner, has worked in the Crimea. I have seen a landscape by this artist capital for studied foreground, brilliant sky, and skilful treatment; the painter is no novice, his art is unusually mature for Russia: his works would stand well in any Western capital of Europe. The drawings made by Mr. Edward Goodall during the Russian war show what excellent sketching-ground is to be found in the Crimea. The coast scenery is specially picturesque, bold cliffs rise from the sea, and the harbour of Balaclava is castle-crowned. In the interior are sheltered ravines prettily wooded; the banks of the river Alma make a lovely picture; poplars grow on the margin of the waters, and above rises a grand array of hills. The villages, too, embosomed in trees, with shining minarets, picturesque figures, and camels bearing burdens in the foreground, make charming compositions. No less effective for play of line and grandeur of position is the monastery of St. George above Balaclava. The Valley of Death near Sebastopol has a dark tragedy all its own.

Perhaps among all living artists in Russia the most famous, the most notorious, the most successful in a commercial sense, is John Ayvasowsky, closely identified with the Crimea. Yet his landscapes are too vague and decorative to pretend to local truth. Ayvasowsky's career is not exceptional; he served a pupilage in the Academy of St. Petersburg, in which at a more mature age he became a professor. Now advanced to his fifty-sixth year he finds himself court painter, and moreover professor in Theodosia, the ancient city in the Chersonesus Taurica, wherein he has taken up his residence. Among his known pictures is a landscape of the neighbouring town of Kertch, the ancient Greek city which yielded the vases, gold crowns, and other treasures now transported to the Hermitage. The pictures of Ayvasowsky are so numerous, and in art quality they take so wide a range from good to bad, that the conclusion seems inevitable that the painter is a trader working for lucre. His monetary success has been great; it used to be said in St. Petersburg that he lived as a prince, and it came as a cheering fact that Russia could place a mere landscape painter in so proud a position. The artist is most prolific: I have known an incredible number of his landscapes scattered over the Hermitage, the Academy, the Winter Palace in St. Petersburg, also I have found his works in Moscow, likewise, as a matter of course, in divers International Exhibitions. When I projected a visit for art purposes to Russia I was told that, at all events, in Professor Ayvasowsky I should find a genius. But when I encountered 'The Creation of the World' and 'The Deluge,' in the Hermitage, I knew not whether to pronounce the painter a genius or

a madman. To compare, as some have done, Ayvasowsky with Turner would be an infinite injustice to
Turner. The two are comparable only when their works
verge on insanity. Ayvasowsky is habitually vaporous
and inflammatory, his highly-coloured landscapes are as
pyrotechnic displays at the Crystal Palace or in the
Surrey Gardens; they are without form, detail, or nature.
Even in small canvases, where there can be no scope for
imagination, such as in 'A Corsair near Mount Athos,'
'A View on the South Coast of the Crimea,' and 'Carters
in the Crimea,' severally present at the International
Exhibition of 1872, the artist shows supreme disdain
for truth. And yet for each of these insults upon nature
Ayvasowsky presumes to ask the modest sum of £200.
Nowhere in the life-labour of the artist have I discovered an approach to the close study which Turner
threw into the 'Liber Studiorum.' Yet Ayvasowsky is
interesting as a phenomenon. He is almost the only
Russian artist endowed with imagination or with a sense
of colour. His landscapes are not realities but phantoms,
his pictures are visions: they are products of the passionate South, and serve to prove that Russian art, like
the Russian climate, comprises contrasts wide as the
poles asunder.

The Russian school, both on its landscape and its
figure side, appeared in exceptional strength in the International Exhibition of 1872. The collection showed
good solid work; a style which, if rarely original, is seldom
immature. Russian landscape painters, as already seen,
though they begin they do not end in St. Petersburg; on
the contrary, for the most part they extend their studies
to Germany, Italy, and France. The Russian Academy
in Rome, as already shown, is well endowed, and successful students are provided with pensions to prosecute

their travels through Europe. The Russians are known
as great linguists and travellers, and although constitu-
tionally apathetic at home, their landscape art, as already
seen, bears sign of enterprise. The International Exhibition of 1872 enabled me to make acquaintance with
a few more painters who will further extend the compass of this Northern school. I found yet another
brilliant scene from the Crimea. A. Bogoluboff, a name
of repute, has fallen upon a subject which vividly recalls
to my mind the scenery of the Bosphorus. A moment
has been seized when the climate is simply heavenly,
and the materials which come to hand could not be
more felicitous : the composition consists of round headlands, houses and forts nestling under rocks, wooden
huts with the ordinary arrangements for coffee, sherbet,
and pipes. On the beach are boats with crews and
cargoes, all expressly made for a picture. The whole
is well painted after the Düsseldorf manner. A diverse
scene, though equally characteristic of the Russian
climate, bearing a truly descriptive title in the one
word 'Thaw,' was contributed by a certain M. Wasilieff.
The subject is a cottage, a peasant, a little child, with
a few black rooks, all set in a dreary snow field with a
leaden sky overhead. The frost of a long winter evidently
begins to break, a gleam of sunlight bespeaks the return
of spring, and the snow under thaw is no longer white,
but murky, dank, and dappled over with dirt, also the
cart ruts are slushy with water. The scene is the reverse
of inviting because so literally true to that change of
season which in northern latitudes, though most eventful,
is least agreeable. It cannot be doubted that Russian
painters have a great faculty for faithful copyism of
whatever exists in outward nature ; they paint what
they see with all the more fidelity because they have

little imagination to put them out. To the artists already
enumerated may be added P. Brulloff, son of the architect who built the new imperial palace in the Kremlin,
and nephew of the painter of 'The Last Day of Pompeii,'
a work which, as we have seen, was the first to gain a
European reputation. 'Rest in the Harvest Field,' by
Brulloff the younger, unites figures to landscape; the
style has the vigour and the realism which distinguish
the Russian art revival.

Even water-colour painting has been domiciled in
St. Petersburg. No fewer than sixty-eight drawings
were sent to the Kensington Exhibition of 1872. The
greater number, it must be admitted, are feeble though
faithful; the style resembles the inartistic work done in
Switzerland. Russians, by virtue of their realistic power,
render with verisimilitude architectural buildings, interiors, and still-life; occasionally, too, they are successful in the delineation of animals. Yet it must be admitted that the view of 'Kief,' by L. Premazzi, is a
childish affair, something in style between the Swiss
and the Chinese. 'A Street Scene in St. Petersburg,'
by A. Lavezzari, is a little better. Also conscientious
but weak are fifteen architectural drawings by M. Shish-
koff. 'A Marine View,' by A. Bogoluboff, as might be
expected, is clever; the artist has used charcoal, and the
effect gained is striking and broad. Also powerful and
well conceived is a Russian cart with a team of horses,
by P. Sokoloff. The animals have great go, and are
capital in character. But by far the most remarkable
among these water-colour works is the 'Migration of
Bulgarians,' by Philipoff, a composition which was conspicuously placed on an easel at the time when I visited
the Academy of St. Petersburg. The subject necessarily
combines figures with landscape. A gipsy kind of rabble,

with cattle and belongings, fly in precipitate disorder before a fire which rages through thick reeds and grass. Here again the interest is greatly increased by the novelty of the subject-matter : for the first time Bulgarians are brought within a picture-gallery ; Russian artists are certainly much to blame when they content themselves with hackneyed and worn-out subjects.

In Russia subjects suited to landscape art are widely scattered, they lie far apart. While in England half a day's journey is sure to bring a painter to his sketching-ground, in Russia, on the contrary, he may travel a thousand miles without the temptation to take out his paint-box. The road from St. Petersburg to Moscow, and even further south, is dreary and monotonous in the extreme. The territory looks forsaken and uninhabitable, and yet when I remarked to a Russian traveller, of the rank known in England as a country squire, on the scantiness of the people, I received for reply the assurance that the country was suffering from over-population. The seeming contradiction might have been explained by Malthus ; the simple fact would appear to be that the inhabitants are in excess of the means of subsistence, a condition compatible with the most scanty population that ever held a desert land. The traveller at long distances encounters wood-built hamlets, but the houses are bare and barn-like as Norwegian tenements. Nature, too, is stunted, starved, and stricken ; the trees struggle between life and death, their topmost branches have been carried away by the storm, and their roots are denuded by biting ice ; it must be admitted that such scenes are not without a rugged and stern grandeur. Forest lands, too, which sometimes stretch from the foreground to the horizon, especially when left to their own wild will, move the imagination equally with the boundless and restless sea. Then at intervals are interspersed, amid arid plains, fertile oases ; spots favoured by nature and fostered by man. Here the colour, especially under sunshine, becomes vivid, and often in these northern latitudes the traveller finds brilliant banks of wild flowers, for almost before the snow has melted away verdure springs into life. I have sometimes stopped to note the colours which nature blends in these foreground studies. Usually the three primaries—yellow, red, and blue—are brought into strong juxtaposition ; indeed the artist is offered more colour than he knows how to manage, and the difficulty of a vivid foreground, out of keeping with the dun greys of the distance, has to be met as best may be. The contrasts are in these regions known to be harsh. And yet the most desolate and uninviting of Russian land-scapes gain grandeur and beauty under hourly changes of atmosphere. When the sky glows with sunset, as the shades of evening gather, as star by star lights a candle in the sky, and the moon makes darkness visible, poetry asserts the universal spell felt in all lands, though perhaps least in Russia. Painters of the North seek to steal a charm from more romantic climes, they rightly strive to mitigate the austerities of long winters and furtive summers. And yet, though Russian painters succeed in casting and concentrating a transitory gleam and glow on their transcripts from nature, the impression remains that they dwell in a land of lengthened shadow and far-stretching snow, that they see the shadow side of nature stern and cold.

Nevertheless artists of ready pencil, such as the brothers John and Peter Sokoloff, find compensating interest in the marked character and the picturesque

costume of peasant life. An empire cannot be uninviting to a painter which offers such capital subjects
as a 'Horde of Bohemians in the Caucasus,' and a
'Village Wedding,' also in the Caucasus : both works
rightly obtained good position in the great Paris Exhibition of 1867, a proof that Russian artists do not
suffer in international competition. I have elsewhere
stated, as one among many indications that art has
already penetrated far and wide through the empire,
that John Sokoloff was born at Astracan on the Caspian, and that he betook himself professionally to the
remote provincial town of Sudscha, in the Government
of Koursk. This is a territory wherein agriculture,
ecclesiastical miracles, and church processions flourish in
combination—a concatenation of circumstances I have
found in Russia, as in Italy, favourable to art. Certainly, as I can testify, in Russia incidents are not
wanting to the art of picture-making, though it must
be admitted that the trade of picture-selling is poor.
In my transit through districts south of Moscow materials for the portfolio thickened. I remember, for
instance, in the course of the journey, which I made
in an open springless cart, called the Imperial Post,
that I came on a company of sportsmen clad in skins
and armed to the teeth. Before them hung on a pole,
as a trophy of the chase, a wolf which had ravaged
the neighbouring hamlet. Nothing was needed to
complete the picture ; the landscape glowed with golden
corn, in the distant horizon was seen a village with
encircling trees, and the foreground, as I have said, was
held by sportsmen with their booty.

The pictorial resources of Russia will never be known
till a John Lewis or a David Roberts, either in the
person of a native or a stranger, shall pitch his sketching-

tent under the shadow of the Kremlin or before one
of the fortress-monasteries, such as Troitza and Kief.
Seville and Grenada are scarcely more lovely in situation, more imposing in architectural grouping, more
tempting to the sketcher in rich and varied accessories
of figures, than are these sacred spots of pilgrimage.
I have looked down upon Cairo from the citadel, I have
seen Damascus from the hills, and Jerusalem from the
Mount of Olives, and yet I have never seen a picture
more lovely than the Kremlin with its golden domes
and dark bulwark towers at sunset. But though neither
Balbec nor Palmyra have been too distant or difficult
of access for David Roberts, Carl Haag, and other skilled
and enterprising painters, Moscow, Troitza, and Kief lie
as yet beyond the frontier of European art. In no
gallery of the West do I remember to have seen any first-
class pictures from these cities and shrines—as sacred
to the Russian Church as St. Peter's and the Vatican,
or as the convent at Assisi, are to the Latin Church.
The reason is easily stated. If Russia possessed even
one draughtsman graphic as our English Prout, who
put upon paper with telling effect the crumbling stone-
work of our old cathedrals, or a single painter in oils as
brilliant and realistic as the Belgian Bossuet, who, over
a period of fifteen or twenty years, has made the sunny
and red brick walls of Cordova glisten in the picture-
galleries of Paris, Brussels, and London, we should not
now have to argue the question whether there be in
Russia a sphere for the painter who delights in the
architecture of ancient cities. But hitherto Muscovite
artists have not been fortunate enough to command a
foreign market; and probably the day is still far distant
when Russia shall be able, like France, Belgium, Germany, and Italy, to open with England an export trade

in pictures. The price doubtless would be low, even though the quality were sufficiently high.

Another reason why the resources of Russia remain undeveloped is, that no one part of the empire has been included within what may be termed the sketching-ground of Europe. Sir Charles Eastlake, in his young days, painted landscapes in Greece, and numberless painters have since brought home portfolios well stored with studies from the East; but, with the exception of my namesake, Mr. Atkinson, the Siberian traveller, scarcely a single landscape painter has ventured across the Russian frontier. Nor can this timidity be cause for wonder. Food, climate, language, difficulties of transit, not to speak of the chicanery of the people, are sufficient to deter from the rash enterprise. In Moscow I said to the landlord, 'I understand you give to your guests Russian dishes.' 'Do you deem me mad,' was the reply; 'every traveller would be in the hands of the doctor at once.' This I could well believe from my experience at the Russian restaurant attached to the Paris International Exhibition. Artists to their cost will find the living in out-of-the-way places in Russia a wholly different sort of thing from the homely but wholesome fare at Bettwys and other sketching-stations in Wales. I met, however, in St. Petersburg with one English painter who had braved the dangers. Climate, again, is in itself sufficient to close the greater part of Russia to the itinerant sketcher. For example, I found the heat of the sun at Moscow in August sufficiently overpowering to make sun-strokes imminent; and I learnt that during the previous winter the cold had been so far intolerable that two passengers were found frozen to death in their seats on the arrival of the train from St. Petersburg. My informant added, that one evening, when on foot, he feared that the cold would have paralysed his walking powers before he could reach home, in which case he must simply have laid himself down to die. Moscow, then, excepting for some few favoured days or weeks, is the last place in the world for outdoor sketching. St. Petersburg and intermediate places are, of course, no better. I need scarcely dwell on the difficulty of language. Those who have travelled or sketched in Egypt, Palestine, or Turkey, will know that a dragoman or some personal attendant is an indispensable companion and protection. In short, Russia cannot be taken possession of by the landscape painter without a complete equipment as for a serious campaign. I have spoken of the chicanery of the people, but I should in justice add that, though they pick a pocket with one hand, they do not plunge a dagger into the breast with the other. If Russian peasants are ignorant, indolent, and dishonest, they are at any rate innocuous and even kindly. Without fear, without protection, without the companionship of even a pistol, I traversed two hundred miles of territory in an open cart. A painter, I believe, might safely trust himself for days or years in remotest districts of Russia, though he would not dare to make a sketch beyond gunshot of Athens.

Southern Russia comes as a surprise upon the traveller who has pronounced the land barren. The stranger, who had previously declared the empire uncultivated and poverty-stricken, suddenly opens upon districts which are as mines of wealth. Vast territories, which had presented geological strata thin and sandy, with a people equally meagre and starved, are exchanged for fertile tracts heaving with golden corn. And naturally the population grows numerically in proportion to the increased fertility of the soil; the fields, or rather the open tracts and undulating steppes, are busy with labourers. Windmills, cottages, and villages enliven the landscape. In the south the peasants gain also in picturesqueness; even when the costumes are colourless, raggedness and ruggedness seldom fail of pictorial character. Occasionally, too, is thrust in, when least expected, an affluence yet subdued splendour of colour which tell that the traveller approaches oriental frontiers. In fact Russia, which on her northern borders may have been pronounced unpictorial, here on the confines of the Black Sea assumes art aspects which recall my experiences in Italy and Greece. It was harvest-time when I left the railway which leads on to Odessa, and then took to posting by stages two hundred miles westward to Chernowitz. An artist armed with sketching-pad, pencil, and colour-box, might have stocked a folio. The rising and the setting sun clothed by turns the landscape in gold, purple, and grey, and on the far track of country, undulating as a tumbling sea from foreground to sky, were marked as on a sun-dial the hours between waking and sleeping. No hedge, no barrier was there; the eye in fact stretched onward without break to the far-off horizon, as in a primeval zone where earth and air are original elements, and the land has not been yet apportioned among the children of men. Were it not for furtive culture and the occasional intrusion of human dwellings, the wide plains in Central Russia would seem, as the broad wastes over which I have ridden in Turkey, to belong to nobody. In the South, as I have said, barrenness is exchanged for fertility. I was there furnished with a passport from the imperial government, which entitled me to travel at a cheap rate in a cart, at the speed of ten miles an hour, dashing, as the case might be, through forests, over mossy hillocks, road ruts, and stones. The forests are not as paintable as Fontainebleau, but apparently as extensive. Presently, after traversing across some miles of solitude, the eye distinguishes in the distance a desolate cluster of dwellings, it may be a village or only a farm. At some risk to the wheels of the rickety vehicle, as well as to the bones of the stranger, the horses tear onwards at rattling speed to the post where they will be unharnessed from their load. The change at these stations is not always made speedily, for sometimes the steeds have to be caught in the open field; but usually by the time the official documents are examined, the formal entries made, and a little refreshment taken, the postboy is mounted, with reins and whip in hand, ready to start on the coming stage at a furious pace. Thus days pass, and with them picture after picture is presented in swift succession.

The painter, too, who can throw figures into his landscape need never lack a subject. Want of colour cannot be felt, at any rate in harvest-time. The hourly track of the traveller lies, as in Spain, between cornfields which, for colour and continuity, I have never seen equalled save along the bridle-road which leads the whole day long across Syrian cornfields to the town of Bethany. The ingathering of the harvest too, with teams and rude agricultural appliances, and labourers decked as for artists' studios, make pictures ready for the pencil. The figures are indeed posed as for pictorial composition: peasants who live and labour in these southern latitudes are ever art objects. The sun burns the skin into hues of gold and copper, as in the heads of the shepherds who went in quest of the Manger at Bethlehem. And when these figures pass from labour to

devotion they make themselves worthy of Zurbaran.
No Franciscan monk by Spanish painter, no Mahomedan
at prayer in the desert, could be more impressive than
these Russian peasants when kneeling at their sacred
shrines. Even beggars are venerable, and especially
devotional ; clothed in rags and wearing beards worthy
of apostles, they group admirably with the surrounding
landscape or the architectural background. Such subjects, if any painter cared to search them out, would at
any rate be commended for novelty. Even Wallachian
peasants have begun to make themselves at home in
picture-galleries ; but Russian peasants in a cornfield or
within a church, although equally paintable, remain yet
to be pourtrayed.

In fine, much remains in Russia to be painted. The
borders of the Black Sea and the mighty rivers which
drain the watershed of Central Russia have scarcely yet
been explored by the artist. There are wild districts
of field and forest bordering on Turkey to which I have
known Englishmen go all the way from London for the
sake of sport ; guns, ammunition, potted-meats, and
other provisions and appliances, have been carried many
hundred miles to kill the wild boar ; but no sketching
books, canvases, pencils, or colours have been brought
to bear on these, as yet, unpainted landscapes. I have
known, in Moscow, Englishmen intent on commerce
pushing their way to the Caspian Sea ; but as yet the
whole of the vast regions held by Russia in Asia are
almost beyond the pale of the artist. Again, the Ural
Mountains have yielded rich treasures of gold and
precious stones ; but I do not recall a single picture
they have furnished to public museums or imperial
palaces. A painter with such spirit of adventure as
animated the late Mr. Catlin when sketching in the

far West inhabited by American Indians, would have much to reveal of the unexplored lands of Eastern Europe. But the pioneer must arm himself as if he were a soldier entering on arduous work. He might need a hatchet to cut his path through the forest, or want a compass for a guide across tracts on which the sun rises and sets as on the wide swell of the Atlantic. That there is an art of the future which, following the footsteps of commerce, shall open up whatever is most beautiful, grand, or strange in the Russian Empire cannot be doubted. Humboldt foretold the time when the forests, the rivers, and the mountains of South America shall be taken possession of by the landscape painter. In like manner, in Eastern Europe, the pictorial arts are destined to extend our knowledge of physical geography and to deepen our reverence for the wonders of creation.

CHAPTER IX.

MOSCOW.

IT is difficult to imagine a stronger contrast than that which is presented by the two chief cities of Russia. St. Petersburg is modern, Moscow is ancient; St. Petersburg rises out of a flat morass, she is moored as a raft on shallow waters; Moscow, on the contrary, is planted among undulating hills, her heights are crowned with the cupolas of churches and the towers of fortresses. Once again, St. Petersburg is planned almost with military precision; streets, straight as a right line, radiate from a common centre, squares laid out with symmetry are surrounded by stately edifices; everywhere the pomp of empire asserts itself over the poverty and parsimony of nature. The ancient city of Moscow, in contrast, rejoices in the ever-varying charm of irregularity; the streets are neither straight nor level, the public places, though spacious, are without state or symmetry; the finest architectural combinations often present picturesque discordances—old Orientalism is mixed up with new Europeanism. The plan and general aspect of the city retain signs of Asiatic parentage; the walls show the irregularity of Syrian towns, which, lying on the confines of desert tracts, are defended by rude fortifications against marauders; the houses, too, instead of being ranged in long streets, are often detached and surrounded by a court or a garden, the streets are labyrinthine as the ways in Constantinople and Damascus; the presence, too, of countless cupolas all the more

enhances the Oriental character of the city panorama.
The stranger in Moscow is subject to pleasant surprises.
There are many towns which, lying on the flat, with
narrow streets and high houses, seem to imprison the
traveller; neither eye nor mind can find outlook or exit.
But here, in a city which undulates between gentle
heights and valleys, the traveller is relieved by constant
change; at one moment he is down in shadow, the next
he mounts into sunshine; in one district he finds himself cribbed, cabined, and confined, in another he is able
to breathe freely among trees and gardens, or to command from ramparts a view of the vast city, with its
multitude of roofs, chimneys, cupolas—the Kremlin as
an acropolis towering above all. Each great capital of
the world has its distinctive characteristics, and Moscow
in her own way is without a rival.

And yet I confess that Moscow disappointed me. In
former days I had passed six weeks in Cairo, a month
in Jerusalem, a fortnight in Damascus, and five weeks
in Constantinople. My eye therefore had become pretty
familiar with the architecture and the general aspect of
Eastern cities, and I own that on entering Moscow,
the most 'Oriental of European cities,' the comparisons
I made were little to its advantage. The greater part
of the town is too modern for the interests of art or of
archæology. Prior to the year 1812 Moscow had been
better worth a visit, but the fires of the French invasion,
which raged for more than a week, reduced to a heap of
smoking ruins the palaces and churches which Napoleon
had from the heights looked down upon with wonder
and with envy. It is true that much escaped, and it
is equally certain that many streets and structures were
speedily restored as near as might be to their original
condition. But a confusion of styles and of dates ensued

which is more curious than strictly artistic. Indeed, owing to the prevailing custom of covering walls with stucco, and then with the further disguise of colour or whitewash, the test of antiquity for the majority of travellers becomes little more than surface dirt and decay. Modern work of the trowel and of the brush intrudes on ancient structures. Thus the Church of St. Basil, in the great square beneath the Kremlin, a building which embodies some of the most ancient masonry in the city, is accustomed to have its bizarre cupolas repainted, in the crudest of reds, yellows, and blues, every three or four years. Moreover, since the great fire, now sixty years ago, the natural elements of destruction have not been in abeyance; yearly recurring frosts render wholesale renovations the serious business of every spring. And what makes the medley of styles and the confusion of dates all the more perplexing, is that the Russian artisan has always been so perfect an imitator that, if he re-touch a wall-painting or restore a moulding, it is hard after the lapse of a twelvemonth to tell where the old work ends and the new work begins. The impression left on my mind was that of universal rottenness, falsity in internal construction, and illusion in external material. Yet if the student will consent to unburden himself of art principles and rest content, in a good-humoured way, to gain amusement out of picturesque incongruities, he may find in the streets of Moscow incitement for many a day. The architect, however, will not meet with much to record in his note-book. The fact is Oriental conceptions and details can be gathered elsewhere in purer form. And as for local or Russian styles, if they exist at all, they are little more than corrupt derivatives from generic roots planted afore-

time in neighbouring nations. But, in speaking thus
plainly, again I must pay tribute to the imposing
pictorial effects which the city panorama presents,
especially when the towers and cupolas of the Kremlin strike against the evening sky.

Moscow, as already said, is picturesque rather than
expressly artistic. The domestic architecture adopts
the common vernacular of modern Europe: square-
headed doors and windows pierce walls without mouldings or other ornamental relief. In vain the eye looks
along the streets for points of detail and decoration
such as are never wanting to the street architecture
of the smallest Italian town. Few indeed are the signs
that the people have a delight in beauty, or a desire
to bring the arts into their daily life; a black Byzantine picture, or a brightly coloured print, seems sufficiently to satisfy their cravings for the beautiful. The
churches in Moscow—said to exceed in number, as
the churches in Rome, the days of the year—have for
the most part little more pretence to art than the private
dwellings. Indeed it may be almost said that the
many purposes to which lath, plaster, and whitewash
are put, supersede the necessity of any art which
may not be easily got by a saw or a hammer, by a
nail or a brush. Russia is a nation of makeshifts,
of piecings and patchings; the late Richard Cobden
was wrong politically when he said that the Russian
nation could be crumpled up as a piece of paper in
a hand, but he would have been right in point of art
had he thus designated and denounced the private and
public structures in her chief cities.

Here in Moscow the contrasts and anomalies are
more striking than even in Constantinople, inasmuch
as in a really Eastern city all is more of one pattern.

In Moscow, porticoes rising in all the pomp of Corinthian pillars adjoin the meanest wooden huts, and colossal public institutions are next door to the smallest shops. Yet, fortunately for pictorial purposes, such incongruities are not incompatible with the element of the picturesque. Prout would have delighted in the negligence and irregularity of these tortuous streets, yet all so much alike that the traveller loses himself several times in the course of a morning. One method which I had tried twenty years before, when wandering in Constantinople, proved here efficient. I placed a pocket-compass on a map of the city, and holding both map and compass in hand was able to steer my course with tolerable precision. And in my perplexed track I had the pleasure of coming suddenly on surprises; thus an apparently blind alley would unexpectedly open on a broad square; or, after threading my way without landmark, a tower of the Kremlin, high in the sky, would pronounce my whereabouts. There are also other boundary lines which may be useful in the navigation of a city whose circumvallation is said to exceed twenty English miles. The Kremlin, seated about the centre, declares itself unmistakeably from whichever side it may be approached; then there is a river spanned by bridges which serves, as it were, as a base for operations; furthermore, there exists an inner and an outer circle, consisting of wide roads, like boulevards planted with lines of trees on the sites of ancient moats or fortifications. I can scarcely describe the pleasurable sensations with which, day after day, I explored on foot, without a guide, the wonders of this strange city. My rule in travelling is never to take a carriage when I can go on foot, and on this principle I once walked from Rome to Florence. In an Empire so

vast as that of Russia pedestrianism is almost impracticable, though the story has recently been told, that
when a certain attaché was transferred, without any allowance for travelling expenses, from Paris to St. Petersburg, he chose to walk the whole distance between the
two capitals. That such pedestrian feats are in these
regions absurdities, seems to be signified by the fact
that the said attaché on reaching St. Petersburg found
his dismissal awaiting him. But when once a traveller
has reached, by rail or otherwise, in the most rapid
way possible, some chief centre of operations, then he
will do well, according to his strength, to trust to his
legs. My experience in St. Petersburg and Moscow is,
that whatever I saw from a carriage in rapid motion was
forgotten, while all that could be deliberately examined
on foot was fixed in the memory, with all the attendant
circumstances of climate, people, and costume. Moscow
thus, day by day, grew on my mind as a living reality.

Moscow is the best coloured city I know—the finest
of all cities when seen in distant perspective, with her
thousand and one golden domes glittering in the sun
against the sky. Cairo viewed from the citadel, and
Constantinople from the tower of Galata, are comparatively grey and colourless. Moscow when illumined
under sunset shines with Oriental splendour ; the eye
is dazzled as by a brilliant stage scene, more like
enchantment than reality. Not that the colour is refined or in strict harmony ; often, indeed, all that can
be said is that the painter has used his paint-pot
generously, that yellow ochres, reds, blues, and gold
are laid on thickly. But anything that may be wanting on the part of the artist is supplied by the hand
of nature ; time brings the harshest of pigments into
tone ; atmosphere casts a delicate veil over the per-

spective vision ; distance, in short, lends enchantment.
It often happens in semi-barbaric structures that what
the artist intended may be commonplace and coarse,
but that what he did not intend, that is, unforeseen
accidents, or combinations which fall out by the happy
chance of circumstance, proves most effective. Such are
the panoramas which arrest the traveller's steps as the
eye sweeps over the housetops, chimneys, towers, trees,
gilded and many-coloured domes which stretch from
foreground to horizon. There are cities which the
stranger should never enter, there are buildings which
the critic can scarcely dare to approach. But magnitude and multitude move the imagination. One minaret
may be mean, one dome insignificant, but the moment
the unit becomes a thousand, and as soon as space sufficiently expands for atmosphere to suggest magnitude
or mystery, then literal facts give place to phantoms,
and poems and pictures are wrought out of even com-
monest materials.

Yet these many-coloured domes, though they float
as a thing of beauty between earth and sky, are rather
bulbous in character ; indeed, sometimes they thrust
themselves upwards and outwards as excrescences. The
construction, too, is rather gimcrack ; in the Kremlin I
examined several cupolas under repair ; when the outer
covering of thin metal is removed, ribs, as of an umbrella
or of a lady's crinoline, are laid bare. A make-up thus
flimsy and slight admits of more easy adaptation than
bricks and mortar to the many varied forms which
fancy may suggest. The curves and outlines assumed
are sometimes graceful, often fantastic ; in some directions the eye seems to look on a number of giant
gourds, in others a group of Turks' turbans may be
suggested, while the smaller domes may be mistaken

for pepper-boxes, decanters, or castors familiar on dinner-tables. In short the variety of forms already in existence is all but infinite, and others might readily be invented. Specially graceful is a common type, not larger in diameter than a minaret, bearing a golden dome as its crown. One pretty effect I observed within the Kremlin. The newly-wrought cupolas of highly burnished surface serve as Claude Lorraine mirrors to reflect the moving clouds, the passing crowds, the trees and encircling landscape. It may easily be imagined how gay and glittering a city looks thus set with jewels and shining with patens of bright gold. The colours, too, are scarcely less varied than the forms : besides gold, there is silver, often blue, and green and red ; sometimes also a green ground is set with gold stars : inscriptions in letters of gold may likewise be seen as friezes around towers. So much, indeed, is Moscow a city of colours, that the walls even of ordinary dwellings are illumined brightly with red and yellow, and the roofs are green. The climax is of course reached by the Kremlin, which dominates over the city lying beneath as a church, a palace, and a citadel.

This stronghold, the acropolis of Moscow, is flanked by massive and picturesque towers, surmounted by rough steep roofs, marked and coloured like the scales of serpents ; also over gateways and at angles are many other towers, which group with domes and pointed pinnacles and golden crosses into ever-varying panoramas as the spectator makes the circuit of the walls, or as the sun, travelling from east to west, alternates light and shade ; the scale is sufficiently extended to gain changeful play of atmospheric effect. One of the towers, that of the 'Spaski' gate, was erected by an Englishman, Christopher Galloway, in 1626. The 'Troitski' tower was also built by him. While the basements are heavy and gloomy, after the Oriental fashion, the upper stories, or sky outlines in infinite fantasy, play with cloudland and seem so to hold themselves aloof from earth as to become creatures of the elements. The Kremlin should be seen by sunset, twilight, and moonlight—no building has such varied moods.

Within the walls of the Kremlin the student will find work for many days. I shall not stop to speak of the big bell, or of the cannon taken from the French; neither will it be needful to describe the immense factory-like façade of the imperial palace which Moscow owes to the genius of Alexander Brulloff, brother to the painter of the same name. But this palace has a magnificent interior, which makes some amends for the poverty of the outside. I had long come to the conclusion that all modern palaces are pretty much alike, yet some exception may be made in St. Petersburg and Moscow on the ground, not so much of better art as of unaccustomed opulence and splendour. Here in the vestibule the stranger is met by the monoliths of marble which ever attend on Muscovite emperors. A handsome granite staircase leads to the state apartments. Vases and candelabra, pilasters of verd-antique, mantlepieces of jasper, and an abundance of pictures, make up that insensate grandeur which delights Russian sovereigns and their subjects. All that is modern is inferior to Parisian fashion and display; but when the traveller turns to the palace wing—occupied by 'the treasury,' he finds himself, not among imported taste or upholstery, but in the company of Russian Tsars and neighbouring potentates, to whom the ancient arts of the East and

of the West were tributes of peace or trophies of war.
Russia, by her geographical position and commercial
relations, has had for many centuries rarest opportunities
of amassing art treasures, which here remain as heirlooms in the reigning family. The collection, though
from time to time plundered and impoverished, is still
a visible token of the historic times when princes came
from far to offer tribute of works most precious, and
when the pomp of courts was swelled by array of gold,
precious stones, and gorgeous apparel.

It is impossible for me to describe within reasonable limits, even did my knowledge suffice, the wealth
of this treasure-house. But I must not forget the room
occupied by the royal insignia—crowns of diamonds and
gold filigree; specially the gold and jewelled 'Bonnet
d'Astrakhan,' and 'le Bonnet de Kasan,' the imperial
globe surmounted by a cross sent from Byzantium to
Vladimer Monomach. This last magnificent work is
enriched by 58 diamonds, 89 rubies, 23 sapphires, 50
emeralds, mounted on enamelled gold. Then follow
crosses, chains, gold and ivory thrones. Some of these
objects might appear at first sight much older than
they are, because in decorative art, as in picture painting, the Byzantine types have been continued into
modern times. One of the ivory thrones was brought
from Greece in the fifteenth century, and as the subjects
carved thereon relate to Orpheus an early date is talked
of. But some of the plaques, at any rate, are admitted
to be late interpolations. Nothing I repeat is so dubious
as the date of treasures found in Russia, and equally
doubtful is the locality whence this work first came.
The Russians, however, claim a distinctive part and
function in the arts of Byzantium; they say that the
Russian pencil and graver may be easily distinguished;

it is stated, moreover, that in the sacred manufactory
on Mount Athos there have been Russians who occupied
all their time in carving and painting images, and that
their work is impressed with their nationality.   Russian
antiquarians lay claim to distinctive characteristics in
works bearing the general Byzantine type produced in
Taurica Chersonesus, now known as the Crimea.   My
time was too limited to form any very definite conclusion
on this difficult turning-point in Russian archæology.

Moscow, still the place of coronation, naturally pre-
serves the imperial vestments of the Tsars, but the
major part are not prior to Peter the Great.   Here also
in the Treasury are gathered from all nations articles
which have served in state ceremonies or for table
decorations at banquets.   Such objects of luxury can
seldom be of home manufacture ; still, by their accumulative mass they attest the growing wealth and power
of the Russian Empire, as well as the love of ostentation
which proverbially belongs to Eastern potentates, who,
in default of taste and knowledge, glory in displays
analogous to the prandial pomp of Manchester and of
the Mansion House in the present day.   It is said that
in this varied and vast Treasury are more than fifteen
hundred old pieces of gold, silver, jasper, crystal, &c.
But here again comes the question of age and of dates.
For instance, there are more than three hundred vases—
silver-gilt, &c.; but the earliest dates established are the
fifteenth, sixteenth, and seventeenth centuries.   Many,
if not the majority, of these works are importations :
for example, a jug and salver came as presents from
Charles I and Charles II of England, and a most remarkable old chariot was a gift from Queen Elizabeth.
Also, Russia is indebted to England for the insignia
of the Order of the Garter, sent by Elizabeth to John

the Terrible. In contrast to these finely-wrought works is the most hideous mass in metal ever seen, due to the munificence of Christian IV of Denmark. Among objects of historic worth is 'a large cup of silver, without any ornament except the following inscription round the edge in interlaced Slavonic characters.' This work is said to date back to the twelfth century, and the inscription runs thus:—'This is the cup of Kniase Vladimir Davidovicz: to the health of him who drinks, and to the praise of God and of the Sovereign Grand Prince.' This treasury, it will readily be understood, contains much on which Russia may look with pride. The arms and armour which dress the walls and corridors are Russian, either by right of capture, of use, or manufacture. I have seen most armouries in Europe—from Madrid to London and Turin—and this in Moscow stands apart by specific characteristics which pertain almost exclusively to the Russian territory. I may mention the damascened helmet of Alexander Nevsky, of the thirteenth century; also grand war banners, especially one of the Tsar, Jean IV, in the sixteenth century, richly embroidered, and bearing the image of our Lord, saints, and seraphim-like beings on horseback, with angels and the heavenly host looking on; all on a star-spangled field. In no country are there banners which can compare in bulk, weight, or strange fantasy of design, with the ponderous erections in Russia, set up in museums and churches, and carried in processions through the public streets.

The House of the Holy Synod, likewise within the precincts of the Kremlin, is the richest treasury in Russia of sacerdotal robes, church-plate, ornaments, and sacred vessels used in the Greek ritual. No sacristy in Europe I can call to mind is its equal; the treasury in the cathedral of Aix la Chapelle is perhaps its nearest approach. This unique collection has been from time to time further enriched by the precious jewels and other possessions which the early prelates of Moscow held as their private property. Many ecclesiastical works naturally came from Constantinople, not only as the great centre of Byzantine art, but likewise as the ancient seat of the Greek Church. A number of these sacred objects are the gifts of Russian sovereigns, anxious either to prove their piety or to make amends for their ill deeds. Thus the most remarkable among the priests' garments is an amazingly rich sakkos, presented by John the Terrible, in expiation of the murder of his own son. Here also are stored up carefully in glass cases the vestments, not only of successive patriarchs of Moscow, but of high church dignitaries throughout Russia. Hence, not only in point of art and of antiquity, but also as a record of the Greek ritual used in Russia for many centuries, the value of this singularly complete collection can hardly be overrated. The Greek Church relies quite as much as the Latin Church upon the effect produced by rich vestments, and it is hard to overestimate the impression produced on the minds of the common people by the use in the offices of religion of these robes, often rich in gold, precious stones, pearls, plaques of silver-gilt, engraved with figures of saints, &c. One such vestment of the fourteenth century is almost without parallel. In another example the embroidery is in design and execution as fine as the carving on the most elaborate of ivories. Here faithful worshippers are able to scan on the back and the breast of their priest pictorial representations of the whole scheme of Christianity—from the Annunciation to the Crucifixion and the Ascension. I am afraid that the age of this

work is not earlier than the end of the seventeenth
century; the style, which is the traditional Byzantine,
affords in this, as in other instances, little or no criterion
of date. As to this generic style, though nothing can
justify poor and inaccurate drawing of the human
figure, I must say, notwithstanding my early prejudices,
I found the ecclesiastical ornament, both in textile
fabrics and metal-work, glorious in colour, strict in the
essential principles of surface-decoration, and altogether
more satisfactory than any of the late work in Western
Europe. I have heard Russians well versed in art contend that the Greek Church would not be wise to depart
from Byzantine precedents sanctioned by antiquity.

Seven patriarchal mitres in this sacred syndicate
would scarcely be known as bishops' mitres in the
Latin Church. Instead of the cleft usual in a mitre
is the unbroken round of a crown or cap; indeed the
earliest of these sacerdotal head-dressings might be
mistaken, as far as the form goes, for a wideawake
hat. But this rudimentary type soon gives place to
more ornate developments. The plebeian brim is cut
away, and the flattened crown becomes elevated into a
dome-like crest, surmounted by a cross more or less
ornate. As in the clothing for priestly shoulders, so
here in the helmet for the skulls of the church militant is
provided a panoply befitting saints. The oldest of these
mitres, hats, or crowns, does not date beyond the end
of the sixteenth century; the work is said to have been
made to the order of the patriarch Job; the material
is blue damask, embroidered with gold and faced with
ermine; the surface receives as its ornament the apparition of the blessed Virgin, and an inscription written in
fine pearls reads thus :—' I put all my confidence in thee,
Mother of God: take me under thy holy protection.'

Also among the surface-decorations are the Saviour, the Blessed Virgin, St. John the Precursor, and at the sides archangels, the apostles St. Peter and St. Paul, with popes and saints. Again, written in fine pearls, is read the further inscription :—'Look down upon us from Thy heavens, O Lord! see and visit this vine which Thy finger hath planted.' Six other mitres are highly decorated with enamels, precious stones, silver-gilt slabs, pearls, rubies, emeralds, sapphires, diamonds. Such are the precious materials which this church of Oriental splendour brings to the enrichment of merely a bishop's mitre. Some of these works are assigned to Russian artisans, and I see no reason to the contrary, especially as the dates come down to the time when the arts had penetrated into Russia. Moreover, as before stated, these Muscovite artificers have for long boasted of special gifts in the workmanship of the precious metals, and in the tasteful adaptation, on an Eastern basis, of surface-ornament. Among the Northern races, even during the pagan period, it has been seen, especially in Scandinavian provinces, that workers in bronze, silver, and gold possessed exceptional knowledge. And down to the present day survives the cunning hand. As already said, not an exhibition opens in Russia or in the West that does not tell of the skill of Muscovite workers in the precious metals. Their art prospers though their talents thrive on a pittance which elsewhere might scarcely save from starvation.

The remarkable crosses preserved in this House of the Holy Synod may be divided into—first, crosses worn on the breast; second, crosses used at the altar; third, crosses carried in procession. The pectoral crosses have such interest as attaches to the Byzantine style :

Christ on the cross, in relief or in chasing, the heads of Christ in niello, together with minor figures and subordinate ornaments, pertain to the style of the Greek Church. Secondly, the altar crosses are mostly of Cyprus wood, carved at Mount Athos, with the usual Biblical subjects. Thirdly, the processional crosses, though of like generic style, do not appear to date earlier than the seventeenth century. I can testify to the use to which in the present day such crosses are put, having witnessed many processions both in the churches and in the streets of Moscow. The pictorial effect of the latter it would be scarcely possible to over-colour or exaggerate, especially when improved by a gale of wind. Then the bearers of crosses and banners are caught as a ship in a storm carrying high masts and heavy canvas; under this sudden stress of weather I have seen the Russian Church compelled to call in the assistance of the laity, by whose conjoined aid the sacred relics were borne to the nearest harbour of refuge. The grand disorder would have delighted Rubens or Pietro da Cortona; and as for the colour, Paul Veronese never in Venice found richer material for his sumptuous panoramas.

It remains to speak, in this Museum of the Holy Synod, of the sacred pectoral images worn by the bishops. Some are lovely as they are rare; indeed the beauty of Byzantine art is often here epitomised in smallest compass. In one specimen is a magnificent sardonyx, bearing the image, in low relief, of the Virgin and Child; in another is a ruby, engraved with the Annunciation, surrounded by gold, chased and set with diamonds; in a third is an onyx, carrying the Holy Trinity; in a fourth is a jasper, encircled with gold and precious stones, the centre being 'The Apparition of the Madonna,' standing among clouds, with arms upraised in prayer, as seen in the Roman catacombs, and bearing on her breast the image of the infant Christ in miniature. Sometimes the inscriptions are impressive; thus a neck-pendant, consisting of an unusually rich composition of rubies, emeralds, and diamonds, enclosing an enamel of the Holy Trinity, with the four Evangelists, has a Slavonic inscription commencing, 'Holy, Holy, Holy is the God of Armies: the heavens and the earth are full of Thy glory.' I am sorry to add that the date is not earlier than the second half of the seventeenth century.

I had the privilege of witnessing, within a stone's throw of this House of the Holy Synod, the use of sacred art-objects like to those just described. Indeed while in Russia I made a point of losing no opportunity of judging of the relation in which the arts stood to the every-day ritual of the Greek Church. In St. Petersburg the ceremonies are dressy, musical, and decorative; the show is almost too modern to be sacred. But in Moscow there is a better chance of getting the real thing; especially here within the Kremlin. Into the venerable Cathedral of the Assumption, where the emperors are crowned, I went one morning in the month of August to witness a high function, the patriarch officiating, and the civil and military authorities not only giving state sanction, but aiding materially by their highly-coloured costumes to the *tout ensemble* of the scenic display. The picture, or rather the moving drama, was forced up by a background of intense colour; the walls and roof of this sumptuous yet cavernous and sepulchral interior, comparable in richness to St. Mark's, are covered throughout with mural paintings heightened by gold glories and gold grounds—even the columns are overlaid with figures and gold. The priests, in rich apparel, stand out as gold in sunlight against gold in shadow. Their robes, of utmost lustre, are enriched by gold, silver, jewels, enamels, and silk brocades. Their head-dresses, which fitly culminate their personal apparel, are not mitres, but rather the high rounded caps I had seen the day before in the treasury of the Holy House; on a ground of gold are wrought designs in pearls, emeralds, and other precious stones. Moreover the mere decorative effect gains intellectual and spiritual expression by venerable heads of a refined and lofty Eastern type, nobler I think than the average run of faces among the dignitaries of the Romish Church. When the priests uncover the head, the aspect, favoured by long thick hair divided over the forehead and falling in ample locks down to the shoulders, is saint-like, almost Christ-like.

But as a set-off to the above description it is fair to state one or two disparaging details. Thus, instead of rich mosaics as in St. Mark's, the walls, vaults, and columns of this chief church in the Kremlin are bedaubed with indifferent pictures, and in place of a floor, also inlaid, as in the churches of Italy, with designs of many-coloured stones, appear blocks of black iron. The dais too has no more artistic covering than a carpet of a large flaunting pattern such as adorned the parlours of our grandmothers before taste and good design had obtained entrance to the household. Indeed Russian churches are still held so sacred, that to improve traditional arts, however low and corrupt, is not permissible, and any consistent revival, such as that which in England has renovated our Gothic churches, seems but a far-off possibility in the future.

To revert to the grand religious function I witnessed within the Kremlin, I may add that the church interiors in Russia, like the Greek churches I have known in Athens, are so small that the stranger is not so much a spectator in the dim distance, looking on from afar, as a sharer in the scene, brought into the immediate presence of the chief performers. And yet beyond the immediate foreground are distances lost in shade and veiled in mystery, only rendered more mysterious by the fitful glimmer of many tapers, which in these Russian interiors make darkness dimly visible. 'The kindling of lamps and tapers,' it has been well observed by the writer in Murray's Hand-book, 'is a pleasing custom; the little flame is so living a symbol of the continued life of the soul, and, beyond all other material things, flame is the best representation of the spiritual. The Russians have so closely adopted this idea that there is no interment, no baptism, no betrothing, in short, no sacred ceremony without lamp or taper; fire is for them the pledge of the presence of the Holy Spirit; and hence illuminations play the most important part in the ceremonies of the Greek Church.'

Specially imposing is the moment when the great doors leading from the holy of holies are thrown open for the grandly-robed hierarchy to come out and show themselves to the people; or when, after certain impressive performances in transept or nave, the whole priestly company retires from profane gaze, and the vast doors, moving without a sound, or with such music as belongs only to celestial spheres, are once more closed, as if, till the Church should again vouchsafe the privilege, all access of the human to the divine was cut off. I have often witnessed the performances in St. Peter's and in the Sistine Chapel, but I have never seen a Church function, from an art point of view, better done than here in the Church of the Assumption within the Kremlin. Nothing could be more histrionic than the walking forth, and then the retiring, of the patriarch and his attendant priests, attired, as we have seen, in gold, silver, and jewels. At a certain point the venerable head of the Church, with two high dignitaries, his helpmates, advanced to the dais set up in the middle of the nave, and there, standing and sitting by turns, read aloud, and then kept silence, and bowed and crossed himself many times in response to the service at the altar. Soldiers, officers of state, and attendant priests stood in waiting or kept the ground open. The ceremony abounded in dramatic situations; there was ever action, contrast, climax. The act of blessing the people with burning tapers in hand specially struck me as symbolic and poetic. The music, the grandest and most effective I have ever known without the aid of instruments, enhanced the rich effect of the colour and the unearthly character of the whole scene. The singing was supremely artistic in light and shade, in advancing relief, and perspective distance of sound; the voices had a sombre tone, and a shadowy colour, in keeping with the rich and deep pictorial backgrounds. The bass voice was ever advancing from dim distance into a pronounced foreground; its march was as the path of thunder, and the domes caught the echo as encircling hills; yet it was too truly musical in tone ever to degenerate into noise. The boy trebles played round this grand sustaining voice in light sportive decoration, which chimed in with the ringing of bells from the towers and the roar of cannon from the arsenal. At other moments the big deep bass stood out alone in the midst of silence, and when the voice of thunder ceased there followed still small voices, which came as beauty amid grandeur. The boys' notes were to me every way more satisfactory than the manufactured trebles in the Pope's choir; the musical quality I prefer, and as to the execution there is more lightness and elasticity. The quality gained indeed was pure, silvery, and transparent, yet it had warmth and passion. The swell and the cadence were as the breezes which pass through an Æolian harp; the melody struck on the ear like music of the elements; it came sweeping, floating, sighing, aspiring, and then it fell and ended. The finale was the most imposing, not to say appalling, I have ever witnessed, either in or out of a church; the voice of thunder again put forth its strength, followed by a full chorus of milder voices, joined by the pealing of bells, and then the cannon roared in climax. I confess that I was somewhat unmanned; I have not known a moment, even in the Sistine or in St. Peter's, when art was so potent. No sooner had the last note been sounded and the closing shot fired, than a general rush was made to the doors. When I reached the outer air a further drama had reached its crisis; the aged patriarch was struggling through a pitiless storm of rain and wind to his carriage. The people blocked his path, eager to kiss the hem of his garment, or to catch benedictions as they fell. At length the tottering old priest gained his chariot, drawn by eight horses, which for a moment threatened to be more unruly than the people or the elements. The venerable patriarch, who is much respected, was thankful to get away. It had been throughout evident how strong a hold the Russian Church, her functions and her dignitaries, retain on the affections of the people. Entering again the church, and returning once more to the scene of the great ceremonial, I was addressed as an Englishman by a Russian lady and her daughter. They said how glad they were to see the interest I took in the functions; they knew there was much sympathy between the English and the Russian Churches, and they looked forward to the day when the two would be in unity. I fear my response was not hearty; I felt that the two Churches, intellectually and artistically, are, and must remain, widely severed.

I have spoken of the Imperial Palace, of the House of the Holy Synod, of the Church of the Assumption, and yet, perhaps, no adequate impression has been given of the Kremlin as a whole. I have generally found that great historic positions, the centres or the strongholds of civilisation, have been planned by nature herself. To this rule the Kremlin is no exception; here it stands, as already said, like a Grecian acropolis, or as an Etruscan city planted on a spur of the Apennines. The plateau is compact, yet sufficiently spacious; isolated, yet in immediate communication with the city beneath and around. While walking on the raised terrace, with hanging gardens and winding paths below, I was naturally reminded of many an evening on the Roman Pincian. It is true that here between the eye and the horizon do not rise structures in magnitude and import comparable to the dome of St. Peter's or to the castle of St. Angelo; and yet the city, in its wide-sweeping panorama, stretches out as a marvel and a show, the like of which cannot be seen till the traveller leaves Europe and enters on Asia or Egypt. Beyond all precedent, even in Cairo, is the multitude of domes; the forms are as fantastic as the colours are extravagant; like fire-balloons or Chinese lamps these cupulas congregate or float in air, and, when the sun catches the burnished gold, shine in glittering light. As said before, Moscow is emphatically a city of colour; Cairo is comparatively bleached as the desert sand. Like an illumined missal or a Japanese screen is this party-coloured panorama; and brighter than a garden is this busy populous field. Many are the cities I have viewed from overlooking heights, but none do I recall more strange and fantastic. I felt it to be somewhat difficult to picture to the mind the lives of the inhabitants in the streets beneath; the structures seemed more for the fantasy of the eye than for daily use, and no noise of traffic, no voice from busy mart, reached the ear. The Kremlin, like other eminences commanding a densely-peopled town, is a place of silence, save when a bell casts its music across the upper air.

The churches of the Kremlin are the resort of the devout pilgrim and of the professional beggar. And just as in Italy peasants turn away from a Raphael to worship before some black Madonna, believed to have come direct from the easel of St. Luke, so here the worst works win the most pence and prayers. In the Kremlin the Russian Church employs lowest art to act on the superstition of the multitude; and so easily are the devout feelings of the people moved, that pictures which would not fetch five shillings in Wardour Street suffice to throw a crowd of pilgrims on bended knees. The three cathedrals on the plateau of the Kremlin do not materially differ in general aspect. In the Cathedral of the Assumption the Tsars are crowned, in the Cathedral of the Annunciation they were baptized and married, and in the Cathedral of the Archangel Michael they were formerly buried. A fourth church, that of 'The Redeemer in the Wood,' is so named from

the wood which here in olden times crowned the summit.
Also must be mentioned the Convent of the Ascension,
if only for the sake of the singing, more lovely than
that of the caged nuns in the Convent della Trinità on
the Roman Pincian. The general aspect of all the
churches, as I have said, is similar. The Cathedral of
St. Michael, which architecturally may be described as
Byzantine with a mixture of Lombardo-Venetian, asserts
its importance by nine gilded domes ; and the other
sacred edifices are in like manner crowned and enriched.
It is also usual for the uppermost archways in the
façades to be decorated with paintings, just as similar
wall-spaces in St. Mark's, Venice, are covered with
mosaics. The interiors too are, as before seen, entirely
clothed with wall-paintings ; the decoration indeed is
alike in the Russian and in the Latin Church ; thus the
interiors of the Kremlin are as much painted chambers as
the churches at Assisi or Giotto's Chapel, Padua. Only
in point of art these Russian wall-pictures differ from
the Italian as widely as darkness is divided from light.
The subjects are often arranged as a biblical series ;
thus the entire west end of the Church of St. Michael
is covered with sacred compositions, in the midst
whereof sits Christ between the Madonna and St. John
the Baptist. The pictures frequently compose together
into a continuous narrative, which may, as in similar
arrangements in Italy, be read as a consecutive and
united story. Thus within the 'Church of the Redeemer
in the Wood' is depicted the life of St. Stephen of
Perm, the first of Russian missionaries and martyrs.
It is usual to apply to these and like wall-paintings the
generic term fresco, but it may be safely affirmed that
'fresco buono et puro' does not exist within the
Kremlin. The method is that of the 'secco' in its

driest and dirtiest form ; instead of transparency is opacity, and in place of translucency is muddiness. These works further suffer from repeated repaintings ; thus the above-mentioned pictures in the Church of the Redeemer were renovated in 1863, and they now wear quite a modern aspect, and are as valueless in archæ-ology as in art.

The traveller will do well to spend as many half-hours as he can spare within these three cathedrals of the Kremlin. As in St. Mark's, Venice, he will spy out, even in odd corners, surface-decoration, metal-work, crumbling tombs, and revered reliquaries. Persons interested in Christian symbolism will discover how in the Greek Church the outward is a sign of the inward ; the intention of course being that the arts shall, through the avenue of the senses, reach the soul. And here again the student will be able to understand how symbolism has never been favourable to art as art : the noblest type of the human form, which is the highest aim of art, has never been striven for under the sway of symbolism. Physical beauty and truth to nature stand in fact in the way of that act of faith and attitude of devotion which the system of symbolism engenders. Here in the cathedrals of the Kremlin, as also in the churches of St. Petersburg, I observed, what I had long noted in Munich, that the modern art, which aims to be true in its drawing and grammatical in its construction, has much less spell over the multitude than the so-called miraculous pictures, though coarse and common as sign-boards. One of such works, the Holy Virgin of Vladimir, said, of course, to have been painted by St. Luke, and now absolutely black, and with features obliterated, receives, as one of the most ancient images in Russia, countless kisses and genuflexions. Here is an instance where Mr. Ruskin's 'lamp of sacrifice'—a principle fine in humanity but false in art—is made to burn most brightly. This holy image is covered with precious oblations; the jewels which bedizen it are said to be worth £45,000, one emerald being valued at £10,000. No reasonable being will contend that this is art : nothing further need be said, for this one example represents the whole.

I have already said that the interiors of the churches in the Kremlin are painted throughout. The number of figures on the walls, domes, and columns of the Cathedral of the Assumption is something prodigious; thus it is calculated that there are 249 full-lengths, some much above life-size, besides 2066 half-lengths or heads; it is also said that 210,000 gold leaves were lavished on the glories and the gilt grounds. The decorations were renewed and the pictures retouched or repainted in 1773; probably not a square inch of the old surface remains anywhere; the pigments are opaque and dirty; indeed dirt in the estimation of the Russian peasantry is almost indispensable to sacred art. In these interiors, as indeed in the churches of Russia universally, the best art is not the pictures, but the metal-work in which they are enshrined. Often the surface-ornament is excellent in character, and the enrichments of jewels and enamels show an Oriental eye for colour; the style of all the purest examples, as already said, is a transcript or an adaptation of the Byzantine.

In the Cathedral of the Assumption is a picture of some interest, covered, after usual fashion, with gold, on the principle that a picture when sacred must not be seen. The work to which I refer is 'The Saviour,' presented to the church by the Emperor Manuel. Only the head, the hands, and the feet are without a covering of gold. The features, as usual in Russia with objects of worship, are almost obliterated ; yet it is possible to recognise a refined and ideal type, differing from the Western type of the head of Christ by being more Eastern and Jewish. The face is not directly Byzantine ; apparently modern elements are present. I again repeat that I searched in vain in Russia for any valuable contributions to that much-vexed theme, the traditional heads or portraits of Christ. I had, not unnaturally, hoped here, in the stronghold of the Greek Church, to find some original materials. Another important picture in this interior is a vast 'Last Judgment,' which covers the west wall. The nearest approach to this and many similar compositions in Russia is found on the west wall of the cathedral at Torcello. The pictorial treatment of 'Last Judgments' in general—comparing the compositions in the Greek with those ·in the Latin Church— I have often thought would form an instructive subject for inquiry. In Russia a leading object is an immense serpent, which coils itself up at least one half of the whole church wall. The creature takes its start from a giant Lucifer, seated at ·the right-hand corner, in the place assigned by Orcagna, in his rendering of the 'Last Judgment,' at Pisa, to Hell and Satan. Within the convolutions of this vast serpent is found space for both saints and sinners—the latter preponderate ; also are brought together strange animals and fishes, with here and there a judicial angel or a flaming seraph thrown in. Above the serpent is set a table with two angels, all placed in the clouds ; a cross stands above the table, and beneath is hung a pair of scales, where occurs the usual tussle for human souls between the agents of Satan and of God. Above this table, at which

St. Michael may be presumed to preside, are usually mounted two tiers, crowded with as many characters and incidents as the space will hold. In the midst of one of the spheres Christ sits, his feet placed on a globe, his head encircled by a rainbow. Over all reigns God the Father, supported by angels and seraphim, and surrounded by the heavenly host. Cheap engravings of such compositions, highly coloured and interspersed with explanatory text, seem to have extensive currency among the people. I purchased one or more versions of this traditional 'Last Judgment' at stalls and under archways in the streets of Moscow. Such works, whether the originals in the churches or the cheap reproductions hung in the peasants' huts, have little claim to attention in point of art ; yet they serve to complete the history of the relation between religion and the arts throughout the world—a history in which, I fear, Russia takes a mean position. The religious arts, Christian as well as Pagan, are beset by strange contradictions. Among the ancient Greeks the art was true while the religion was false ; among the Christians it often happens that while the religion approaches to the true, the art degenerates into the false. The highest art and the truest religion have never been brought together ; this perfect union is a hope for the future which must be indefinitely postponed, at least in the Russian empire.

The museums in Moscow bear no comparison with those in St. Petersburg. The gallery of old masters, for example, consists of but weedings and gleanings from palaces and other national collections. Dr. Waagen, when arranging in St. Petersburg the Hermitage, found that it was possible to spare works which would make for Moscow a representative collection of the leading schools. Of more importance in this museum are the modern pictures by Russian artists, among which, as a masterpiece, stands 'Christ Appearing to the People at the Baptism of St. John.' This and its companion works have already obtained distinctive notice. The collection again proves that Russia has for more than a century boasted of painters who have produced very respectable works in the several departments of portraiture, history, landscape, and genre. Stchedrin deservedly ranks as one of the very first landscape-painters in Russia; indeed his position would be fairly good in galleries of the West. Some of these artists improved themselves in England, while, in turn, one or more English painters came to advance their fortunes in Russia. In this museum, for instance, are portraits by George Dawe, a Londoner, who was elected into the Academy of St. Petersburg, and as court-painter executed many portraits of the imperial family. Dawe lived till the year 1829.

The Moscow Museum likewise comprises a curious ethnographical collection; a large hall is here occupied by life-size figures, in full costume, of the various races who inhabit the Russian Empire. Another hall is devoted to Slavonic tribes not yet subject to Russia. These dummies are scarcely sufficiently good to serve as lay-figures in an artist's studio, yet, as will be readily imagined, they do not fail to attract crowds of gaping townsfolk and peasants. But by far the most interesting department of this heterogeneous museum is in the four rooms devoted to Christian antiquities. In St. Petersburg I had been fortunate to fall in with a Loan Museum, wherein was collected all that is held most sacred in the Russian ritual. In the Great Paris Exhibition of 1867 were also brought together a multitude of original works or reproductions which served further to attest how rich Russian churches, monasteries, libraries, and museums have been and are in illumined books, panel-pictures, vestments, pectoral crosses, and other ornaments. The peculiar interest attaching to these works, as already said, is that they embody the Greek or Eastern phase of Christian art. At the same time the drawback is known to be finality, universal sameness; in other words, the incessant repetition of stereotyped forms and fixed ideas. The art in fact has been reduced to the fixity of a manufacture, hence less surprise need be felt at the multitude of works produced. Italy was wondrously prolific, but she falls far behind the productive capacity of Russia. In Muscovite factories one artist paints a hundred heads, another a hundred glories, a third a hundred legs. Thus a picture is put together like a pin or a mosaic, by pieces, and accordingly there is little to choose between one picture and another, though all are hand-made. Yet Christian art obtains in this museum valuable illustration; I would, for instance, have given much for an early mosaic of the head of the Saviour, attributed to the eleventh century. But though the work be now in Moscow it is not necessarily Russian : local archæologists naturally strive to claim native nationality for every object they can lay their hands on. This is the fallacy against which the student has to guard.

Little more in the way of art collections would merit notice, even were further space at my command. Yet just a word may be given to the Galitsin Museum of pictures and curiosities, although every object might exist as well in Paris as in Moscow. Certainly the art student would expect to find in France or England, rather than in Russia, a Biberon of Henri Deux ware.

The work has certainly not been over-valued at £1000. Only fifty-five specimens of this rare fabric exist, and this Biberon is the sole example which falls to the lot of Russia.

CHAPTER X.

ART-EDUCATION IN MOSCOW.

I AM enabled to give some details which may not be without interest concerning a large and efficient School of Design established in Moscow. It will easily be understood that the former seat, and the present centre, of the great Muscovite empire affords a good station at which to plant a School of Art. When the extended system of Russian railways shall be completed, Moscow will be the focus from which five trunk lines will radiate ; thus she must become more than ever the centre at which may meet the varied and somewhat heterogeneous nationalities of 'all the Russias.' Moscow will, on the south, be brought into immediate communication, not only with the vast corn-growing districts which border on the Black Sea, but with Kertch, in the Crimea, and other colonies of ancient Greece, rich in remains of classic art ; also she may establish intimate relations with Circassia, Georgia, and the Caucasus, whence the bazaars and great fairs are supplied with ornate fabrics, Oriental in design and colour. Again, Moscow on the north and the west will be brought into direct correspondence with the trade of the Baltic, with the art and commerce of Western Europe, with the undeveloped resources of Scandinavia and Finland. Lastly, the railways already projected towards the eastern frontiers must render more available the vast mineral treasures of the Ural Mountains—mines of gold, silver, malachite, lapis lazuli, and precious stones, which, from time immemorial, have given a kind of barbaric magnificence to the regalia of the sovereign, and even to the jewelry of the peasant. At the same time these increased facilities of communication will tend to make Moscow the European terminus for the commerce of Asia, the emporium of Eastern manufactures, the seat of those arts of design which for centuries have been pushing their way westward from China, India, and Japan. These considerations point to the conclusion that for Moscow are reserved important developments in arts and manufactures. Moreover, her prestige is great; her history pregnant with art-associations: unlike her modern rival, St. Petersburg, she is so placed in the empire, that she can rally around her whatever is national and historic. The existence of the Kremlin, with its unrivalled treasury, the possession of museums, public and private, indicate that if Russia has in the past, or can create for herself in the future, a school pretending to nationality, that school will find no more appropriate resting-place than under the sacred shadow of the Kremlin. Therefore 'L'École Stroganoff' at Moscow— the chief art-school in Russia—already an institution active and useful—will, if duly supported by the State, supply those æsthetic wants which are never more keenly felt than at the turning-point when a nation is passing out of barbarism into nascent civilisation.

The School Stroganoff in Moscow takes its name from the Count Stroganoff, an enlightened nobleman, among the first in Russia to entertain the idea that the nation's manufactures might be advanced by the education of the people in the elements and principles of design. Accordingly the school was founded by the Count in 1825, and for eighteen years supported at his expense.

In 1843 it passed over to the Government, and in 1860 an imperial ukase was issued, which defined the organisation and prescribed the future action of the institution. The director, M. Victor Boutovsky, in a pamphlet entitled ' De l'Education artistique appliquée à l'Industrie en Europe et particulièrement en Russie,' describes the school and its allied museum as follows :—

' This establishment, with its museum of art and of industry, is nearly all that has been done in Russia, down to the present day, towards associating art-education with the industry of the people, The epoch of its foundation coincides with the general art-movement in Europe. The instruction of the school is divided into five classes, of which three are preparatory, and two special. In the first division the pupils are instructed in those elementary truths of art and of science, which are equally necessary to industrial artists as to mankind at large. The second section is formed of two subdivisions: the one prepares designers for printing and weaving patterns on textile fabrics; the other trains artists for decoration in general, especially for gold and silver work, leather and wood work, and for the modelling and engraving of bronzes, porcelains, precious stones, and other objects, wherein is required elegance in form.'

I may add, from the statements both of Director Boutovsky in Moscow and of M. Grigorovitch in St. Petersburg, that the Russian scheme of art-education already tried—and let us hope about to be further developed—is expressly based on the system at South Kensington.

The director makes the following returns of the pupils receiving instruction, during a single year, in the Stroganoff School. In the classes of design there are 504 pupils, to which number may be added 19 amateurs, who gladly take advantage of the instruction offered. Furthermore, there is a class for women, numbering 35 students. Also must not be forgotten a Sunday-school for the teaching of design, which has on its books about 200 pupils. A Sunday drawing-class sounds as

an innovation; in England reading is taught on the
Sabbath, but not drawing. The Russian Church seems
more tolerant of art-education on the Sunday than the
Anglican, or even the Roman Church. These Sunday
art-classes are composed chiefly of the labouring population. The school, which is under the Minister of
Finance, seems well appointed; the building assigned
to it is spacious; the class-rooms are furnished with
usual appliances; the educational staff consists of a director and about twenty 'professors' or assistants. The
pupils are admitted between the ages of twelve and
fifteen years upon examination; the course extends over
five years. The general, as distinguished from the specific instruction, comprehends 'academic design, landscape, flowers, drawing from nature, linear design. The
pupils also enter for courses on religion, the Russian language, writing, geography, history, arithmetic, and geo-
metry.' The special classes, as before stated, have for
their object the practical application of art to industry;
moreover, æsthetics and the history of the arts are comprised in the general curriculum. The pupils end with
a kind of apprenticeship; having made choice of a trade,
they at first try their hands within the school, and afterwards enter some manufactory as apprenticed designers,
modellers, ornamentists, or art-workmen. On leaving
the school each student undergoes an examination, and
receives a brevet or certificate according to his merit.
Since 1860 more than thirty students have been found
qualified to take the duties of masters in schools of
design. The above sketch will indicate that, though
much remains to be done, already a good work has been
set on foot. From personal inspection I can testify to
the order and the energy of the administration. In
a country where the need of popular art is scarcely as

yet felt, the director has had uphill work; among a people singularly indifferent to beauty in any form, it has been difficult to plant the elements of art or the principles of correct taste.

The persistent and well-intentioned work commenced in the Stroganoff School has obtained recognition in Western Europe. And yet the official reports of national and international exhibitions tally with the judgment at which I arrived on personal examination, namely, that Russia is in art still a desert land, producing, save in some few favoured spots, little that can by utmost courtesy rank as fine art. In the exhibition of 1851 it became evident that the Russians did not know how to turn to good account the precious materials nature had placed at their disposal: the malachite, lapis lazuli, porphyry, jasper, &c., at their command were often so wrought as to outrage pure principles of taste. And again, the position taken by Russia in 1862 showed the country still in the rear of civilisation. Thus, while England obtained 1639 medals, France 1390 medals, Austria 504 medals, Prussia 330 medals, Italy 322 medals, Belgium 251 medals, Russia gained only 176 medals, whereof more than 100 were due to 'animal and vegetable substances used in manufactures,' 'substances used for food,' 'mining, quarrying, metallurgy, and mineral products,' and 'skins, furs, feathers, and hair.' This enumeration at once indicates that the strength of Russia lies, as is well known, in raw materials, not in art-manufactures. However, in the last Paris Exposition, and, more recently, in the Exhibition of St. Petersburg of the year 1870, Russia proved, by the progress made, that she had arrived at that stage in her history when everything is to be gained through technical schools of science and art. And it is satisfactory to know that there exists the nucleus of a national education which might easily be made to embrace the arts. Russia is already provided with seven universities, fifty-one provincial head-schools, besides district-schools. Education, moreover, receives support from the State. Yet in the report of General Morin and of M. Tresca on industrial education, as represented in the Paris Exhibition of 1867, it is stated that 'En Russie, l'Institut Technologique de St. Petersbourg et l'Ecole des Métiers de Moscou sont les seuls établissements dans lesquels le travail manuel entre pour quelque chose dans l'enseignement professionnel.' The School Stroganoff, however, justified the expectations of its founders by obtaining as her reward three medals; one for 'art applied,' another for 'technical instruction,' and a third under the section 'History of Labour,' 'for designs and models from Russian antiquities.' I may be excused for here transcribing the notes I made upon the designs exhibited in 1867 by the School Stroganoff, especially as more recent experiences confirm the judgment then arrived at :—

'In designs for paper-hangings, &c., in common with other art-products from Russia, I observe the conflict between two opposing schools—the old and the new—between the traditional Byzantine and a directly naturalistic treatment. And it is interesting to note that while in the province of oil-painting the naturalistic is the best, so, on the contrary, within the sphere of decorative art the traditional treatment is the best. Adaptations of Byzantine ornament, and even of the Scandinavian Runic Knot, are successful. The colour, as frequently happens in Russia, though rather crude and violent, is happily mindful of Oriental practice.'

These notes may lead the way to the discussion of what national or historic style it is wise for Russia to espouse in her schools of design.

This question of a national style for Russia was almost set at rest in the very remarkable display made by the

School Stroganoff in the last exhibition at St. Petersburg. Specially good were the designs applied to ceramic manufactures ; also the drawings based upon historic styles, which lay claim to be Russian. Moreover, in the compartment assigned to this Ecole Technique of Moscow, were exhibited illustrated works intended to serve as grammars of Russian ornament for the use of Russian schools of art. Moscow, indeed, has taken honourable position in the literature of historic arts : thus, in the great Paris Exhibition, under 'Histoire du Travail,' I find mention of 'Antiquités de l'Empire Russe : ouvrage en 446 planches chromolithographiées accompagnées de texte—Oroujeïnaïa Palata, à Moscow.' I also found an instructive work, 'Manual of Christian Iconography,' the illustrations taken from ancient MSS. in the Greek Church. I had the advantage of the guidance of M. Boutovsky through the Museum of Art and of Industry, which, in imitation of the doings at South Kensington, Lyons, and Vienna, has recently been set on foot in connexion with the imperial school in Moscow. The museum comprises three divisions—artistic, industrial, and historic. The artistic department comprises plaster casts ; the industrial part is represented by ceramic products, textile fabrics, enamels, glass, &c. ; the third section is dedicated to monuments of Sclavo-Russian and Byzantine art, both originals and reproductions. The series of historic works here collected in illustration of decorative art in Russia is valuable as wholly without example elsewhere. On asking the director upon what ground designs evidently Byzantine in style had been appropriated by Russia, the reply was, that a MS. when in Russian characters was presumed to be of Russian origin. The answer, though open to objection, has force. In corroboration of the argument, I was shown in the Syndic Library of the Kremlin a series of Russian MSS., commencing with the eleventh century, and ending with the sixteenth century, which in good degree substantiated a claim to historic and national art. The impression, however, left 'on my mind was, that Russia at all times has imported her art from foreign, though neighbouring countries, and that the utmost she can claim is to have impressed upon Byzantine and other styles some distinctive character of her own. A handsome volume, 'Histoire de l'ornament Russe du xᵉ au xviiᵉ siécle d'après les manuscrits,' has been published by Morel of Paris. The letterpress is furnished by M. Boutovsky. The object of the work is to show to Russian artists and artisans the types of a truly national style. For this end are produced facsimiles, to the number of one hundred, of illuminations from ancient Greek and Sclavonic MSS., selected chiefly from the Syndic Library at Moscow and the Imperial Library in St. Petersburg. A second folio, termed ' didactic,' contains a hundred plates representing the ornamental designs which may be derived from these sources.

The letterpress revives the discussion how far these ornaments are Byzantine and how far Sclavonic. It is argued, that so far as they are Sclavonic they embody a national Russian element. Moreover, M. Boutovsky contends, that in Russia is found a village art of the people, essentially local, and therefore distinct from Greek and Oriental styles. It is also asserted that the history of architecture corroborates like conclusions. Thus, over and above Byzantine and Lombard types, there are forms which expressly pertain to Russia. But the argument receives its chief support from the numerous Sclavonic-Russian manuscripts which still survive the ravages of time. These manuscripts, which are the recipients of ornamentations as beautiful as they are peculiar, extend from the eleventh to the eighteenth century. The most characteristic period is from the twelfth to the sixteenth century.

A pamphlet, which M. Boutovsky, the director of the Moscow school, has forwarded to me since my return to England, contains an interesting programme of proceedings. In addition to details before given, it may be stated that the Moscow school has been instrumental in collecting ethnographic and archæologic data in the north-western provinces of the empire. Of the important bearings of these departments I was the better able to judge on a visit to the Moscow Museum, which contains a remarkable ethnographic collection, as well as a series of Christian antiquities elucidating the history of the Russian Church. That the Government has yet to perform arduous and imperative duties may be judged from the following requisitions, condensed from the manifesto of M. Boutovsky: the desiderata are—(1.) To introduce the teaching of design in its A B C in all the establishments of general instruction throughout the empire; (2.) To encourage special schools in manufacturing centres; (3.) To frame a scheme or programme of art-teaching best suited to the wants of the nation; (4.) To encourage in manufacturing centres the formation of museums of art and industry, and to establish in connexion therewith Sunday and evening classes for the teaching of design; (5.) To organise in chief towns societies, composed of master-artisans and amateurs, for the general management of schools of design and local museums of art and industry; (6.) To establish normal schools for the training of art-masters.

M. Boutovsky has at various exhibitions put to the

proof the practical results of the teaching in the Moscow school. He has done well to select such products as bear most closely on the historic styles which claim Russian origin. That he is fully alive to the exigencies of the case becomes evident from the pamphlet he has published on 'art-education.' It is therein stated that Russian manufactures are beginning to assume in form and ornament a national character ; that this has become inevitable and imperative from the zeal which the Government and the people evince in the study of the ancient monuments of the country. Historic and pre-historic times open vast storehouses whence Russian artists and artisans may draw inspiration, enter on spheres of invention, and invoke styles national and independent.

Russia, as we all know, has long made up her mind to take a foremost place among the great powers. Her material resources are vast, her empire extends over a sixth part of the *terra firma* of the globe, her population amounts to 70,000,000, her revenue to £50,000,000 sterling. In the course of a few years a grandly conceived system of railways will further develop her all but exhaustless resources. The future of the empire must now greatly depend upon the intellectual forces brought into the field, upon the sphere which shall be open for mental growth, for scientific advance, and artistic development. The rulers of the land are fortunately alive to the pressing emergency. The civilisation of the country will not be worth much in the eyes of other nations if it remain, as now, the servile transcript of the habits and customs of Western Europe ; if sciences and arts are still imported from France, Germany, and Italy ; if even language and fashion in highest circles remain Parisian. Russia will show culpable lack of energy and patriotism if she do not assert intellectual independence, and establish her distinctive nationality.   In the arts, at all events, her line of action is clearly defined. Assuredly her physical geography, national products, ethnography, and religion, are sufficiently distinctive to form the basis of a national art.   Her antiquarian remains, comprising Northern antiquities in Finland, classic works in the Crimea, metal-work of Scythia, aboriginal and primitive, Byzantine illuminations in monasteries and churches, and Eastern phases of ornament from Circassia and Georgia, furnish rare and rich material out of which to form styles original yet historic.

These treasures in St. Petersburg, Moscow, and the great monasteries, seem to indicate a possible threefold development.   First, in the direction of 'Northern anti-quities,' as exemplified, for instance, at the St. Peters-burg Exhibition by jewelry designed from ancient Finnish metal-work, not dissimilar to the jewelry which in Dublin has been adapted from ancient Irish designs. A school thus formed would train up skilled workers in filigree, modelling, and chasing. Then, secondly, Byzan-tine art having through ages grown almost as a second nature among the people, Russia may, I think, with reason appropriate the Byzantine style to her own use. Moreover, as Byzantium is practically extinct, Russia, for more reasons than one, has the power, and possibly the right, to usurp the heritage of the empire of the East. Already the best decorative art in Russia is directly Byzantine. Russian artisans are most happy when they imitate, emulate, and adapt that style which, having originated in the Eastern Roman empire, has become the sacred art of the Eastern Church. The third, last, and possibly fittest sphere for development is still more Eastern or Oriental. Russia not only borders upon ancient Byzantium, but she is the close neighbour of Persia, India, China. In her public marts the most artistic goods — embroidered silks, carpets, rugs, and even printed cottons—are in style Oriental. Russia in fact, if she be wise, will constitute herself the exponent and champion of the Eastern arts. This line of action she might, with advantage to the world, make her mission. She has, too, as the head of the Greek or Eastern Church, to maintain in art a commanding position. But this question is far too complex and difficult for discussion in a single paragraph. In conclusion, I would simply point out that the 'Northern,' 'Byzantine,' and 'Oriental' arts above dispersed over three divisions have manifest points of contact. What is decorative and useable in 'Northern' antiquities is due, I believe, to an Eastern origin; and as to the Byzantine school, it did not exist till the Romans made Constantinople their Eastern capital. Therefore I think it were wise for schools of design in Russia to seek for a national style in the direction of the East. Any such style could, of course, only become conterminous with a vast empire and varied races by making itself widely representative. Wholly to exclude light from the West would throw Russia into a position behind the age; and yet her strength manifestly lies in her vantage-ground in the East. The problem to be worked out becomes obviously complex; and the policy which the Government ought to pursue, though imperative, is far from simple. The temptation, judging from documents before us, seems to be to copy South Kensington wholesale. This course, as to organisation, may be sound; but, on the other hand, Russia simply commits suicide if she barter her historic birthright, and take in exchange hybrid arts of Western Europe, the corrupt progeny of the Italian Renaissance.

CHAPTER XI.

KIEF, the Jerusalem of Russia, is by nature marked for distinction; she rises like an Etruscan city from the plain; she is flanked by fortifications; she is pleasantly clothed by trees, and height beyond height is crowned by castle or by church. Fifty thousand pilgrims annually, many of whom are footsore from long and weary journeying, throw themselves on their knees as they see the sacred city from afar: her holy places shine in the sun as a light set upon a hill which cannot be hid. Three holy shrines which I can recall to mind—Kief, Assisi, and Jerusalem—are alike fortunate in command of situation; the approach to each is most impressive. In Kief particularly the natural landscape is heightened in pictorial effect by the picturesque groups of pilgrims, staves in hand and wallets on back, who may be seen at all hours of the day clambering up the hill, resting under the shadow of a tree, or reverently bowing the head at the sound of a convent bell.

Kief is not one city, but three cities, each with its own fortification. The old town, strong in position, and enclosing within its circuit the cathedral of St. Sophia and the palace of the Metropolitan, was in remote ages a Sclavonian Pantheon, sacred to the Russian Jupiter and other savage gods. The new town, separated from the old town by a deep ravine, stands on a broad platform which rises precipitously from the banks of the Dneiper. The walls are massive, the fort is strong, and the famous monastery, the first in rank in Russia, with its gilt and coloured domes, shines from out the shade of a deep wood. The third division, 'the Town of the Vale,' situated between the hills and the river, is chiefly devoted to commerce. Without much stretch of fancy it might be said that Kief, like Rome, Lisbon, and some other cities, is built on seven hills. And thus the pictorial aspect changes almost at every step: a winding path will bring to view an unsuspected height, or open up a valley previously hid. The traveller has in the course of his wanderings often to feel thankful that a kind providence has planted sacred places in the midst of lovely scenery. The holy mountain at Varallo, the sacred hill at Orta, are, like the shrines of Kief, made doubly pleasant for pilgrimage through the beauties of nature by which they are surrounded. It is said that at the monastery of the Grande Chartreuse the monks do not permit themselves to look too much at the outward landscape, lest their hearts should by the loveliness of earth be estranged from heaven. I do not think that Russian priests or pilgrims incur any such danger. When they are neither praying nor eating they are sleeping; in short, I did not among the motley multitude see a single eye open to the loveliness of colour in the sky above, or to the beauty of form in the earth beneath. It is singular how obtuse these people are; I have noticed in a crowded railway carriage that not a face would be turned to the glory of the setting sun, but if a church tower came into view on the distant horizon, every hand was raised to make the sign of the cross. While taking my observations among the pilgrims at Kief I was struck with the fact, not only that a superstitious faith, but that a degraded art blinds the eye to the beauty of nature. It is one of the high services of true art to lead the mind to the contemplation, to the love and the better understanding, of the works of creation. But, on the contrary, it is the penalty of this Byzantine art to close the appointed access between nature and nature's God. An art which ignores and violates truth and beauty cannot do otherwise than lead the mind away from nature. This seemed one of the several lessons taught by Kief, the city of pilgrimage.

Sketchers of character and costume will find excellent studies among the pilgrims at Kief. The upper and educated classes, who in Russia are assimilating with their equals in other nations, and are therefore not tempting to the pencil or the brush, do not, as we have already seen, come in any numbers to these sacred shrines. It is the lower orders, who still preserve the manners and customs of their ancestors, that make these church festivals so attractive to the artist. The variety of races brought together from afar—a diversity only possible within an empire, like Russia, made up of heterogeneous materials—might serve not only to fill a portfolio, but to illustrate a volume; the ethnologist equally with the painter would find at the time of great festivities curious specimens of humanity. I remember some years ago to have met with the French artist, M. Theodore Valerio, when he had brought home the 'Album Ethnographique' from Hungary, Croatia, and the more distant borders of the Danube. It was quite refreshing, after the infinite number of costume-studies I had seen from Italian peasantry, to find that art had the possibility of an entirely new sphere among the Sclavonic races. A like field for any painter of enterprise is now open in Russia. The large and famous composition, 'The Butter Week (Carnaval) in St. Petersburg,' by C. Makowski, already described in previous chapters, may serve to indicate the hitherto undeveloped pictorial resources of the empire. When the conditions are new there is a possibility that the art may be new also. The ethnology, the physical geography, the climate, the religion, the products of the animal and vegetable kingdoms, so far as they are peculiar to Russia, will some day become reflected into the national art. It is true that the painter may occasionally feel a want of colour, the costumes of the peasant are apt to be dull and heavy, yet not unfrequently rags and tatters bring compensation by picturesque outlines and paintable surface-textures. At Kief, however, the traveller is sufficiently South and East to fall in with warm Southern hues and Oriental harmonies, broken and enriched moreover among the lower orders by that engrained dirt which I have usually noted as the special privilege and prerogative of pilgrims in all parts of the world. The use of soap would seem to be accounted as sacrilege on religious sentiment. What with dust, and what with sun, the wayfarers who toil up the heights leading to the holy hill have gained a colour which a Murillo would delight in. The face and neck bronzed by the hot sun tell out grandly from a flowing mass of hair worthy of a patriarch.

Beggars, who in Russia are as thick about the churches as the pigeons that pick up crumbs in front of St. Mark's, are almost essential to the histrionic panoramas at these places of pilgrimage. I have never seen so large or so varied a collection of professional and casual mendicants as within and about the sacred enclosures of Kief. Some appeared to enjoy vested rights; these privileged personages would as little endure to be driven from a favoured post as with us a sweeper at a crossing would

tolerate a rival broom. Several of these waiters upon
charity might be termed literary beggars ; their function
is to read aloud from a large book in the hearing of the
passers-by. They are often infirm, and occasionally
blind, but they read just the same. Another class
may be called the incurables ; in England they would
be kept out of sight, but here in Russia, running sores,
mutilated hands and legs, are valuable as stock-in-trade.
Loathsome diseases are thrust forward as a threat, dis-
torted limbs are extortionate for alms ; it is a piteous
sight to see ; some of these sad objects are in the jaws
of death, and come apparently that they may die on
holy ground. Another class may be called the pious
beggars ; they stand at the church doors ; they are
picturesque and apostolic ; long beards and quiet bearing, with a certain professional get-up of misery and
desolation, make these sacred mendicants grand after
their kind. Such figures are usually ranged on either
side of the chief entrance ; they are motionless as statues,
save when in the immediate act of soliciting alms; indeed
I have sometimes noticed how beggars standing before
a church façade are suggestive of statuary, the want of
which is so much felt in the unsculpturesque architecture
of Russia. Pilgrims and beggars—the line of demarca-
tion it is not always easy to define—have an Oriental
way of throwing themselves into easy and paintable
attitudes ; in fact posture plays a conspicuous part in
the devotions of such people ; they pray bodily almost
more than mentally—the figure and its attendant costume become instruments of worship.

The cathedral of St. Sophia, which dates back to the
eleventh century, is of interest from its resemblance to
St. Mark's, Venice, in the plan of the Greek cross, in the
use of domes and galleries, and in the introduction of

mosaics as surface-decorations. I saw the galleries full
of fashionable worshippers ; the galleries in St. Mark's,
on the contrary, are always empty and useless, though
constructed for use. In the apse are the only old
mosaics I have met with in Russia : it is strange that
an art which specially pertains to Byzantium was not
turned to more account by the Greco-Russian Church.
There is in the apse, besides, a subject composition—a
noble female figure, colossal in size, the arms upraised in
attitude of prayer, the drapery cast broadly and sym-
metrically. In the same interior are associated with
mosaics, frescoes, or rather wall-paintings in 'secco.'
On the columns which support the cupola are frescoes
which, though of no art value, naturally excited curiosity
when they were discovered some few years since, after
having been hid for two or more centuries by a covering
of whitewash. Some other wall-pictures are essentially
modern, and others have been restored, after Russian
usage, in so reckless and wholesale a fashion as to be
no longer of value as archæologic records. In the staircase leading to the galleries are some further wall-
paintings, said to be contemporaneous with the building
of the cathedral ; the date, however, is wholly uncertain.
These anomalous compositions represent a boar-hunt
and other sports, with groups of musicians, dancers,
and jugglers, intervening. In accord with the secular
character of the subjects is the rude naturalism of the
style. Positive knowledge as to date being wanting, it
is impossible to speak of these works otherwise than
to say that they cannot be of Byzantine origin. If of
real antiquity they will have to join company with other
semi-barbaric products in metal, &c., which prove, as we
have seen, that Russia has two historic schools, the
Byzantine, on the one hand, debilitated and refined,

as of periods of decline, and, on the other, a non-Byzantine and barbarous style, strong and coarse as of races still vital and vigorous. A like conflict is found in the North of Italy between the Byzantine and the Lombard manner; and even in England the west front of Wells Cathedral presents the same unresolved contradictions. It would seem that over the greater part of Europe, Eastern as well as Western, these two hostile arts were practised contemporaneously: at all events the same buildings are found to display the two opposite styles. It would appear probable, however, that the respective artists or artisans belonged to at least two distinct nationalities.

The Pecherskoi Monastery or Kievo-Pecherskaya Lavra at Kief, the Kremlin in Moscow, and the grand monastery of Troitza, have this in common, that the situation is commanding, the site elevated. Also, these three venerable sanctuaries are strongholds, for though the holy places at Kief are not on all sides fortified, yet the approach from the old city, which is the most accessible, lies along bastions and walls. In fact, here we have again a semblance to the ancient idea of a church, a citadel, and a palace united, as in an acropolis—the Church and the State being one; the arm of the flesh sustaining the sword of the spirit—a condition of things which has always given to the world its noblest art. The walk to this most ancient monastery in Russia passes pleasantly by the side of a wood, then opens a view of the vast plain beneath, intersected by the river Dneiper, over which is flung the great suspension-bridge built by the English engineer, Charles Vignolles, at the cost of £350,000. The immediate approach is lined with open shops or stalls for the sale of sacred pictures, engravings of saints, and other articles which pilgrims love to carry back to their homes. Within the enclosure trees throw a cool shade, under which, as in the courtyards of mosques in Constantinople, the hot and weary may repose.

The cathedral dedicated to the ascension of the Virgin has not the slightest pretence to external architecture. The walls are mostly whitewashed, and some of the windows have common square heads crowned by mean pediments; the intervening pilasters and floral decorations in relief, and all in the midst of whitewash, are of the poorest character. The seven gilded cupolas or domes may be compared to inverted cups surmounted by crosses. The form resembles the cup commonly combined in the fantastic towers and spires of Protestant churches in Germany, where, however, it has been supposed to signify that the laity partake of the chalice. These domes are made further decorative at the point of the small circular neck which connects the cupola with the upper member, or finial; around this surface is painted a continuous series of single saints standing; the effect of these pictures against the sky, if not quite artistic, is striking. Other parts of the exterior may indicate Italian rather than Oriental origin, but the style is far too mongrel to boast of any legitimate parentage. Here, as in the Kremlin, are external wall-paintings of saints, some standing on solid ground, others sitting among clouds: the Madonna is of course of the company, and the First and Second Persons of the Trinity crown the composition. The ideas are trite and the treatment is contemptible—the colours pass from dirty red into brown and black. These certainly are the worst wall-paintings I have ever met with, worse even than the coarsest painted shrines on the waysides of Italy ; indeed no Church save the Greek Church would tolerate an art thus debased. A year after my journey to Kief I travelled through the Tyrol on my way from the Ammergau Passion Play. The whole of this district abounds in frescoes, many being on the external walls of private dwellings. This village art of the Bavarian Highlands, though often the handiwork of simple artisans, puts to shame both the external and the internal wall-paintings at Kief, Troitza, and the Kremlin. Yet this contrast between Russia and Southern nations does not arise so much from the higher ability of the artists, as from the superiority of the one school to the other school. The pictorial arts fostered by the Western Church are fundamentally true, while the arts which the Eastern Church has patronised and petrified are essentially false and effete.

The scene which strikes the eye on entering this party-coloured Cathedral of the Assumption, though strange, is highly picturesque. To this holy shrine are brought the halt, the lame, and the blind, as to the moving of the waters. Some press forward to kiss the foot of a crucifix, others bow the head and kiss the ground, a servile attitude of worship, which in the Greco-Russian Church has been borrowed from the Mohamedans. The groups which throng the narrow, crowded floor, are wonderfully effective ; an artist with sketch-book in hand would have many a good chance of catching graphic heads and costumes, and all the more easily because these pilgrims are not so lively as lethargic. Still, for grand scenic impression, I have never in Russia witnessed any church function so striking as the piazza in front of St. Peter's on Easter Day, when all Rome flocks to receive the Pope's blessing from the balcony. Yet the whole interior of this cathedral is itself a picture, or rather a countless succession of pictures; as to the architecture there is not the minutest space that has not been emblazoned by aid of a paint-pot.

But the greatest marvel in this Cathedral of the Assumption is the 'iconastas,' or screen for the sacred pictures, a structure indispensable to all Russian churches, of which I have withheld the description till now, when I find myself in front of a larger and more astounding erection than can be found in St. Petersburg, Moscow, or Troitza. In small churches these sacred placards, bearing the character of drop-scenes, are apt to be paltry, indeed the irreverent stranger may even be reminded of painted caravans at village fairs. But in large cathedrals the screen which stands between the people in the nave and the priests in the holy of holies, presents a vast façade, upon which are ranged, in three, four, or five stories, a multitude of sacred pictures covered with gold and decked with jewels. These elaborate contrivances correspond to the reredos in Western churches, only with this important difference, that they are not behind the holy place but in front of it. They might, perhaps, with more correctness be compared to the rood-screens which in our churches stand between the altar and the people. The sacred screen now before me mounts its head into the dome, and presents an imposing and even an architectonic aspect, but certain details, such as classic mouldings of columns, and a broken entablature, pronounce the edifice to be comparatively modern. The summit is fitly crowned by a crucifix, almost in the flat, in order not to evade the law of the Russian Church, which prohibits statues in the round; the figure of Christ is silver, the cross and the drapery of gold or silver-gilt. On either side of the crucifix stand at their prescriptive stations the Madonna and St. John. On the story beneath comes the entombment, all covered with gold and silver, in a low-relief which indicates the forms of the figures beneath ; the heads, which are not in relief but merely pictorial, are the only portions of the picture actually visible.

These altar-screens, which in Russia are counted not by tens but by hundreds and thousands, are highly ornate. Silver and gold and jewelry are conjoined with painting after the nursery and doll-like fashion approved in the south of Spain and at Naples. Only in the most corrupt of Roman Catholic capitals does ecclesiastical art assume the childish forms common in Russia. Resuming the description of the above altar-screen, we find next in range below the entombment a large composition, comprising God the Father surrounded by cherubs, with two full-grown seraphs, encircled by six gold wings, standing on either side. Again, the only parts of the picture permitted to be seen are heads, crossed hands, black legs and feet. Christ with the open book of judgment is another conspicuous figure ; also a companion head, gigantic in size, is the Madonna, directly Byzantine in type, though its smooth and well-kept surface gives little sign of age. The Christ, too, must be accounted but as modernised Byzantine ; here is none of the severity or of the tenuity of the early periods. The type is poor though refined, debilitated though ideal. The hair, parted on the forehead, falls thickly on the shoulders. The face is youthful, not more than thirty, and without a wrinkle ; the cheeks are a little flushed, the prevailing expression is placidity. The accessories of glory, drapery, and open book are highly decorative ; here embossed patterns on the gold coverings enhance the richness of the surface-ornament. Once again the

Russians appear supreme in metal-work, especially in the elaboration of decoration in the flat. Most of the pictures before mentioned are evidently supremely holy; they are black and highly gilded; moreover they move most deeply all sorts and conditions of men, women, and children.

I may here again mention that one purpose of my Russian journey was to discover whether there were heads of Christ in the possession of the Russian Church older or nobler than the ivory carvings, the frescoes, or easel pictures which are found in Italy and other Southern or Western nations. And I was, I confess, disappointed not to meet with any data which could materially enlarge or enrich this most interesting of subjects. As to priority of date, it seems to be entirely on the side of the Roman catacombs and the Latin Church; moreover, in Russia, as I have before frequently remarked, chronology is untrustworthy, inasmuch as comparatively modern works assume and parody the style of the most ancient. The heads of Christ in Russia, one of which has been just described, are, as already said, more or less servile reproductions of Byzantine types. Still the typical form is found under varying phases; the general tendency in these replicas of anterior originals would appear to be towards the mitigation of the asperities in the confirmed Byzantine formulas. Thus the more recent heads of the Saviour in the churches of St. Petersburg, Moscow, Troitza and Kief, assume a certain modern manner, and occasionally wear a smooth, pretty, and ornamental aspect. In these variations on the prescriptive Eastern type, the hair usually flows down upon the shoulders, as with the Greek and Russian priests in the present day. As to the beard, it is thick and full, or short and scant, but the cheeks are left uncovered, and show an elongated face and chin.

These Russian heads of the Saviour in softening down the severe and aged type common to Byzantium, assume a physiognomy not sufficiently intellectual for the Greatest of Teachers. These 'images' in fact inspire little reverence except with blind worshippers; they are mostly wrought up and renovated, so as to fulfil the preconceived conditions of sanctity: undefined generality, weakness, smoothness, and blackness, are the common characteristics of these supposititious heads of the Saviour. It will thus again be easily understood how opposite has been the practice of the Eastern and Western Churches; it is a striking fact that at the time when, in Italy, under Leonardo da Vinci, Raphael and others, the mystery of a God manifest in the flesh had been as it were solved by a perfected art, this Russian Church was still under bondage to the once accepted but now discarded notion that the Redeemer ought to be represented as one who had no form or comeliness. Art in the Western world gained access to the beautiful, the perfect, and the divine, as soon as it was permitted to the painter or the sculptor to develope to uttermost perfection the idea of the Man-God. All such conceptions of the infinite, whether it be that of Jupiter in pagan periods, or of Christ under our divine dispensation, have always been the life and inspiration of the arts. But in Russia ignoble heads of Christ convinced me that such life and inspiration were denied. And I look upon the head of Christ as the turning-point in the Christian art of a nation. If that head be conceived of unworthily there is no possibility that prophets, apostles, martyrs, shall receive their due.

CHAPTER XII.

RELATION BETWEEN THE RELIGIOUS ARTS, THE
RUSSIAN CHURCH, AND THE RUSSIAN PEOPLE.

THE religious arts in the Russian Church are greatly
prejudiced by the prohibition under the second Mosaic
commandment of the use of statues. It is true there
has been a partial evasion of this restriction, inasmuch
as though figures in the round are not admissible, no
veto is put upon low-reliefs or even on high-reliefs,
especially if the enclosing border or frame is made
to project to the outermost limits of the encircled
figure. It were beyond my purpose to show how
unreasonable is this distinction. I will merely take
things as I find them, and shall at once proceed to
point out in briefest terms how injurious has proved
this prohibitory edict on the arts of the Russian Church.
Whatever derogates from the use of the human
figure degrades art : the noblest periods in architecture, whether we recur to the time of Phidias, or to
those subsequent ages when Gothic cathedrals received elaborate carvings under portals and niches, have
always been identified with great works in sculpture.
And one reason I take it why the church architecture
of Russia remains flimsy and false, thin and flat in
surface, and weak in shadow, is that the plastic arts
have been ignored, that modelling has been neglected,
and that in place of the sculptor's chisel has been
substituted the painter's brush. In fact architecture

is by the Greek Church denuded of ennobling sculpture, for though statues, when external or not used in worship, are not absolutely forbidden, they are so seldom seen that they can scarcely be said to exist. Milan Cathedral, with its company of saints thronging the upper sky, were wholly out of place within the Russian dominions. And yet the Milanese school of sculpture, which down to the present day holds a distinctive position in Italy, has been reared and kept alive by the continuous demand, over a period of centuries, for the many hundred statues needed for this apotheosis of the sculptor's art. No such patronage subsists in Russia. Yet architecture without statues is as a city without inhabitants—it is silent, solitary, soulless. The saints who night and day keep guard over the shrine reared in Milan in honour of the Madonna, are not merely art objects, they are as pilgrims of the sky, ambassadors of heaven, a Te Deum of angel voices, a connecting link between two worlds. The substitute in Russia is a gilt dome, or at best a dome, blue as the midnight sky, set with stars of gold. The idea is not without beauty, especially when these forms and colours are indefinitely multiplied, so that a whole city has its upper air illumined; yet the type possesses little value in the rank of intellectual or creative art. Of such architecture we may say, as used to be asserted of our Regent Street of shops, that it can stand neither criticism nor climate.

The traveller, when he turns from exteriors without either saints or gargoyles to the interiors, finds like need of the auxiliary aid of statuary. Even the tombs are wanting in effigies, the figures of emperors do not recline on their sepulchral monuments, a Tsar is buried with almost quaker baldness, the churches are not peopled with the dead slumbering in stone; that presence of the great departed, which makes the interior of Westminster Abbey soul-moving, is a negation in the cathedrals of Russia. A like vacuity in sculpturesque form and personal presence is felt at the situation which answers to the choir or altar in Roman Catholic churches. Instead of a perspective led off from transepts flanked by statues, and including within view a baldacchino sculpturesque in details and attended perchance by cherubs, angels, saints, all catching light, casting shade, and giving substance, reality and personality to the creations of imagination, and to the spiritual longings of faith, there is put up a painted screen smartly gilt.

Again I say that I do not wish to argue questions of creeds, neither do I call in question the principles or prejudices which may abjure art altogether in a church, chapel, or meeting-house, but this position at least seems undeniable, that if art be permitted at all it should be the best and not the worst of its kind. The debased character of the pictures which crowd the altar-screens in these Russian churches has been already described, though in terms not sufficiently severe. Yet it does not seem easy to improve on the unsatisfactory state of things. It is understood that emperors and empresses, when they planted Western arts and sciences in the midst of Russian barbarism, desired at the same time to renovate and revolutionise the sacred arts which had for centuries danced attendance on the illiterate clergy and commonalty. But the deep affections of the people were not to be thus uprooted so suddenly. The utmost advance effected has been the substitution in St. Isaac's, and other comparatively modern churches in St. Petersburg and Moscow, of pictures in the style of the bastard Italian decadence in place of works of Byzantine inanity. And, when in Kief and other sacred places I had the opportunity of observing the conduct of devotees, I found that this low art became a mental degradation instead of an elevation as true art ought to be. The pilgrims were as heathen who bow down to stocks and stones, the art was not high or strong enough to emancipate from superstition. When I compare the effect produced on the worshippers by this holy but abject art with the power of the great masterpieces in Italy, I feel that I am placing ignorance against knowledge, deformity against beauty, the debased in opposition to the divine. Again, to guard against misconstruction, I repeat that I speak as an artist, not as a theologian. Thus speaking, I once more gladly attest to the supreme impressiveness of the vocal part in the ceremonials of the Russian Church, and this I do most earnestly, even after making considerable subtraction on account of dreary monotones. In Russia the truest and least trammeled of the arts is music, and that apparently because musical sound is more free to do what it listeth than constructive architecture or pictorial form.

On the whole I take a discouraging view of the present and future relation between the arts and the Russian Church. The imposed conditions all but preclude the possibility of emancipation and improvement : the Church degrades the arts, and in turn the arts are fetters on the intellectual development of the people. As naturally might be anticipated, the religious services satisfy the aspirations of the ignorant classes chiefly ; I did not observe among the pilgrims at Kief the higher orders, or scarcely the well-to-do middle classes. Indeed the most devout worshippers might almost be mistaken for gipsies.

Cheap religious prints, brightly coloured, and often highly sensational, are in great favour with the Russian people. The trade in these pictorial wares is considerable. In Moscow may be found, under the shelter of an arch, a whole gallery of Madonnas, Christs, Crucifixions, Last Judgments, all selling for a few pence a piece. In the outskirts of the same city, too, is held every Sunday morning an open market where these devotional compositions are mixed up with stolen goods. At the great entrance, also, to the Troitza Monastery there are stalls where may be purchased at popular prices rudely-coloured woodcuts from the pictures which in the adjacent churches are held in greatest veneration. Within the monastery likewise is a studio or workshop, where cheap religious pictures are manufactured wholesale. It is a pretty sight to see this large room full of diligent manipulators, one painting a head, another a blue drapery or a golden glory, all repeating ordained types and prescriptive compositions, from which there is no desire for departure either on the part of the artist or of the public. It seems to be considered a part of the appointed duty of a religious fraternity to supply to the faithful an orthodox art which may be enjoyed without danger. The traveller at once naturally reverts to Italy of the middle ages, when monks illumined choral books and covered their cells with frescoes, but in the Greek and Greco-Russian Churches, out of the nameless multitude of painters there has not risen to distinction a single Fra Angelico or Fra Bartolomeo. The art manufactory at Troitza is of interest as a sample of the mode of work which, practised on Mount Athos, has naturally been diffused over the territories held by the Russian Church. The method precludes either originality or progress : a copy is set before an artisan, who reproduces with dead routine and mechanical precision ten or a hundred replicas. As I watched the workers, it again became evident how well fitted the Russians are for this servile and persistent drudgery, they are faultless as copyists ; and one reason no doubt why the arts of the Church remain stationary is that the Russian painter has no natural impulse towards progression. At the monastery in Kief I was disappointed not to meet with a studio as at Troitza, but a printing-press and a publishing establishment were shown, which are employed in the multiplication of illustrated books. And round about the churches and within the sacred enclosure there was no lack of shops and stalls, where pilgrims obtained to their heart's content pictorial aids to their devotion. I availed myself of this privilege largely : in Moscow, at Troitza, and Kief, I lost no opportunity of securing these popular religious prints, these people's editions of compositions held sacred in the Church. The most complete and characteristic collection is in the Museum of Moscow.

Again I was greatly perplexed in the matter of chronology. A large number of these cheap prints however were unmistakably modern ; the art of engraving has naturally in its prevailing style followed the art of painting, in both alike are seen certain modernising tendencies which are comparable to the just conceivable case of a Cimabue assuming the prettiness and softness of a Carlo Dolce. Still the original Byzantine basis remains, except in some extreme works which seem to owe quite as much to Paris as to Moscow or Kief ; in other exceptional instances also the designer appears to have consulted even nature. Indeed these popular religious prints indicate, as I have before said, that the sacred arts are at the present moment in a transitional state, that they are vacillating between archaism and naturalism ; that, in fact, a new school has arisen, which, though in a minority, moves in response to the prevailing styles in modern Europe—a school which is willing to surrender the artists of Byzantium to the post-Raphaelite painters. I have before me highly-coloured lithographs of the three angels who visited Abraham, also of a Christ, which are severally afflicted by this degenerate modernism, the infirmity whereof is that it lacks the severe dignity of archaic styles, the ideal beauty of Raphaelesque schools, as well as the vigour of healthy naturalism. There is not an art more contemptible in Europe. The measure of its debasement is in the degradation of the human figure, a degeneracy which, as already indicated, is strangely associated with a true system of ornamentation. Thus I have now before me one of the many well-known personations of St. Nicholas, altogether abject in the drawing of the figure, and yet the surrounding glory, breast-plate, and metal background, heightened by pearls, jewels, and enamels, is a fine piece of decorative art. And in this subordination of the figure to ornamental accessories, it is interesting to trace that close relationship with the Oriental systems to which, geographically and otherwise, Russian art is obviously allied. In Indian, Persian, and Saracenic schools, the human figure is either subordinated or positively excluded, while colour and decorative design are triumphant. It might seem that the union of the two elements were incompatible had not Italy, about the time of Cellini, given proof that the perfect figure is reconcilable with consummate ornament. But Russia is, and always has been, far away from this faultless combination.

The sacred and legendary art of Russia will reward the attention of the careful and curious student; the differences will be found to be considerable between this phase of Christian art and the forms common in the Western Church. For instance, I have eight pictures before me, wherein the infant Christ is fully dressed, and in four of these compositions the Child wears a crown as well as a glory. The glories of the Madonna are sometimes not only gilt but decorated with precious stones; in fact the Russian Church is seldom content with the primary and spiritual conception of a divine effulgence, a radiance of light around the heads of the elect and precious; the idea evidently is that the glory shall be as a head-dress, or as a rich and solid piece of plate, manufactured, engraved, and jewelled by a goldsmith. This treatment is but one of the many examples of how poetic and pure conceptions are brought down to materialism, and made to subserve mere decorative ends. How low and even revolting are some of the ideas which this semi-barbaric art promulgates may be seen in a religious print, 'The Virgin with Three Arms.' In this picture three distinct hands are shown. That the most blessed of women should be represented with such deformity is a sad proof that arts divinely appointed as the educators of the people pander to the lowest tastes.

This Russian art jumps at the supernatural in any form: winged beings abound, sometimes as small cherubs, at others as larger creatures with wide expanding pinions, or again as the six-winged seraphim, or often as what may be called the angels-of-all-work, ready to mourn with those who mourn, to comfort the afflicted, or to reprove the transgressor. These winged beings fitly serve as the ministers of God, and, were they not often ugly and deformed, their presence would tend to

elevate the scenes in which they are frequently the chief
actors. The principle of evil is also copiously personified; wicked spirits are properly clothed in ugliness; but,
though some inclination is shown towards the grotesque,
and though a busy mischief-making prompts to animated
action, yet the grandeur of archangels ruined, as seen in
Spinello of Arezzo and in Luca Signorelli at Orvieto,
is never reached. A really noble form of the grotesque
does not exist in the Russian Church. Imp-like demons,
with wings of a bat, horns of a goat, tail of a monkey,
and claws of a scorpion, are but active little creatures,
doing as much harm as they can, and coming into sharp
and continuous conflict with God's winged ministers of
mercy. Now before me is a rude print of the parable
of the rich man : below the table lies Lazarus with dogs
licking his sores. The chief story is further carried out
through three accompanying compositions. In one the
rich man is seen in his grave, an angel leaves in sorrow,
while three devils seize on their prey ; in a second, Dives
lifts up his voice in hell, being in torment of flames and
torture of demons ; in a third, Lazarus is borne by a
company of angels to the bosom of Abraham, who
stretches out his arms in attitude of welcome. The art
is here about the lowest of the low, yet the narrative is
as clear as in the old woodcuts known in the West as
the 'Bible of the Poor ;' in fact these popular prints serve
as the Bible of the people.

The parable of Lazarus and Dives from its highly
dramatic character is evidently a favourite theme, but
there are other narratives, biblical or legendary, which
are deemed equally cogent in the pictorial appeal made
by the Church to the people. Here is a picture of a figure
floating in a bath of liquid fire ; from the ribs issues a
tree, as in representations of ' the root of Jesse;' but on the

branches, instead of descendants grouped in comfortable
condition, are figures hanging by the neck or heels consumed in devouring flames. On a hill which commands
this tragic scene, worthy of Blake or Dante, appears an
angel leading by the hand an aged man, who looks
down with sorrow on fellow-creatures suffering under
the penalty of sin. Again the conception reads better in
words than in forms and colours ; the moral taught, too,
is sounder than the art displayed ; indeed the art teach-
ings of this Church are not so much to be despised on
the ground of ethics as of intellectual imbecility. Another
subject, rendered more than once, represents a dead
woman stretched on a bier, a man, apparently the mur-
derer, intercedes for mercy at the feet of a winged angel
bearing a drawn sword. Above the bier stands Christ,
holding in his arms the spiritual body of the deceased
fully draped, as spirits find it comfortable to be in the
Russian climate. Over all presides God the Father—
but what a God ! We have only to compare the First
Person of the Trinity in the Eastern Church with the
grand creations of Michael Angelo and of Raphael in
the Sistine Chapel and the Loggia of the Vatican, to
know how vast is the interval which divides the arts of
the Latin and of the Greek Churches. I may here observe that the point of faith on which the two Churches
diverge—the procession of the Holy Ghost—does not
appear to necessitate any difference in art formula. The
Divine Dove in St. Petersburg, as in Rome, floats mid-
way between the Father and the Son.

I mention yet another print for its supreme sensa-
tionalism. A youth is stretched on a sumptuous couch
in death's agony. Money-bags by his side, which claim
his last concern, are already grasped by a hydra, while
devouring dragons, with open mouths and flaming tongues,

rush forward on their prey. But the brand is snatched from the burning; a guardian angel watches over the bedside; in the upper sky Christ appears cross in hand, and from the Divine Presence dart lightnings, to the discomfiture of the satanic host, who had already made sure of their victim. I should infer, by the presence in the foreground of a lyre, a music-book, and a mask, that the youth had been guilty of fine-art indiscretions, something worse, no doubt, than Tennyson makes full much of in 'The Palace of Art.' I need not add that the conception is puerile and extravagant : the appeal here made is to vulgar fear. In concluding this brief notice of the sacred and often scenic arts in Russia, I may be permitted to recall a remark once made by a stage manager : that if in a theatre they could not do things better than in the churches, the whole concern must pass through the Bankruptcy Court.

Another species of religious art obtains extended currency among the people ; the material is brass, enriched frequently by blue and white enamel ; the subject may be a crucifix or some other sacred composition ; the shape is that of a rectangular plaque, or perhaps more frequently the arrangement assumes the form of a triptych. In St. Petersburg, Moscow, and Kief, I spared no pains to get a fully representative collection of these ecclesiastical brasses. But, before speaking further of these bas-relief tablets, I may say a word about the old curiosity shops in the bazaars and elsewhere, which offer sad temptations to travellers with art tastes. The contents of these stores are miscellaneous yet monotonous ; Russian home-treasures are here evidently turned out wholesale ; the household gods are put up for what they will fetch, and the strangest objects imaginable get into the market. Yet these art medleys are, as I have said, monotonous from the endless repetition of all but identical forms; the ideas are few and often poor. Perhaps the Russian pectoral crosses, in silver and silver-gilt, are among the most interesting objects: the four arms are equal, as in the Greek cross; around is a circlet; the whole arrangement admits of much play of symmetric line and ornament, and the surface is decorated with inscriptions. Likewise may be found varieties of the type of spoon known as the apostolic, often inlaid with floral and other ornament, usually good in style; indeed, as before said, Russian artisans are most skilful and tasteful in metal-work, whether ecclesiastical or domestic. I may here say that the act of purchasing is usually a tedious process unless the traveller submits cheerfully to imposition. It is not safe to make a first offer at more than a third of the sum asked, and then the bargain may be struck at a half or two-thirds. The vendor is usually full of lamentations; he pretends that he sells for less than he gave, and that he is a ruined man; and yet, in the next breath, he will offer something else, and does not let the customer go without promise of return. It struck me that, in the old curiosity shops or stalls, there was no certain standard of value, except when the object is in a precious metal, and then, of course, the price can never be less than the sum declared by the weight. But, when the article is of a fancy character, the value is capricious, sometimes because the merchant or huckster has caught it up for less than it is worth; thus, no doubt, an experienced traveller may meet with bargains; yet I generally found the Russian tradesman keen and sly; certainly any person not alive to his own interests is the exception. Above all, the traveller should be on his guard against haste; it is best to walk about leisurely to see what the bazaars present,

to inquire into prices deliberately, to make a few casual
offers on the safe side, and so to judge of the strength
of the market. I knew of an Englishman who would
thus keep several transactions on hand from day to day,
closing a bargain sometimes after a week's negotiation.
He thus amused himself, learned a little of the language,
and became acquainted with the manners and customs
of the people. I have usually found these tradesfolks
more good-tempered than truthful; indeed it seemed to
me almost impossible to give them offence or to rouse
them to anger. On one occasion, in Moscow, when
bartering for some religious brasses in the Sunday
market for stolen goods, I greatly feared that the keeper
of the largest stall would refuse more dealings with me;
but, on the contrary, when I walked through the market
on the following Sunday, I was agreeably surprised to
find that he had brought out for me his most precious
stores. We did some business to our mutual satisfaction, and parted the best of friends; indeed a traveller
who leaves behind him in Russia enemies can have little
tact or courtesy, so kindly is the nature of the people.

The religious brasses in my possession furnish subject
for a brief description, which will serve to elucidate the
sacred narratives and the art treatments most in vogue
in the Russian Church. The brass crucifixes are sometimes pectoral, but occasionally they reach a size suited
for domestic or processional uses; one of the latter may
be described for the sake of peculiarities which, though
habitual in Russia, are unknown in the crosses of the
Latin Church. In the first place, the board for the feet
to rest on is not only slanting, but so far prolonged as
to constitute a second cross, and then above the head
comes another lateral projection; thus the cross has
three arms. In the spaces hereby obtained appear the

head of St. Veronica, two angels, the sun and the moon, a couple of castles, and Golgotha with a skull. A smaller and possibly pectoral cross, greatly worn away, and giving indication of a date unusually early, is similar in general arrangement. Here, however, the Christ is draped, and above the head appear the Holy Dove and God the Father : thus the Trinity is present.

Among numerous brass triptychs one is remarkable for its size, enrichment, and theologic dogmas. In the central compartment stands Christ, with open Book of Judgment, a glory, enriched with gold and white enamel, encircles the head, a foliated background has similar enrichment, and the right hand is raised after the Greek manner of benediction. The Blessed Virgin, who occupies a second plaque in the triptych, is equally in the Byzantine style both as to type of face and cast of drapery ; the accessory floral decoration is also of champlevé enamel in blue and white, the brass serving for gold. A problematical and exceptional character occupies the third leaf in the triptych—the figure I have found in Russia but not elsewhere. A winged man, rather than a winged angel, on the same scale as the Christ and the Madonna, occupies the whole of this third plaque ; a jewelled glory is round his head, and in one hand he holds a small vessel wherein floats an infant, also with a nimbus round the brow. The infant stretches forth the right hand as Christ in attitude of benediction ; the austere man, old enough for a grandfather, also holds up the right hand, apparently in the action of baptism ; that this strangely venerable being is intended for the Baptist may be inferred from a shaggy garment, as of camels' hair, but then, on the contrary, a large space is given to a pair of mighty wings ; also, it may be objected that a discrepancy of forty or fifty years between the baptiser and the baptised is wholly incompatible with the assumption so often made the most of by Raphael and other artists in the West, that the infants Jesus and John were playmates. Perhaps the discrepancy may here, as in other perplexed cases, be resolved by the supposition that the scene is laid in heaven, where chronology becomes naught, because time has been swallowed up in eternity. Other triptychs are decorated with varying series of Biblical subjects in bas-relief. St. Nicholas, the patron saint, and the character most often repeated, sometimes occupies the central position. In another triptych the middle compartment is filled by a Madonna and Child; the mother represented with arms upraised—a favourite attitude—as in figures in prayer found on the walls of the Roman catacombs.

It may be here worthy of remark, that neither in the religious brasses, nor in the religious prints, is found a single instance of what in Italian art is known as a 'Holy Family,' as distinguished from 'The Mother and Child.' The latter abounds everywhere in varying form; four different arrangements are now before me. But the fuller composition, associating with the Madonna and Infant, St. John, St. Joseph, and sometimes St. Anne also, is not included in these popular phases of sacred art. Another chief subject in these triptychs is Christ visiting the souls in Hades; above sits the First Person of the Trinity, with outstretched arms. A further composition is Elijah carried to heaven in a chariot, attended by an angel; the divine hand reaches forward from the upper sky,—a favourite symbol with Giotto and other early Italian painters; indeed this very subject, with a difference, has been painted

by Giotto. The two wings or shutters to these triptychs are often each divided into three compartments,
wherein are usually repeated routine compositions.
Thus, in duplicate, are now before me, 'The Annunciation,' 'The Flight into Egypt,' 'The Presentation in the
Temple,' 'The Resurrection of Lazarus,' ending with
'The Ascension of Christ.' Among other familiar
incidents are 'The Nativity,' 'The Baptism,' 'The Transfiguration,' 'The Crucifixion,' 'The Supper at Emmaus,'
'The Assumption of the Virgin.' In one plaque 'The
Madonna and Child' appear four times within a gold
frame, and numerous saints are grouped around in
adoration.

These works are suggestive of a few observations.
The first is the general resemblance between the
Biblical series ordained in the Russian and in the
Latin Churches, a resemblance which naturally arises
out of common points of contact in creed. But then
comes the contrast, often before insisted on, between
the progressive art of Italy and the stationary art of
Russia. These plaques are multiplied down to the
present day; sometimes the old moulds are used, in
which cases the new castings in style necessarily correspond to the time when the mould was made; but
often new moulds are wrought, still even then the old
designs are more or less closely adhered to, and so
dates and places of manufacture are thrown into confusion. It is even said that some of these brasses are
brought out in Birmingham; and the story goes that
a Brummagem manufacturer, travelling in Russia, had
some of his own sacred wares offered him at a bargain.
I see, however, no reason to doubt that these brasses
are, at least for the most part, home-made; indeed often
it becomes evident how much the moulds have been

worn by long use ; forgers, moreover, would be apt to overlook accidental defects such as here appear. The rudeness, too, of the execution is another mark of native origin; the handling in fact belongs almost to barbaric times. Tula is usually named as the site of manufacture, a town south of Moscow, termed the Birmingham or Sheffield of Russia, and famous for silver - niello snuff-boxes, also for brass tea-urns, which are at least quite as indispensable to the Russian commonalty as sacred brass triptychs. As to dates, all within certain limits is in doubt, for the reasons already assigned. A brass, corresponding in style with several works in my possession, is now on exhibition in the South Kensington Museum under the following description :—'Brass Poliptych of four tablets, with scriptural subjects in low-relief, blue enamel ground, Russo-Greek work, seventeenth century; lent by Mr. Beresford Hope.' The subjects, twelve in number, offer little variation on the routine before mentioned ; they begin as usual with the Annunciation. The date of the seventeenth century here assigned I take to be somewhat conjectural, for the causes before stated. How uncertain are the internal evidences of date is often proved by the tricks of dealers ; thus an old work will be made to appear smart by rubbing up and sharp surface-tooling; in other instances, age is simulated by the common custom of feigning old designs and archaic execution.

Religion throughout Christendom is confessedly the sphere of the supernatural, and religious art for the Russian people, in default of being supernatural in the high sense of attaining a truth, beauty, and goodness beyond the common reach of nature, commits itself to a phase of the supernatural which belongs to ages of ignorance and superstition—it assumes the abnormal, the monstrous, and even the diseased. St. Basil, it is said, became a saint because born imbecile; and in such reverence for infirmities, mental and bodily, the Russian Church but shares the faith of Mahomedans, among whom the custom prevails of raising sacred shrines to that class of people whose first claim upon the laws of England is a commission of lunacy. And this grave intellectual mistake reflects itself inevitably from the religion into the art of the Russian people. Forsaking the only true idea of the supernatural in art—based either on the perfecting of types existing in outward nature, or in the visible realisation of the soul's inborn longings for perfection—forsaking, I say, the formula established by all great schools, whether Pagan or Christian, this Russian school makes sacred the blemishes and abortions of humanity. But, again, some tribute is due to the technique of this art. The system of surface-ornamentation, and even of colour, in these sacred brasses, is comparable to the floral symmetry and the chromatic harmony which we are accustomed to admire in Indian shawls and other Eastern fabrics. That the Russians are Christian artists at all seems to be somewhat of an accident, but that they are skilful decorators comes as a necessity of race and geographic position. These rude triptychs, the largest and best of which do not fetch more than from £5 to £10, are remarkable as examples of that system of enamelling on metal which, though for a time almost extinct among Western nations, has ever been kept alive among Eastern peoples. Enamelling seems to be as indigenous in Russia and other territories eastward as fresco-painting is in Italy—indigenous in this sense, that the produce is native to the soil, that no special culture is needed, but that the common

artisan can, as a matter of course, turn out good work ;
not superfine work it is true, as that of Limoges, but
yet good, even in its imperfections ; the colours, though
in outline blotched, blend as in Eastern fabrics ; they
consort together, as predisposed to harmony, and the
balance in the end comes apparently by unconscious
intuition rather than by calculating forethought.   These
brasses, which serve in the cottages of the peasant for
altar shrines or domestic gods, are in Kief and other
towns sold from the same stalls as the silver-gilt chains
supposed to be dug up by villagers as treasure-trove.
But as with the brasses so with the chains, the spoons,
the buttons, and the prints, the new are intermingled with
the old, the times that are past and the days that are
present appear as one.   Emperors may decree reforms,
nobles may affect the fashions of Paris, but the bulk
of the people refuse, at least in the arts, to move
onwards.   Thus ignorance and superstition are cherished
as the triumph of faith and the safeguard of the religious arts.

The remainder of my journey leaves little to record.
From Kief I travelled by the Odessa railway south-
wards 200 miles, then, as already stated, I went by
carriage 200 miles more.   On arriving at Czernowitz,
the frontier of Austrian Poland, I was glad to find
myself again within the confines of a civilization, which
contrasted pleasantly with the semi-barbarism which
I had left behind me in Southern Russia.